Crowds,
Power, and
Transformation
in Cinema

CONTEMPORARY APPROACHES TO FILM AND TELEVISION SERIES

A complete listing of the books in this series can be found online at http://wsupress.wayne.edu

General Editor

BARRY KEITH GRANT
Brock University

Advisory Editors

PATRICIA B. ERENS
School of the Art Institute of Chicago

LUCY FISCHER
University of Pittsburgh

PETER LEHMAN
Arizona State University

CAREN J. DEMING
University of Arizona

ROBERT J. BURGOYNE
Wayne State University

TOM GUNNING
University of Chicago

ANNA McCARTHY
New York University

PETER X. FENG
University of Delaware

Crowds, Power, and Transformation in Cinema

LESLEY BRILL

WAYNE STATE UNIVERSITY PRESS   DETROIT

10 09 08 07 06   5 4 3 2 1

Library of Congress Cataloging-in-Publication Data

Brill, Lesley, 1943–
   Crowds, power, and transformation in cinema / Lesley Brill.
       p. cm. — (Contemporary approaches to film and television series)
   Includes bibliographical references and index.
   ISBN 0-8143-3275-7 (pbk. : alk. paper)
   1. Crowds in motion pictures. 2. Power (Social sciences) I. Title. II. Series.
   PN1995.9.C67B75 2006
   791.45'6552—dc22
   2005020939

Much of the chapter titled "Packs, Predators, and Love in Hitchcock's
North by Northwest" first appeared in *Arizona Quarterly* 56.4 (2000).
Reprinted by permission of the Arizona Board of Regents.

∞ The paper used in this publication meets the minimum requirements
of the American National Standard for Information Sciences—
Permanence of Paper for Printed Library Materials, ANSI Z39.48-1984.

Contents

Acknowledgments

This book incurred its greatest obligations at the beginning and end of its creation. The late Steve Rosen of St. Peter's (New Jersey) telephoned me one memorable day to suggest that I might find the multitude of ideas in Elias Canetti's *Crowds and Power* well suited to the study of film. Like most Americans, I had scarcely heard of Canetti; but when I opened that volume, I found a conception of the world in which not only film but everything else human appeared clarified and more deeply coherent. At the end of the work that led to this study, Barry Grant of Brock University suggested that I add a chapter on populist comedy and that I organize the chapters into broad sections according to general topics, both of which I did. Neither Steve nor Barry—need I add?—are in the least responsible for the misuses to which I may have put their ideas; the faults and foolishness that escaped the eyes of other readers, to whom I also owe considerable debts, are mine alone. Among those readers, the most influential—in this as in most things—is Megan Parry, a penetrating and tactful editor. George Toles offered sustaining encouragement along most of the route that led me to this point. Jim and Sue Palmer, as always, were generous and perceptive in reading the chapters I inflicted on them, and a number of anonymous readers of various drafts for Wayne State University Press offered carefully considered, useful suggestions for additions and corrections. My gifted professor of German and colleague at Wayne State, Alfred Cobbs, led a middle-aged student of no particular talent into the lovely language in which Canetti wrote, enabling me to catch glimpses of the flights of Canetti's originals—which is not to denigrate Carol Stewart's essential (for me) translation of *Masse und Macht*. The director of Wayne State University Press, Jane Hoehner, and acquisitions editor Annie Martin have been steadfastly confident in the potential of this study; I am deeply grateful to them. Maya Rhodes and John Crowley assisted in the making of the frame captures that illustrate some of my arguments. Eric Schramm has been a judicious copyeditor. An earlier, somewhat different version of the chapter on *North by Northwest* appeared in *Arizona Quarterly,* and a half-dozen pages of the writing on *The Silence of the Lambs* are scheduled to appear in a chapter on that film in *After Hitchcock,* forthcoming from the University of Texas Press. The overwhelming influence of Elias Canetti on the study that follows is obvious; I hope that my appropriations of some of the ideas of that curious, formidable, playful *Dichter* are not entirely unworthy of him.

Preface

This study attends to aspects of the cinema that have been mostly ignored or have proven difficult to categorize and analyze. Although it draws on diverse scholars to inform its approach, it primarily enlists Elias Canetti's *Crowds and Power,* bringing to the study of motion pictures Canetti's understanding of crowds and their relation to individualistic power and transformation. Frequent as representations of crowds have been in movies, they have received surprisingly little study; nor have they been systematically related to the portrayal of power, another of the great, pervasive subjects of the cinema.

The introduction discusses crowds both within films and as audiences in the theater. It focuses on Canetti's conceptions of crowds and packs and what he sees as their obverse, the paranoia that characterizes seekers of power. Succeeding chapters on individual films, divided into sections on "Power versus Crowds" and "Predation versus Transformation," analyze themes and imagery that have proven elusive, even in classic movies that have been extensively studied.

In part 1, two silent classics, Eisenstein's *Potemkin* and Griffith's *Intolerance,* illustrate the affinity of the cinema for representations of crowds. *Potemkin* is precisely organized around the formation of a crowd and its subsequent transformations. For *Intolerance,* dense with representations of power, crowds, and crowd symbols, Canetti's thought does not so much simplify our perception as assist us to understand the complex unity of Griffith's work. Preston Sturges's comedies emphasize throngs of people as central images and brilliantly embody the affinity between film comedy and affirming crowds. The isolation afflicting seekers of power is at the center of Kurasowa's *Throne of Blood.* Ultimately triumphant, however, is the crowd of the dead that shall finally conquer all living ones. In *Citizen Kane,* the conflict between crowds and power takes place as much within the protagonist as between him and the people he attempts to master.

Part 2, "Predation versus Transformation," begins with *North by Northwest,* a movie rich in hunters and predation, agencies of power, crowds, and what Canetti called "crowd symbols." Transformation in that film functions as the primary means by which its protagonist attempts both to escape and to defeat the figures of power who pursue him. Burnett's *Killer of Sheep* exemplifies predation, packs, thwarted transformation, and melancholia. Its archetypal groups—men and women, predators and quarry, adults and children—are at once conflicting and mutually reflective. *The Silence of the Lambs* shares with *Killer of Sheep* more than a title species; all its central figures desire to metamorphose into something stronger and more beautiful, and all are at once predator and prey.

Following these chapters on individual films, the body of the study ends with a conclusion that summarizes the preceding chapters and extends some of their central ideas. An afterword on *Crowds and Power* discusses its genre, modes of argument, and relation to some other social thinkers. Finally, the appendix provides a summary of *Crowds and Power.*

Attention to issues of gender, class, and race as well as the introduction of the perspectives of Freud, Lacan, and cognitive psychologists (among others) have broadened film studies during the past several decades. The subjects and arguments of Canetti's work will, I hope, further broaden and deepen our understanding of one of the dominant art forms of our era.

A rhythmic
crowd gathers
in Forman's
Loves of a Blonde

Introduction

Movies are crowd machines. They doubtless do other things as well, but most of them excel at gathering crowds and presenting images of them. Like all mass media, film creates, communicates with, and represents masses. Having seen specific movies and having opinions about them constitutes an all-but-indispensable credential for joining or counting oneself among certain groups. Obviously, all films made in hopes of wide distribution seek to attract audiences; that is, to generate crowds. Film companies, stars, directors, and the industry at large desire not only to attract as large an audience as possible but also to maintain it through time, to keep people coming back.

A great many films prominently represent crowds in their plots, sounds, and images. Within moving pictures, indeed, the representation of crowds is commonplace, and the stories of many narrative films, like other stories, establish for the protagonists a central goal of joining, creating, or restoring a sympathetic crowd. Even movies that lack crowds frequently make implicit appeals to a fictional crowd off-camera or to an assumed real audience in the theater. Simultaneously, films invoke crowds through the sort of imagery that Elias Canetti called "crowd symbols," multitudinous natural or man-made objects like flocks of birds, forests, or rows of houses.[1] Both through crowd symbols and through direct representations of masses of people, cinema shows its audiences reflections of themselves (however idealized or otherwise distorted), not just as individuals but also as groups.

As Canetti discovered in creating his monumental *Crowds and Power* (the central ideas of which loom large in this study), to discuss crowds in a revealing way one needs to understand their psychological and social components. As regards the psychology of crowds, Canetti inquired what in the human psyche makes crowds possible and what other expressions those psychic predispositions might produce. His answers, respectively, supply the other two central concerns of this study: transformation and power. Transformation, the imaginative ability to feel oneself as another, makes possible one of the fundamental qualities of all crowds, equality. In a crowd, Canetti writes, "Suddenly it is as though everything were happening in one and the same body" (16). There is no difference of station, status, age, or even sex. The ultimate motive for the formation of crowds, the deep fear that all humans have of suffering an unknown, unexpected touch, can give rise not only to the impulse to form crowds but, pathologically, to a profoundly dangerous alternative response, the drive to seek and exercise power. I go into these matters more deeply in the afterword on *Crowds and Power*, but for the moment the point is that Canetti's comprehension of crowds cannot be separated from his ideas of transformation and power. Those concepts are as important to crowds as understanding mediums of transmission and the possibility of distortion are to the reproduction of music. As regards social contexts, for Canetti they are extremely broad, encompassing all the human societies with which this massively erudite man was acquainted and extending into their most durable institutions. The variations that masses exhibit in different times and places are critical to completing the picture of crowds as a fundamental human quality. The basic kinds of crowds and their metamorphoses from one kind to another may be especially well seen in the precursor of crowds, namely, packs.

The twentieth century, by many accounts the century of the crowd, was also a century of motion pictures, encompassing virtually all the history of cinema and its growth into a dominant global medium. Movies are so full of crowds that one is tempted to suppose that cinema is suited by its very materials to their representation. So thought Felix Mesguich, a cameraman for Lumière, about "the true domain of the cinema," in which he prominently includes "the crowd and its eddies."[2] Siegfried Kracauer, to whom I owe the Mesguich quotation, notes "the attraction which masses exerted on still and motion picture cameras from the outset,"[3] and Stanley Cavell writes of "film's . . . natural attraction to crowds."[4] My wife, a painter, imagines the pleasure of early photographers when they understood that they could portray multitudes of people without having to invent and draw each individual. A sometime photographer, I visualize the rushing, jerky stream of individual exposures—approximately 150,000 to 175,000 for feature films of average length—along with the clumps of silver halides or the dye clusters that make up photographic grain in a single exposure, the host of molecules that constitute each individual grain, and the still greater number of photons to whose passage they bear witness. The physical basis of cinematography thus replicates the status of the objects that Canetti called crowd symbols. As media become digitized, the bytes recording visual and aural information maintain the crowd qualities of earlier materials.

Surprisingly, we have not thought very much about movies and their audiences with respect to crowds. Film theory largely addresses itself to viewers as collections of individuals, while practical movie criticism usually considers particular characters, actors, and directors. Studies of movie genres have mostly adopted similar assumptions. The Freudian and Lacanian underpinnings of much film theory focus on speculations about individual psychic development and its implications for the understanding of motion pictures. Theorists who think about film in terms of its physical and formal properties—Rudolf Arnheim and Andre Bazin, for example—also tend to assume an individual viewer or interpreter. But as Vanessa R. Schwartz asserts, "The history of cinematic spectatorship cannot be recounted simply in terms of the connection between an individual spectator and a film. For it is necessarily among a crowd that we find the cinematic spectator."[5]

There does exist a prominent line of film theory oriented toward the movies as mass media. It has a distinguished ancestor in Walter Benjamin's famous "The Work of Art in the Age of Mechanical Reproduction" and includes some prominent theorists, among them Siegfried Kracauer. More recently and emphatically, it extends to Marxist and other politically oriented critics who regard movies as conscious or unconscious purveyors of "the dominant ideology" for a vulgar, exploited, or self-satisfied herd. Such a view of cinema distrusts both mass media and the masses. It aims at revealing the quasi-concealed, manipulative messages by which movies putatively justify the social status quo and pacify gullible, oppressed groups—the proletariat, ethnic or racial minorities, women, old people, children, and so on. This strain of film theory, which overlaps several others, may accurately be called anti-crowd. It aspires to free an imperceptive mob of consumers from the hegemony of a smaller group of oppressors and to restore their autonomy as individuals.

Because of their hostility to mass media and their willingness to accept widely held assumptions about crowds, politically inclined commentators have rarely analyzed the groups that make up movie audiences. Nor have scholars or critics of any persuasion often concentrated on the representation of crowds within movies, important as that has been for the making and marketing of numerous films ("With a Cast of Thousands!"). Insofar as film studies has thought about crowds, its conception generally fits Lenelis Kruse's description: "What is common to the progenitors of crowd psychology in the late 19th century, but not much less common to many contemporary theorists[,] is their 'description' of mass behavior in dramatic and highly negative terms, such as extraordinary, exaggerated, bizarre, chaotic, evil, and disgusting"[6]—and, above all, suggestible and easily manipulated. Film studies generally continues, in short, to view crowds as Le Bon, Tarde, and their followers have done.

As even those who regard them as destructive and atavistic agree, however, crowds have their own qualities and dynamics; they are more than a setting for the individuals who constitute them. Like individuals, particular crowds have their own characteristics. This study largely attends to filmic representations of crowd qualities and dynamics and to representations of the crowd's usually evil twin, power. I also speculate, mostly in this introduction, about film audiences; but the principal focus of this book is on the analysis of movies themselves.

Perhaps the most ambitious attempt to understand crowds as crowds, rather than as agglomerations of individuals, was published in 1960 as *Masse und Macht* (translated as *Crowds and Power*, 1962) by Elias Canetti.[7] I do not suppose that Canetti has put down everything of consequence about crowds, power, or the transformations crucial to understanding both, nor that all his arguments will be equally convincing for all readers. He does provide an organized and deeply thought-out set of conceptions about crowds and their relation to power that helps us to focus on those phenomena as they appear in motion pictures. Consequently many of my arguments will draw on Canetti's ideas, and occasionally on those of other crowd theorists and social psychologists. Since Canetti's work is less well known in North America than in England and Europe, I have added an afterword and an appendix, the first briefly summarizing Canetti's life and discussing the genre, main ideas, and intellectual affiliations of *Crowds and Power,* and the second summarizing that work via a précis and adding a bit of further commentary. Readers unfamiliar with *Crowds and Power* or especially interested in how Canetti's work can apply to the humanities generally may wish to go to these sections before continuing to the readings of individual films.

In the following essays on individual movies, *Crowds and Power* is less frequently "applied" than enlisted to direct our attention to aspects that might otherwise go unnoticed or that have proved difficult to describe or categorize. That is, *Crowds and Power* serves at least as much to offer clues about where to look as to provide suggestions about the meaning of what we find. Put another way, Canetti allows us to ask some questions more precisely than we have done and to ask some others that we have not asked at all. His work also supplies coherent models that help to organize our thinking about such things as the relation among various crowds or between representations of masses and those who oppose them. In many films, delineations of crowds and power conform to a remarkable degree to Canetti's analyses. The insights and observations that he systematized during decades of thinking and reading have frequently been given narrative and imagistic embodiment in the more intuitive work of directors, writers, and others who make movies.

A concentrated, comprehensive meditation of approximately five hundred pages, *Crowds and Power* looks back to early nineteenth-century anthropological sources for glimpses at the origins and transformations of masses, witnesses their scope in the twentieth century, and analyzes the human passion for power as a paranoid disease that directly reverses the energies of crowd formation. Unlike most other crowd theorists, who tend to equate masses with mobs, Canetti neither identifies them with demagogic leaders nor assumes that they represent a savage or decadent regression against which civilized societies must struggle. Nonetheless, he does not idealize them or overlook their destructive history and potential. "For me," he wrote, "the crowd is neither good nor bad but simply *is.*"[8]

Canetti's social psychology is far ranging, and his understanding of power is fundamentally integrated with his understanding of crowds. The impulse to form crowds and the impulse to accrue power share the underlying motive of the desire to escape the threat of death. Within crowds, people feel safe from most sources of attack; they feel equal to and united with one another. By contrast, seekers after power, *die Überlebenden* ("survivors" or "outlivers"), dangerously invert the dynamics of crowd formation. Whereas crowds are characterized by density and equality, power seeks isolation and a sense of inequality so radical that it finally denies human status to its adversaries. The full realization of a crowd occurs when its members feel complete identification with one another, when they experience transcendence of an isolated self, and when in their equality with the other crowd members they feel safe. The human capacity for transformation, the ability to feel the body of another as one's own, makes crowd formation possible. Command and secrecy, on the other hand, are the instruments of power. Far from experiencing a sense of safety, even the mightiest feel themselves to be constantly under attack. Instinctively, the power seeker will attempt to prevent or pervert transformations, which overcome the distances upon which power depends.

The most intense feeling of power is experienced when a survivor surveys the corpses of everyone else. "Horror at the sight of death," Canetti writes, "turns into satisfaction that it is someone else who is dead. . . . Whether the survivor is confronted by one dead man or by many, the essence of the situation is that he feels *unique*. He sees himself standing there alone and exults in it." As the general played by Adolphe Menjou in Stanley Kubrick's *Paths of Glory* says, "There are few things more fundamentally encouraging and stimulating than seeing someone else die." The peril to humankind of this exultation, writes Canetti, is multiplied by the circumstance that survival "can become a dangerous and insatiable passion" (230).

Like the impulse to form crowds, power is motivated by the desire to escape known or unknown threats. Francis Ford Coppola, a shrewd cinematic dissector of power, creates Canettian portraits of those who seek it in the *Godfather* trilogy (1972, 1974, 1990), *Apocalypse Now* (1979), and, in a different key, *The Conversation* (1974). All five films detail the growing alienation and paranoia of central figures who struggle to control others. Kubrick also returned regularly to portrayals of power and its paranoia, and one finds the same complex of themes across all of film history, from F. W. Murnau's *Faust* (1926) through its satiric retelling in Stanley Donen's *Bedazzled* (1967) and Taylor Hackford's *The Devil's Advocate* (1997)—to trace one small strand. Luc Besson's widely misunderstood *Messenger* (1999) portrays the inevitably tarnished origins of power and the temptations of its realization.

Movement toward tragedy in films, as in other narrative forms, generally emphasizes the increasing isolation of protagonists, an isolation that almost always parallels their pursuit and gaining of power. Predominantly comic stories, by contrast, move protagonists toward social integration—toward establishing or joining benignant crowds—and portray them successfully resisting or escaping power. Tragic heroes die alone. Their comic counterparts wind up with spouses and companions, families and communities. Witnessing such narratives, the audience itself is turned into a crowd whose members come together in both desire and gratification—their laughter and applause confirming their unity.

As in life, power in movies is often embodied in a threatening group: mobsters, a corrupt police force or other government agency, the dead (or the "living dead"), the "so and so gang" of innumerable westerns, and so on. The wickedness of these groups, which are usually packs rather than crowds, strongly tends to be concentrated in their leaders. They may be opposed by a more virtuous group with whom the audience is encouraged to sympathize or by heroes who do not flee evil—as ordinary, prudent people do—but seek to confront it. Yet even when heroes do battle as solitary protectors—Alan Ladd in *Shane* (Stevens, 1953) or James Arness almost weekly during the 1950s and 1960s on *Gunsmoke*—we understand them to be fighting on behalf of some crowd: "the people" (often "good," "decent," or "little"), society and its laws, homesteaders, or honest farmers. In their most peaceful forms, plots that evolve around conflicting double crowds lead to the ascension of an invigorated new group that displaces a declining one which has diminished crowd characteristics. The old group has ceased growing, dispersed, lost its sense of equality, or betrayed its goal—growth, density, equality, and direction, according to Canetti, being fundamental features of all crowds.

We might pause here to note one of the advantages Canetti offers for thinking about crowds in movies. For most viewers, one film crowd looks pretty much like another, and the energies that govern its behavior appear specific to the plot of the narrative in which it plays a part. As we see in the following chapters, Canetti's understanding of the fundamental qualities and dynamics of crowds allows us to discriminate among the often chaotic-appearing movie masses and relate them more precisely both to conflicts particular to their narratives and to representations of crowds in other films. The crowds at the beginning of *North by Northwest,* for example, display obvious growth, density, equality, and direction. But their direction, like the obscure motives of the movie's hero, doesn't seem to be leading anywhere more meaningful than into underground subways. When Roger Thornhill cuts ahead of a woman to commandeer her cab, he implicitly violates the principle of equality upon which crowds depend. Most of what threatens him thereafter occurs because of his removing himself from the protection of the masses. In Kurosawa's *Throne of Blood,* two Canettian insights into crowds are especially illuminating: the dynamics of antagonistic double crowds, and the governing drive of all open crowds toward increase. The masses in *Potemkin, Intolerance,* and *Citizen Kane* can be understood more clearly for Canetti's exposition of the relation of crowds to power. At the same time, they can be compared in ways made possible by the discriminations among differing groups that *Crowds and Power* sets forth. The central actions of rejoining and reuniting crowds in the films of Preston Sturges confirms that the warmth and generosity of their endings is not meretricious but follows logically from their understanding of their characters and of society.

If one believes what one reads and what one sees at the multiplexes, violent "action films" are targeted at and largely attended by people in their second decade of life. Such an audience has not yet experienced the complications and traps of power, which still appeals to them as an effective solution to human evils. They are perhaps particularly attracted to what Canetti called a "baiting crowd" and also to the idea of war as an instrument of justice. At this point, *Crowds and Power* offers a suggestive insight. Underlying the onset of violent mass hostilities, Canetti declares, we may discover the following train of thought: "I wish to kill, therefore I can be killed" (72). The violence of action movies can be seen as equivalent to rituals of sacrifice and power, rituals constructed to mollify the dreadful intimations of mortality that most people increasingly experience as they enter adolescence—and with which many of us, as Ernest Becker argues, never come to terms.[9] Like Becker, the literary critic Irving Massey laments that "our tepid consciousness is fully employed in disguising the truth about our destiny [death]."[10] As we shall see, the human terror of death and attempts to deny or evade its inevitability have profound, sometimes disastrous, consequences both individually and culturally.

Although a considerable number of movies cater to fantasies of force, many also enact the restoration or creation of what are portrayed as just and proper crowds. Even movies of revenge by single heroes or small groups typically end with some kind of social affirmation, a group or society welcoming back, acknowledging, or coming into being around the now-justified protagonists. Such social reintegration is signaled by the crowd scenes that make up the concluding or next-to-last sequences of a surprisingly large number of films. When the public confirmation occurs as the penultimate action, the final one is likely to show lovers at last alone, as at the end of Hitchcock's *Strangers on a Train* (1951) or Sturges's *The Lady Eve* (1941), and most of that director's other films as well. Often such endings have it both ways, with the now firmly established pair untroubled by other people but on a set dense with crowd symbols or with implied crowds nearby. The end of *Singin' in the Rain* (Donen and Kelly, 1952), with its crowd-invoking billboard behind the lovers, or of Ramis's *Groundhog Day* (1993), with the formerly alienated Phil having been at the center of the Punxsutawney celebrations, are typical examples of such conclusions.

Social confirmation and witnessing by crowds also occur at intermediate climactic moments. *The Truman Show* (Weir, 1998) and *Hero* (Frears, 1992), characteristic of recent movies in this respect, use images of television audiences and broadcasts to authenticate especially important turning points in the midst of the action, as well as at or near the conclusion. Among classic films, *Grand Illusion* (1937) and *Rules of the Game* (1939) exemplify Renoir's instinct to involve social groups during and around crucial events. Such appearances of crowds at critical narrative points occur frequently and function quite variously; all act, however, both to insert crowd dynamics into the film and to prompt the actual audience to "identify with" the crowd on screen, or to recall its own status as a crowd. An analogous example of inducing such identification is constructed near the end of the play *Marat/Sade* (Peter Weiss, 1964) when the spectators in the theater find themselves unwittingly conscripted into playing the part of the fictional audience at the asylum.

While movies mirror their audiences by presenting them with fictional ones, they also frequently encourage us to feel that plots resolve *because* the crowd (the one within and/or the real one watching) wishes it. Such a feeling solidifies both the crowd of the fiction and that in the theater. As Alfred Hitchcock's practice demonstrates, an audience's identification with the figures on the screen can be so strong that not only can it be encouraged to hope for the triumph of protagonists, but it can also be induced to desire the success—usually in the form of escape—of criminal antagonists of whom it simultaneously disapproves. The request in *Peter Pan* that we save Tinkerbell's life by declaring our belief in fairies explicitly addresses the audience's feeling of empowerment.

Movie viewers may be encouraged to feel that their wishes for power are being gratified by the elimination of a villain or the destruction of a numerous enemy. They are then appealed to as a crowd united in opposition. Audiences may also be prevailed upon to wish for the death of protagonists as well as antagonists. In such cases, death is shown as constructive because it effects integration into a succoring, sometimes overtly heavenly, crowd. John Huston had a particular fondness for stories in which dying frees characters from their loneliness or anguish and restores them to a peaceful, understanding group of people whose ultimate equality lies in their common mortality. He often represented such rejuvenating deaths symbolically, as by the sea and clouds at the end of *A Walk with Love and Death* (1969) or the snowy countryside at the end of *The Dead* (1987). At the conclusion of *Moulin Rouge* (1952), the sequence of Toulouse-Lautrec's perishing directly rejoins him to society, first through his father's report that his work is to be hung in the Louvre and then through the apparitions of his long-gone demimondaine acquaintances. In his determination to follow his genius as a painter, he exemplifies "the individual [who] gives himself to the group because of his desire to share in its immortality; [who] is willing to die in order not to die."[11]

As I have suggested, the exhibiting of movies, like their content, can often be understood as designed to create and sustain crowds. Identifying with people and their actions comes about through crowd dynamics as well as through individual fantasy. Common experience suggests that movies and television have in many societies become one of the preeminent creators and definers of crowds. There are "must see" movies every year and certain films—*Rebel without a Cause* (Ray, 1955), *The Graduate* (Nichols, 1967)—have been considered to speak for American youth of entire decades. Social subgroups, if they are not exactly defined by the motion pictures and television shows they watch, can be identified by them. "Must see" programs and movies will generally be quite different for suburban teenagers, conservative middle-class couples, liberal intellectuals, or born-again Christians. A film like *Forrest Gump* (Zemeckis, 1994) sets about in its narrative, and therefore in the audience it aspires to address, to include pretty much everyone.[12]

The egalitarian inclination of most narrative film—whether directed toward a broad audience or toward a subgroup—accounts to a considerable degree for its power to form crowds. The audience's feeling of equality goes in two directions, toward the figures on the screen and toward other people in the theater. "The most important occurrence within the crowd," Canetti writes, "is the *discharge*, . . . the moment when all who belong to the crowd get rid of their differences and feel equal" (17). For a motion picture audience, the discharge begins when the feature begins, the patrons hush or are shushed, and the crowd is unified in its expectations and behavior for the next two hours. If the movie successfully engages the audience, this sense of group concord will increase as the show runs, sometimes culminating in an apparently pointless outburst of applause. We may understand such applause as directed not toward the absent filmmakers, but rather as a concentrated expression of audience unity, a climactic discharge after which the crowd disintegrates and disperses. (These observations are equally true, I suspect, for concerts and other live performances. The applause and the increasingly frequent standing ovation express the accord of the auditors at the same time that they offer tributes to the performers—though in practice these aspects are inseparable. The demand for encores that protracted applause communicates may come as much from the crowd's desire to persist as a crowd as from its desire to hear more music—though again the two aspects are not easily separated.)

Among different audiences, conventions of spectatorship vary; but the relevant point is that such activity conforms to conventions observed by the overwhelming majority of those in attendance. The strong inhibition many people feel about leaving a movie during the show may well originate in the inclusive crowd feeling expected of the audience. Similarly, refusing to applaud or stand after a live performance when others are doing so marks one as rejecting membership in the crowd.

The discharge, the powerful moment of total equality, at once creates a crowd and anticipates its dissolution; for such equality is usually bound to a particular occasion and cannot long persist in the wider world with its differences of background, occupation, sex, economic status, and social affiliation. Because open, relatively spontaneous crowds typically lead short lives, those that wish to persist may convert to closed crowds, which limit their capacity for growth in exchange for increased longevity. Canetti analyzes this tactic in a section of *Crowds and Power* titled "Domestication of Crowds in World Religions." After a period of explosive growth and unbounded ambition, the movies, like religions, came to "see how difficult it is to hold one's ground" (24). Consequently, a good deal of the later development of the film industry has been devoted to attempting to sustain its crowds through time. Almost from the point at which attending films achieved the status of respectable leisure time entertainment, the idea of movie theaters as temples and moviegoing as similar to religious ritual has suggested itself. Jeffrey Richards asserts that "the neighborhood cinema had come to assume a place in the life of the community analogous to those other foci of leisure time activities, the church and the pub."[13]

Repetition becomes as important as growth; filmmaking companies aim to produce movies that will appeal to and build loyalty in certain audiences. Entertainment theme parks constitute an extreme manifestation of the desire to hold what were originally crowds of moviegoers. On a smaller scale, repertory-like production groups around directors like Sturges, Bergman, Truffaut, Woody Allen, or the Coen brothers do much the same thing, as do sequels and serials like the *Rocky* or *Flash Gordon* series. Fans of cult films, besides the regular repetition of their cinematic devotions, also define themselves as a small group of cognoscenti and serve as "crowd crystals," Canetti's term for a limited number of persons attached to a cause that might eventually attract a crowd when conditions become favorable. The occasional abrupt return to popularity of a classic or largely forgotten movie confirms the latter function of their devotees.

Ceremonies surrounding "going to the movies"—a phrase that bespeaks repetition—intensify one's sense of belonging to a defined group that repeatedly comes together. Driving to the theater, standing in lines at the ticket window and points of entrance, purchasing and consuming traditional food (for most Americans, popcorn) and drink, perusing reviews and advertisements, forming and joining fan clubs, and reading stories about stars all combine to emphasize the element of repetition. In the case of cult films, the social ritual may well be the most important aspect of the activity. About one such film, Bruce Austin writes, "By definition, veterans and regulars are devoted *Rocky* [*Horror Picture Show*] followers. The reasons for repeat attendance that they reported were largely social rather than related to qualities of the film itself."[14]

Canetti notes that mature religions have "a strong tendency to collect the faithful in separate units" (24); that is, to discourage them from forming open crowds. The regularization of show times and the end of the practice of allowing people to stay in movie houses for as long as they wish have obvious economic benefits for exhibitors and also seem to favor repetition over crowd growth. At the same time, however, the potential for an open, explosively growing crowd lurks deep in the soul of any domesticated one; and anticipation of a blockbuster picture—an anticipation that is itself now somewhat ritualized—continues as part of every summer and holiday season.

Whether the growth of home theater via VCRs, DVD players, and elaborate sound systems is part of such a trend remains to be seen. A recent article in the *New York Times* suggests that the tendency of movies to attract crowds—or at least packs—may be persisting in this relatively new form of consumption. In home theaters, watching movies and sporting events on TV "is becoming more of a communal ritual, shared with family and friends."[15] To one home theater installer, the old equation of movie watching with religion continues into this domesticated form of consumption: "It's an American temple and the screen is the altar."[16]

The impulse to form crowds, Canetti argues, arises from the primal terror of an unknown touch. The film theater palliates that fear. We sit concealed in a crowd of equals, able to see everything on the screen but safely unseen and untouchable by anything we are watching. Cavell writes that "the movies permit us to view [the world] unseen . . . not to need power."[17] At the same time, the dark sequestration of the auditorium protects us from outside threats, as does the sheer number of viewers. The unified sense of an audience can be effectively shattered by abruptly turning on bright lights, and most people of my acquaintance feel more secure in a crowded cinema than in a largely empty one. In *The Westerner* (Wyler, 1940), Roy Bean (Walter Brennan) makes himself fatally vulnerable when he buys out an entire performance of Lillie Langtree's opera, then watches it alone. Wyler emphasizes the point by cutting at a crucial moment outside to Bean's men, who mistake the sounds of the desperate gunfight inside for theatrical effects.

We might ask whether we feel the same security watching a film alone or in a small group on video as we do in a crowded theater. Does the very act of sitting in front of a movie imply that we are joining an audience, however dispersed in space it might be? Will current and future electronic technologies vastly multiply the opportunities for crowd formation, to the extent that they will have unprecedented power to affect or even direct events? The authoritarian society depicted in *Fahrenheit 451* (Truffaut, 1967) vividly portrayed some of the more alarming possibilities of such a society.

Such questions and my preceding speculations about how Canetti can inform our understanding of film audiences might be susceptible to testing, both by directly observing movie viewers and through continuing research in reception history. While I am neither a sociologist nor a specialist in the history of movie audiences, the relevant research with which I am familiar suggests that Canetti's ideas of crowd formation, especially as such formations are expanded by mass communications, are consonant with the history of early cinema and its growth into a global industry and cultural force. Looking at the history of moviegoing in one of the most carefully theorized recent studies of cinema audiences, the authors remark, "There is a strong sense that the importance of cinema lay in its social and community function as much as, if not more than, in the films it presented."[18] The title of another volume declares the intimate relation between modern social history and the movies: *Cinema and the Invention of Modern Life.*[19] Current research on movie audiences and on the social history of film exhibition and reception, however, has little to say about theorizing the film audience as a crowd. It is to that issue that Canetti may most usefully speak.

As David Bordwell has remarked, "In the writing of film history, the distinction between the humanities and the social sciences can become fairly thin."[20] Even if I were competent to dissolve that distinction, this book would become excessively long and diffuse if it attempted to cover both the economic-social applications of crowd theory to moviegoing and its use in what is known as practical criticism. The historical and social settings of any work of art and its interpretation as a relatively self-contained object are mutually dependent, of course, and I have attempted to give some sense of that mutuality in this introduction. I hope that there might be useful substance in my suggestions of how Canetti's ideas about crowds are relevant to the study of movie audiences and reception. The focus of this study, however, will be on the themes of crowds, power, and transformation as they are represented in particular films. At the same time, of necessity, those analyses will add some central ideas of *Crowds and Power* to the varied perspectives of current film studies.

Like literature, painting, and sculpture, film is wonderfully well suited to representing the sort of transformations that many critics and aestheticians identify as occupying the center of the human imagination. Movies are a literal art of image-ination. Their power to transform people and the world, moreover, is directly connected with their ability to represent crowds. Underlying that tight connection is the equality, the profound empathy that both transformation and crowds require. For either crowds or transformations to be fully achieved, people must experience others as themselves.

Cinematic set designers and choreographers have instinctively grasped the deep attachment between the cinema's facility for metamorphosis and its ability to represent crowds. No one realized that capacity more vividly than Busby Berkeley. Among numerous examples, the celebrated production number near the end of *42nd Street* (Bacon, 1933) shows as well as any Berkeley's practice of transforming rhythmic crowds of people into crowd symbols (here, blocks of buildings). Cinema typically makes concrete the close association between literal crowds and symbolic ones: the shots of ripe apples and grain associated with the villagers in Dovzhenko's *Earth* (1930); the warring double crowds of cattlemen and farmers associated respectively with the symbols of fire and corn in *The Westerner,* symbols assigned to the same conflicting groups in *Oklahoma!* (Zinnemann, 1955); and the "Sorcerer's Apprentice" section of Disney's *Fantasia* (1940), in which transformation, crowds, and crowd symbols become inseparable. These examples are quite arbitrarily chosen; thousands of other films contain similar fusing of crowds with their symbols.

As movies create and represent crowds, they also catalyze transformation. Their ability to reshape existential audiences or make them more empathetic may be best investigated by sociologists and psychologists, but representations of transformation fall into the critic's domain. The capacity of the cinema to show metamorphoses could hardly be more striking, as filmmakers and audiences have understood since motion pictures began. In the movies,

Dancers trans-
formed into
crowd symbols
in *42nd Street*

people can turn into other people, animals, or even objects. Charlie Chaplin can become a chicken in his famished partner's eyes and can transform dinner rolls into dancers in his own dream (*The Gold Rush*, 1925). Buster Keaton can enter into the film that he is projecting and become a great detective in *Sherlock, Jr.* (1924) or be "the whole show"—musicians, ticket-taker, audience, and performers—in *The Playhouse* (1921). Cocteau repeatedly explored the transformative power of the cinema. *The Matrix* (A. and L. Wachowski, 1999) and *Being John Malkovich* (Jonze, 1999) are among a host of recent films centered on transformation.

Crowds and Power offers two especially fertile sets of conceptions toward a deeper understanding of cinematic transformations. First, as we have seen, it connects the processes of transformations with the dynamics of crowds. Second, Canetti distinguishes transformation from partial- or pseudo-transformations. The dreadful metamorphoses of countless horror films can be understood as false transformations because they are not additive or reversible; that is, people either entirely lose themselves to the new personality (*Dr. Jekyll and Mr. Hyde*) or are unable to return to their original, single identity and remain fixed in a double existence. Discussing "clean transformations" among the Bushmen, Canetti writes, "The individual identity which the Bushman gives up is preserved in the transformation. He can become this or that, but 'this' and 'that' remain separate from each other, for between transformations he always becomes himself again" (341). Failed transformations may be aborted or arrested before they are complete. Faked ones serve the ends of power; they constitute dissimulation rather than true metamorphosis.

The primacy of transformation recalls Aristotle's assertion in *The Poetics* that poetry derives from the innate human instinct for imitative representation (*mimesis*). In *The Conscience of Words,* a collection of his essays, Canetti wrote, "The true essence of myths is the metamorphoses practiced in them. It is through them that man has created himself. It is through them that he has made the world his own, through them that he takes part in the world."[21] Where does one find metamorphosis more often or more strikingly than in the movies? Movies are engaged in creating us, as all art does, continually and anew. They are re-creation, indeed. Films characteristically ponder, sometimes explicitly and often implicitly, their own wondrous power of mimetic transformation. As a character in Canetti's play *The Comedy of Vanity* remarks, "Without his own image, man amounts to nothing."[22] Movies, preeminently in our time, show us our own image. To understand the cinema is to understand what the cinema makes of us.

Crowds and Power provides richly suggestive ideas about the qualities, dynamics, and transmutations of various kinds of crowds and a precisely articulated terminology for analyzing them. Although it can hardly aspire to be the last word on crowds—and Canetti himself insists on this point—it offers a multitude of clues as to where and how we might look at their representation in the cinema. It provides at least a preliminary set of ordering principles, a provisional template, for considering the heretofore rather neglected topic of crowds and movies. It also sets forth an original, fertile understanding of power, an alternative or supplement to those of individualistic psychologies and structuralist or post-structuralist cultural conceptions. Through his analysis of the imaginative metamorphosis that Canetti calls "transformation," moreover, his understanding of the motives and manifestations of power is fundamentally integrated with his understanding of crowds. *Crowds and Power* thus also serves to direct us toward connecting aspects of film narratives that have only rarely been regarded as strongly related.

A brief explanation may be in order regarding my reasons for choosing the films discussed in the following chapters—a selection that is deliberately eclectic. First, the films and fragments of films to which I turn in this study have, for the most part, neither slumbered nor slept in popular and academic consciousness. On the contrary, many have been repeatedly analyzed. Certain shots, patterns of images and themes, and broadly unifying conceptions, however, await fuller comprehension. Many of these ignored, bewildering, or dubiously understood aspects come into clearer focus when we turn our attention to their representations of crowds, power, and transformation. Second, I have tried to select films that illustrate different aspects of the themes to which *Crowds and Power* points: various sorts of crowds and crowd dynamics, power in different guises and in different relations to crowds, transformations that are successful, partial, deceptive, or thwarted, and so on. Since these three central terms are intimately connected in practice, all appear to some degree in the explications of the movies that are analyzed. Among the different films, however, those themes appear in different manifestations and with different degrees of emphasis. The films discussed in the first section illustrate in quite diverse ways the complementary and frequently antagonistic relationship

18

between crowds and power while those in the second section share especially emphatic emphases on predation and transformation. As I have already noted, however, all those elements are found to some degree in all the films that are analyzed in those sections.

North by Northwest, for example, is impressively stocked with images of predation, images that become even more prominent in the last two films this study analyzes. At the same time, however, while on its surface it may seem to have little to do with crowds, it is centrally concerned with the relation of the individual to both the masses of people that make up society and to the smaller precursors of crowds, packs. Two silent classics, *Potemkin* and *Intolerance,* exemplify the importance of crowds in cinema from its early period. The progression of the narrative in Eisenstein's famous work follows to a remarkable degree Canetti's description of how crowds come into being, grow, reshape themselves, and spread. Griffith's great film consistently sets the workings of multiple crowds in opposition to the masters of power. He places the heroines and heroes of the four narratives between those two forces, generally (but not always) showing them attacked by the powerful and supported and protected by the masses of common people. The comic heroes of the four Sturges comedies discussed in the first section lose or reject crowds, the regaining of which is immensely significant in the happy endings they at last achieve. An especially threatening crowd, that of the dead, plays a central role in *Throne of Blood,* which also powerfully uses its forest imagery as a crowd symbol. Welles's revered *Citizen Kane* embodies the conflict of crowds and power within a single individual, a conflict that gives it much of its tragic energy. The least known of these films, Charles Burnett's poignant *Killer of Sheep,* shows people who live much of the time as prey—the very condition that, according to Canetti, humans form crowds or seek power to avoid. *The Silence of the Lambs,* the last of the films analyzed, continues that focus on predation at the same time that it provides a fertile text in which to explore varieties both of successful transformation and metamorphic failures.

As I have observed, all but one of these movies comprise cinematic ground that has been much surveyed; new configurations in them will become evident only through a genuinely new perspective. These films, moreover, vary sharply among themselves in terms of genre, historical period, country of origin, and circumstances of production. They represent a considerable cross-section of filmic kinds, and therefore they test what we might call the explanatory breadth of the ideas with which this study approaches them, the degree to which those ideas enable perception into very diverse works. At the same time, the various times and place of production and of genre of these movies also serves to some degree to test the universalist aspects of Canetti's humanist thought.

Such a radically diverse selection of films, however, must appear—indeed, be—somewhat arbitrary. This study has a number of goals—among them to introduce a thinker, Elias Canetti, who will be new to most of its readers and at the same time to say something about his thought that might interest those familiar with his writing; to extend our understanding of films that have attracted much of the best analysis that film studies has produced; to suggest some further directions for audience and reception studies; and to address not only film studies students and professionals but also others interested in ideas that can lead to a more profound understanding of the humanities and the subject that label implies. As Kantians might say, this work must be propaedeutic, a preliminary to deeper, more detailed thought. Regarding the selection of the films that serve as case studies for these objectives, recall what Chabrol and Rohmer wrote in their groundbreaking book on the director around whom film study's most prolific industry has since flourished: "The number of Hitchcockian stories in the world is certainly very large . . . a good third if not a half of all those that have been written until now."[23] Analogously, a startlingly large proportion of the movies that have been made to date exemplify ideas and dynamics that could be understood, one way or another, as Canettian. I have chosen to analyze a few that seem especially well suited to open a path for such thinking about the cinema, but I have no doubt that another selection of works could have served nearly as well.

Nonetheless, all the movies analyzed in the following chapters seem to me to be worthy of continuing attention; all still have a good deal to teach us about our societies and ourselves. In my experience of them over a number of years, they have maintained their depth, liveliness, beauty, and mystery. Approaching them from another angle does not "explain" those qualities; rather, it intensifies and expands them.

PART I

POWER VERSUS CROWDS

Crowds and Power in Two Silent Films:

Eisenstein's *The Battleship Potemkin* and Griffith's *Intolerance*

Moving pictures have an affinity for crowds, both in their imagery and in their distribution and consumption. That affinity made itself evident early in the history of the cinema and was well understood in the practice of many filmmakers by the middle of the silent era. Vachel Lindsey wrote, "While the motion picture is shallow in showing private passion, it is powerful in conveying the passions of masses of men."[1] In this chapter we look at two enormously influential silent films, Eisenstein's *The Battleship Potemkin* and D. W. Griffith's *Intolerance*. The first of these films illustrates with remarkable aptness the four qualities of crowds that Canetti identified as fundamental: their drives toward growth, equality, and density, and their clearly defined "direction" or goal. The second both illustrates the same fundamental crowd attributes and embodies a more complex imagining and anatomizing of crowds. Many of the crowds of both *Potemkin* and *Intolerance* fit Canetti's description of principal types—double crowds, "*Festmassen*" (translated by Stewart as "Feast Crowds" but more generally understood in *Crowds and Power* as festival crowds, crowds in a holiday mood), Prohibition Crowds, Baiting Crowds, and so on. Griffith's sprawling movie also quite strikingly illuminates the often antagonistic relations between crowds and power.

Potemkin

A consequence of the affinity between film and crowds, again early perceived and acted upon, is the suitability of motion pictures for the creation of propaganda—or, more generally, politically tendentious stories and spectacles. Eisenstein was one of many Soviet film-makers in the 1920s who conceived their films as celebrations, advertisements, and justifications of the Russian revolution. *Potemkin* clearly fits into that category. It has long been most famous for its remarkable editing and design; the action on the Odessa Steps, indeed, may be the best known and most imitated single sequence in motion picture history.

The rhetoric and architecture of *Potemkin* as a whole, however, can be seen with greater clarity through an inspection of it both as a tour de force of montage and as an honoring of the Russian Revolution conceived as the development of crowds and their transformations. The valorization of the masses in Eisenstein's film was noticed by most reviewers worldwide during its first showings. Of the dozens of reviews collected in Herbert Marshall's *The Battleship Potemkin: The Greatest Film Ever Made,* the majority point out that Eisenstein's heroes are not individuals but crowds.[2] Typical are "He knows that the Revolution *is not a personality but the masses*" and "In *Potemkin* there is no individual hero. . . . The mass acts."[3] Twenty-five years later, looking back at Eisenstein's masterpiece, Pudovkin wrote, "The masses of the people in this film ceased to be a gray, general background for the actions of a small number of special heroes. They pushed forward and became themselves the hero of the film."[4] Similarly, Parker Tyler: "*Potemkin* was at once revolutionary Russia's notice to the world of its 'populist' philosophy—that collective man, not merely an individual may be projected as a hero."[5] Although everyone acknowledges *Potemkin* to be a film of the masses, only David Bordwell has followed that perception further, relating it to Eisenstein's creation of types as constituents of his "mass protagonist."[6] If we invoke Canetti's analysis of crowds, however, we will be able to discover in considerably more detail *how* the film organizes its structure and figures forth its meanings through its progressively transforming masses.

The five parts of *The Battleship Potemkin* are divided according to their representation of crowds coming into being and metamorphosing into other forms. Part 1 portrays the development of a "Prohibition Crowd," which in part 2 becomes a "Reversal Crowd." Part 3 witnesses in Odessa the growth of an enormous throng, which arises in response to rumors of rebellion on the battleship *Potemkin* and then becomes a "Lamenting Crowd" when it encounters the body of the seaman Vakulinchuk. Part 4 stages two crowds, a "Feast Crowd" that carries food to the *Potemkin* and that cele-

Crowd symbol
and crowd in
Eisenstein's *The
Battleship
Potemkin*

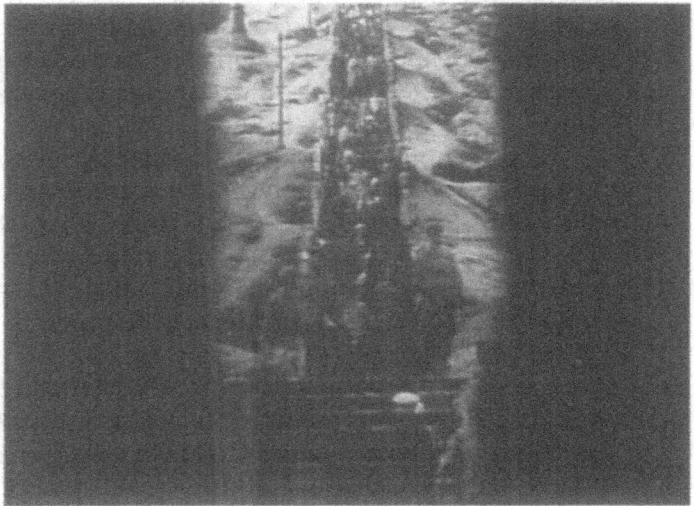

brates the liberation of its recruits, and the "Flight Crowd" into which it abruptly changes when the Cossacks begin their massacre. In part 5, the group of liberated sailors who have ascended to command of the battleship acts as a crowd crystal and leads the rest of the squadron to join it in revolution. The sailors' uprising had a similar function with respect to the citizenry of Odessa. The fifth part functions as both a coda and, by implication, as part 1 for the greater story to which *Potemkin* serves as prelude.

As is common in cinema, the imagery of crowds in *Potemkin* appears both as literal congregations of people and as crowd symbols. For *Potemkin* the most frequent crowd symbols are the sea and several flights of masonry stairs in Odessa. The latter are always associated with masses of people, which usually cover them. In a particularly explicit equation of steps with the citizens who tread them, Eisenstein dissolves a vignetted shot of a long flight of empty hillside stairs into a shot of the same stairs covered by a streaming crowd.

The opening shots of the film alternate between waves crashing against a breakwater and other waves rolling onto rocks backed by a wall. As early as 1915, Vachel Lindsay had observed, "The sea of humanity is dramatically blood-brother to the Pacific, Atlantic, or Mediterranean."[7] Not only do such images of the sea function as crowd symbols, but they also reflect the mood of the action. Bordwell notes, "Like the waves that crash on shore in the opening shots, rebellion steadily gathers force."[8] Discussing the much longer work that Eisenstein originally projected, of which *Potemkin* was to have been only a part, James Goodwin relates that the waves were to have been preceded by another crowd symbol: "The mutiny in June was to link parts three and four, with a cut from wind-tossed fields of grain to a stormy sea marking the transition."[9] The waves at the beginning of *Potemkin,* then, suggest the turbulence of the times (as does the turbulent river at the end of Pudovkin's *Mother*), an equation that was made all but explicit in the epigraph that Eisenstein selected to precede the marine images in the original release prints: "The spirit of insurrection hovered over the Russian land. Some enormous and mysterious process was taking place in countless hearts. The individual was dissolving in the mass, and the mass was dissolving in the outburst."[10]

Other prominent aquatic crowd symbols include the mist that overspreads the harbor after Vakulinchuk's killing and reinforces the subdued, solemn mood of the film after that event. The small waves of a calm sea the night before the *Potemkin*'s possible fight with the rest of the squadron are succeeded by a stormy sea as the battleship approaches its likely foes. In a shot whose content and composition recall the dissolve from empty to thronged stairs, we see a long sea wall covered not by crashing waves but by people. Related to the imagery of sea and mist, repeated shots of a simmering broth made of rotten meat at once express the simmering anger of the seamen who will be asked to eat it and portray one of the causes of their rebellion. The sailors define themselves as a crowd in opposition both to their commanders and to the masses of maggots infesting their meat.

In *Potemkin*, as in *Crowds and Power*, armed forces are regarded not as a form of crowds but as contrasting with them. Hierarchical military discipline is constructed on commands, and armies must avoid becoming crowds in order to function effectively. The equality of crowds, on the other hand, releases its members from command and social stratification. Of all the conflicts in Eisenstein's film, most can be seen as arising between an elitist, alienating military and democratic, fraternal crowds. Part 1 makes this opposition between army and crowd abundantly clear, and it will be reiterated throughout the film, most obviously on the Odessa steps. The seamen's defiance of the commands of their officers initiates the revolution that the Lenin quotation at the opening of prints subsequent to 1935 declares to be "the only lawful, rightful, just, and truly great war."

As many have pointed out, wars are always started by the other side—in *Potemkin*, the tsar's officers. Most implications that the officers initiated the conflict involve crowd symbols. The teeming maggots are a crowd symbol of a particular sort, one that Canetti identifies with the fantasies of paranoiacs and others who suffer from the disease of power. The larvae typify the conceptions that warring crowds have of their foes. Such vermin represent a crowd whose individuals have nothing to do with true humanity, who can be destroyed with impunity and deserve only contempt. That the ship's doctor and the officer with him assign maggot-infested food to the men and assure them that it is, for them, "good meat" represents something very like a declaration of war in itself. As is implied by the title of part 1, "The Men and the Maggots," the sailors are identified by their superiors with worms. Such an identification moves them outside the pale of human sympathy; it renders them in the eyes of their commanders no better than vermin and therefore fit for slaughter. The dehumanization becomes explicit at the beginning of Part 2 when the captain tells restive sailors, "I'll shoot you down like dogs!" He then orders them covered with a tarpaulin before they are to be shot, thereby lowering them further to no more than an animated mound of canvas.

As Eisenstein indicts such behavior by the officers, he nonetheless applies the strategy cinematically to his villains. The officers who stand by awaiting the execution are represented not by their faces but by their legs and coat bottoms. From the early shots of sleeping men in their hammocks through the numberless but individualized faces of the crowds of Odessa, Eisenstein carefully emphasizes the diverse human identities of those on the "rightful, just" side. By contrast, the Cossacks are mostly so many mannequins in uniform and weapons: trousers, boots, backs of military coats, rifles and bayonets. More individualized characterizations of officers and, notably, the cowardly, hirsute ship's priest at the same time dissolve their identities into villainous stereotypes. By cross-cutting, the priest's crucifix is equated with swords and guns, and he prays that "the unruly may be brought to reason"—presumably by murdering them. Consistent with such characterization, the throwing of officers overboard amounts to feeding the fishes with garbage; Vakulinchuk, on the other hand, is "murdered" by a "butcher." The defeat of the commanders is equated with their total destruction.

The rebellion finds its seed when some of the men on the *Potemkin* begin to change from sailors into members of a prohibition crowd. "A special type of crowd is created by a *refusal:* a large number of people together refuse to continue to do what, till then, they had done singly. They obey a prohibition, and this prohibition is sudden and self-imposed" (55). Under the disapproving eye of a fastidious-looking officer, a group of seamen inspect the rotten meat destined for them and declare that they have had enough of such food. Despite assurances that the maggots are harmless and can be washed away, they refuse to eat the soup made from the meat and instead buy canned goods from the ship's store. Eisenstein then cuts among numerous sailors talking angrily, presumably about the rotten meat. The moment at which we see unequivocally that they have become a prohibition crowd occurs when a sailor washing dishes smashes a plate, outraged by the writing on its brim, "Give us this day our daily bread." Such an act gives a crowd its voice; the noise of breaking crockery can be for a crowd "the applause of objects. . . , the destruction of a hierarchy which is no longer recognized" (19).

The refusal to eat the soup leads, at the beginning of part 2, to an assembly on deck, where the behavior of the sailors is treated as insubordination. At the same time, the men increasingly act as a crowd rather than as members of an army. When the guard is called, Matyushenko passes the word for the sailors to meet at the turret and they begin to wander toward it. It is important to note that the genesis of this rebellion precedes Matyushenko's leadership and the crucial intervention of Vakulinchuk a few minutes later. We know from an early scene that these two are ready to join the proletarian revolution that has begun to sweep Russia, but they do not create it. It arises on the *Potemkin* (and, by implication, elsewhere) without an identifiable provocateur. Contrary to the common view of crowds, including Freud's, as creations of their leaders, Eisenstein here portrays the revolution as arising spontaneously from a mass of people that suffers the same provocations and finds its leaders slightly later. Such a dynamic is very much in accord with Canetti's understanding of crowds. They are, as he says, "a mysterious and universal phenomenon . . . suddenly there" (16). Similarly, in his book on English soccer mobs, Bill Buford argues, "A crowd can never be formed against its will, and it is the great fallacy about the crowd that it can be: this is the leadership fallacy, the rabble-ready-to-be-roused theory."[11]

When Vakulinchuk shouts, "Brothers! Who are you shooting at?" he at once restores humanity to the huddling creatures beneath the tarpaulin and inspires the riflemen to join the prohibition crowd of the recruits. Immediately thereafter, as the officers attempt to compel the riflemen to fire, the prohibition crowd abruptly transforms into a reversal crowd. Key to such a reversal is the throwing off of restraints, a point emphasized in the film by shots of the rescued men coming out from under the tarpaulin and, as the rebellion becomes active, further images of the vacated canvas fluttering on the deck. Low camera angles of men rushing over barred walkways give further emphasis to the action of casting off restraints and crossing boundaries. (Thirty-three years later, Akira Kurosawa imitated these shots in a similar context, the rebellion of the slaves in *The Hidden Fortress*.)

In *Crowds and Power* Canetti turns to packs in order "to explore the origins of the behavior of crowds" (94). Of particular importance for understanding the dynamics of packs, and therefore of crowds, is the tendency of various kinds of packs "to change into one another" (127). *The Battleship Potemkin* portrays a series of such transmutations. Restrained and provoked, the prohibition crowd turns into a reversal crowd. Of prohibition crowds Canetti writes, "If it is assailed or besieged, the negative crowd tends to revert to a positive and active one" (57). The commands—many of them manifestly unreasonable—to which the sailors are subjected lead them first to form a prohibition crowd, then a reversal crowd. The latter accounts for most revolutionary activity: "A revolutionary situation can be defined as this state of reversal, and a crowd whose discharge consists mainly in its collective deliverance from the stings of command should be called a 'reversal crowd'" (59).

With the announcement of victory for the uprising, the reversal has achieved its aim and we would expect the crowd to disperse. But a lingering officer shoots Vakulinchuk, whose fatal wounding precipitates the formation of a "Lamenting Pack." This pack comes together immediately after Vakulinchuk has been wounded; as Canetti notes, the lamenting pack often arises before the actual death of the sick or injured person (105). With his death, the lamenting pack carries him away from the ship, an act that will allow him to become an effective martyr for the cause of the revolution. The mist that condenses around the harbor and the body that has been left on the pier by Vakulinchuk's honor guard prefigures the crowd that will soon appear.

Attracted by rumors of the uprising on the *Potemkin* and of a dead sailor, people in Odessa begin to gather. Eisenstein's portrayal of their coming together vividly illustrates the most fundamental attributes that Canetti ascribes to the formation of "natural" crowds: growth, direction, density, and equality. Growth and direction are embodied by a four-minute sequence entirely devoted to the swelling crowd, to its streaming along streets, up and down stairs, and across bridges and breakwaters as it moves toward the waterfront. Its density increases enormously, as Eisenstein emphasizes at the end of the sequence with a shot looking straight down on the mass of people packed around the tent sheltering Vakulinchuk's body.

After documenting the Odessa crowd's growth, density, and direction, Eisenstein turns to the fourth of the characteristics that Canetti identifies as fundamental to crowds, equality. Besides individualizing the members of the Odessa crowd, he emphasizes their diversity and, therefore, the mass's inclusiveness: workers and members of the middle class; the old, middle-aged, young adults, and children; fashionable women in white dresses with parasols and well-dressed men ("shoulder to shoulder," as an intertitle redundantly informs us) beside peasant women in dark shawls and men in rough working clothes. This breaking of social barriers, one of the principal attractions of a crowd, expands on the Odessa Staircase to include an amputee and—famously—an infant.[12] At the end of the earlier sequence that shows the throng in Odessa, further intertitles underscore its unity and equality: "Mothers, sisters, brothers!" declares one. "Let nothing divide us!" Men and women sing, "One for all and all for one," while the image alternates between their faces and repetitions of the high-shot of the crowd surrounding Vakulinchuk's makeshift tomb.

For Canetti, as for *The Battleship Potemkin*, equality is the signal virtue of the natural crowd:

> One might even define a crowd as a state of absolute equality. A head is a head, an arm is an arm, and differences between individual heads and arms are irrelevant. It is for the sake of this equality that people become a crowd and they tend to overlook anything which might detract from it. All demands for justice and all theories of equality ultimately derive their energy from the actual experience of equality familiar to anyone who has been part of a crowd. (29)

Recalling these words on equality and equity, we should note that part 3 of Eisenstein's film, the section devoted to the gathering and transformation of the crowd in Odessa, is titled "A Dead Man Calls for Justice."

An incident near the end of part 2 emphasizes the determined concord of the crowd. A cigarette-smoking, cynical-looking middle-class man calls out, "Kill the Jews!" His attempt to divide the masses produces not a burst of anti-Semitism but outrage. People pummel him to the street and the crowd, in its cohesiveness, closes over him.[13]

"The inner, or pack, dynamics of war are basically as follows," Canetti writes. "From the lamenting pack around a dead man there forms a war pack bent on avenging him; and from the war pack, if it is victorious, a triumphant pack of increase" (138). These dynamics are played out in the sequences described above and in those that immediately follow them. The lamenting pack brings both

A crowd of boats "streamed to the battleship"

tidings of the shipboard uprising and Vakulinchuk's body. Its coming leads, as we have seen, to the gathering on the shore of a crowd. When the crowd reaches its maximum density, the message on the corpse, "Killed for a plate of soup," galvanizes it to cry for revenge and to move from lament toward war. It understands itself to be joining the rebellion of the sailors. Back on the ship, the sailors now explicitly consider themselves part of a war crowd: "Together with the workers of Russia, we shall fight and win." The multitude in Odessa cheers from the great staircase and the war pack seems to feel that by its very act of defiance it has triumphed.

The beginning of part 4 continues to follow the transformational outline that Canetti sketched thirty-five years after Eisenstein's film. The war crowd in its premature celebration of victory transforms into a feast/increase crowd. "Boats streamed to the battleship" from the harbor and in so doing add yet another crowd symbol to those saturating the film. (This crowd of boats anticipates another one, the naval squadron at the end of the movie, which will join with the Potemkin to form further seaborne images of crowd unity.) Carrying fowl, pigs, hams, eggs, and other food-stuffs to the *Potemkin,* the sailboats are intercut with shots of people streaming to the harbor and waving in celebration from the great staircase.

At the height of the festivities, however, the multitude undergoes yet another transformation, this time into a flight crowd as it is attacked by the tsar's anonymous, merciless soldiers. In a way, the fleeing throng on the steps brings the main plot full circle. The action began with sailors who refused to eat their soup and who then wished to flee their sentence; but some were blocked and confined under the tarpaulin. That death sentence gave rise to the reversal crowd aboard ship, to the lamenting crowd that gathered around Vakulinchuk and that metamorphosed into a war crowd and then a feast crowd. But the attack on the gathered people of Odessa returns them to what Canetti finds to be the most fundamental crowd, one easily observable in all social animals including humans, the flight crowd. Partly cut off from escape by fences and mounted soldiers, the Odessa crowd begins to disintegrate into a panic. Those who fall behind die. When the crowd loses its unity, it loses its strength. The attempt of a few women to stem the panic and talk the soldiers out of their slaughter does not have the success that Vakulinchuk had with the ship's guard, and the peace-makers are gunned down.

The Potemkin's guns revenge the massacre by destroying the symbols of the antagonistic crowd, its headquarters in the opera house and its stone lions. At the same time, the demolition of the building and its statuary serves the purposes that Canetti details in a section early in *Crowds and Power* entitled "Destructiveness." "The crowd particularly likes destroying houses and objects," he notes. It hears the crashing of destruction as "the robust sounds of fresh life," "the cries of something new-born" (19). Thus the naval bombardment declares the revival of the war crowd that the events on the *Potemkin* have precipitated, applauds its growth, and anticipates its expansion to the fleet in the final section of the film, "The Meeting with the Squadron."

That meeting is energized by suspense and is packed with crowd symbols: the machinery of the ship; the waves of the sea (small the night before the encounter then breaking against the ships as the possibility of battle looms); the fleet of ships and the smoke that streams from their many stacks; and finally the decks

"Fresh life" in *The Battleship Potemkin*

dense with sailors. For a while, it appears that the only crowd remaining is a hostile one; a title inverts the earlier slogan of unity
into "All against one." But the sailors of the flag squadron join
those of the revolutionary ship and the last minute of the film is
devoted to triumphant images of the new, greater crowd that results, with shots of throngs of sailors waving from the decks and
turrets of the squadron intercut with the familiar crowd symbols of
sea, smoke, and ships. When the *Potemkin*'s appeal to "join us" succeeds in extending the uprising to the sailors of the oncoming fleet,
the crew of the battleship again functions as a crowd crystal and as
fathers to their own new "brothers."

For all the energy of part 5, it remains not so much the conclusion of the film as its coda. It represents the propagation of the
tidal surge unleashed by the uprising on the battleship and in
Odessa, a widening social storm anticipated by the oceanic imagery
of the opening sequence. The growth of a small refusal pack into a
massive war crowd stands as a metonym for the Russian Revolu-

tion. Retrospectively, the inheritors of that revolution create their film to celebrate its success and to memorialize its martyrs.

That *Potemkin* represents the revolution as a triumph of the masses hardly comes as news. Its structure and the rhetorical force of its message are clarified, however, when we apprehend Eisenstein's rigorous portrayal of the formation and transformations of crowds as the keys to its narrative sequence and the organization of its imagery. Because of the striking consonance of Eisenstein's representation of crowd dynamics with Canetti's analyses in *Crowds and Power*, we not only understand better the internal logic of the film's crowds but also begin to account for the sense of universality that arises from its semihistorical details. Although critics generally devote their attention to such formal aspects as montage, composition, and rhythm, *The Battleship Potemkin* does have a plot, the specific shape of which a detailed understanding of its crowd images helps us to perceive. The linked creation of two crowds and their subsequent metamorphoses compose the Aristotelian imitation of an action that gives *Potemkin* its unity. As we have seen, these transformations occur neither randomly nor simply in response to the pressures of the action. On the contrary, they drive the action as much as they are determined by it. The transmutation of the masses in *Potemkin* takes place in accordance with identifiable, characteristic generic and kinetic patterns. Developing a typology and a physics of such crowd transformations composes most of the first half of *Crowds and Power*. With its aid, the specific shapes and energies underlying the crowds in Eisenstein's film come into sharp focus. They appear familiar, almost inevitable.

The artist here precedes the scientist. Eisenstein implicitly anticipates in his film the anatomy of crowd qualities and transformations that Canetti was just beginning to analyze at almost the same time. That fact is far from rendering *Crowds and Power* redundant for our understanding of *Potemkin*, however. We see Eisenstein's film more sharply with the added light of *Crowds and Power*, just as we comprehend *Crowds and Power* more vividly and practically by interleaving its ideas with the images and events of *The Battleship Potemkin*.

Intolerance

David Wark Griffith's massive *Intolerance* is dense both with the crowds of its proverbial cast of thousands and with the crowd symbols of its elaborate sets. Moreover, its structure, its multiplication of plots, multiplies by four the number of its crowds. Like the film as a whole, crowds in Griffith's sprawling epic are more complex than in Eisenstein's compact, unified *Potemkin*. Nonetheless, crowds and their precursors, packs, play central roles in each of its four parallel stories. So does power, often labeled in the intertitles as "ambition." If Griffith's portrayal of crowds in *Intolerance* does not precisely duplicate Canetti's understanding, it comes remarkably close. His portrayal of power—isolated, without the capacity for imaginative empathy, and usually characterized by force—also matches Canetti's in most respects. As in *Crowds and Power*, neither crowds nor power are simple matters in Griffith's film. Canetti does not so much simplify our perception of Griffith's teeming work as help us to organize our understanding of its complexity.

The introductory titles announce that the parallel plots of Griffith's film will "show how hatred and intolerance, through all the ages, have battled against love and charity." "Hatred and intolerance," as we shall see, are approximately synonymous with power. The loving, forgiving adversaries of intolerant enmity, on the other hand, are associated with the positive qualities of crowds. Power in *Intolerance* generally originates with individuals who are isolated from other people and whose normal fear of death, whether straightforward or sublimated, has assumed pathological forms. "Love and charity" are usually associated either directly with crowds and crowd symbols or with what Canetti specified as the fundamental crowd attributes of growth, density, and equality. Direction, the fourth of the basic crowd attributes, has a more equivocal status for Griffith. It is often associated with modalities of power: force, a penchant for viewing opponents as sub-human, self-righteousness, and paranoia. As a consequence, even though his vision of love and charity tends to reproduce the dynamics of democratic masses, Griffith does not romanticize crowds. Crowds in *Intolerance* can variously be antagonistic to power, independent of it, or corruptible and exploitable by it.

Generally speaking, the crowds of Griffith's "Sun Play of the Ages" are on the side of love and charity, and opposed to intolerance. Crowd symbols have similar associations. The sociable streams of workers going to the mill early in the modern story leave behind them the reassuring crowd symbols of vine-covered cottages; and Griffith shows the most important single figure, "the Dear One," in a yard which, besides the usual twinkling foliage, also includes an animated mix of chickens, geese, and goslings.

The Dear One "having the time of her life"

Later the mill workers will form a rhythmic crowd of celebration at their annual dance. When they join hands and skip about the floor, they form an exuberant line that the Dear One, "having the time of her life," excitedly joins. The line dance in particular emphasizes the crowd's capacities for growth, density, and equality. The happy conclusion of the modern story, like that of most comedies, features the restoration of a sympathetic crowd gathering around reunited lovers and emblematizing the rejuvenation of society.

Early in the same story, Miss Jenkins, still hopeful of belonging to the world of youth and love, sponsors a ball, an activity she will abandon and even persecute when she exchanges an amorous social world for the suppressive power of the Uplifters. The wage cut that her brother imposes to support her censorious activities leads to the transformation of the happy, productive mass of workers into a prohibition crowd of strikers. Then, as in *Potemkin*, they become a flight crowd when they are fired upon by Jenkins's company guards.

Despite the fact that the French story will be characterized largely by betrayal and blood, Griffith shows at its beginning benign crowds "celebrating the betrothal of Marguerite of Valois, sister of the King, to Henry of Navarre, royal Huguenot, to insure peace in the place of intolerance." The noble procession through the streets creates an especially dense crowd, similar to the doubly closed crowd that fills an arena and that, in its concentration only upon the spectacle before it and the rest of the crowd around it, has an intense homogeneity. Shots of several young women add overtones of increase to the unified festive mass of celebrants. Ironically, this crowd will soon be divided into a pair of double crowds, far less happy ones, the slaughterers and the slaughtered.

The most refulgent of the fertile, life-affirming crowds of *Intolerance* lights up the Babylonian story. In contrast to many of the big-budget epics that followed Griffith's film and some that preceded it, the sexy, pleasure-celebrating crowds in Babylon embody not decadence but the springing up and increase of life. This sense of joy and fecundity underscores Griffith's instinctive disposition in favor of crowds.

With their profusion of detail and ornamentation, the Babylonian sets multiply crowd symbols that rhyme visually with the rhythmic masses of people who prance through them. Like the crowds themselves, the crowd symbols of carved icons, magnificent sculpture, friezes, and gates decorated with images of priests and warriors exhibit themselves for the admiration of a sympathetic camera, without a hint of puritan disapproval. The audience is encouraged to see Babylon's crowds as pious; one performs "the sacred dance in memory of the resurrection of Tammuz" before the Temple of Love; another, the "Hand maidens from Ishtar's Temple of Love and Laughter," dances joyously through the great carved doors of the city. The erotic celebration of Tammuz's resurrection connects sexual love with life and opposes it to death.

The repeated image of the life-renewing cradle rocking in front of the three Fates during transitions between one story and another expresses the same opposition between increase and death. (The Fates themselves, divided traditionally among birth, destiny, and death, also contain this opposition.) An early intertitle in the modern story, "Age intolerant of youth and laughter," announces a variation on this theme. The Fates are invoked again by the three men who cut the cords in a test of the gallows on which the Boy in that story is scheduled to die.[14]

For the Babylonian story as well as for the other narratives, crowds often are and always ought to be the sites of love. *Intolerance* integrates individuals as sexual creatures into the egalitarian environment of the crowd. In this respect, Griffith is in accord with Freud, since the crowds in the Babylonian story often appear to be united by a shared libidinal attachment to Belshazzar. Again, the difference between Griffith's practice and that of most other film-makers reflects his predisposition in favor of crowds. As a broad tendency, lovers in screenplays are contrasted with and frequently opposed by crowds—at least until the conclusion, when there is often a reconciliation between the amorous central couple and their social opposition. This tendency is especially emphatic, as we shall see when we come to *North by Northwest,* in many of the movies of Hitchcock, who might be considered something of a de-mophobe. There are indeed a number of scenes in *Intolerance* where lovers are persecuted by hostile crowds—notably in parts of the modern story and the French one—but the conjunction of crowds and lovers is more often presented as both possible and preferable.

Even the crowds of virgins behind Belshazzar are intensely erotic, women whose capacity for sexual love has been nurtured, not renounced—a point emphasized by their minimal, all-but-transparent clothing and by the flowers with which they are frequently associated. When intolerant death, through the betrayal of the jealous Head Priest, finally overthrows the forces of life and Babylon bows before Cyrus, the dying virginal Mountain Girl remains faithful to her vow of love to Belshazzar. Doves towing flowers halt before her; behind her we see floral tapestries. Here as elsewhere in *Intolerance* the imagery of birds and foliage function as fecund crowd symbols set against the forces of repression and death.

Birds and verdure proliferate in the bucolic yards of the Dear One and the Boy and, in accordance with the pattern of imagery of the film as a whole, anticipate crowds that are sites of happiness and increase. The mass of people in the city, on the other hand, degenerates into a predatory pack. In the socially fragmented city, the naïve wish of the Dear One to walk so that "everyone" will love her ironically parodies her joyous participation in the mill workers' dance and inadvertently signals something approaching prostitution—a code that the Boy understands, even if she does not.

In consonance with the association of birds, love, and increase packs (strongly linked, according to Canetti, with transformation), Christ approaches the scene of the wedding in Cana utter-

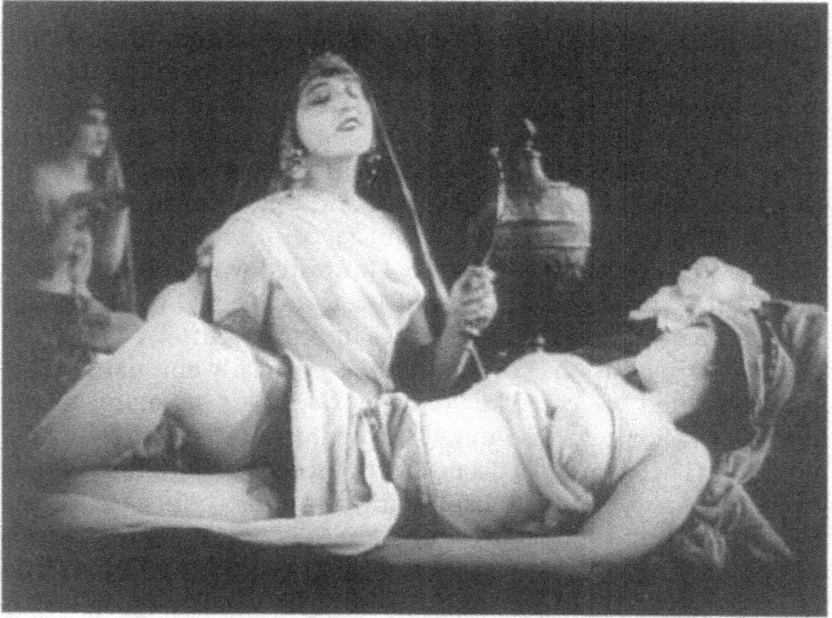

Erotic purity in *Intolerance*

ing the words, "Be ye harmless as doves," and Griffith cuts to a shot of seven white doves. Jesus perpetuates both the joy and the piety of the wedding crowd by performing His first miracle, the transformation of wine into water. (Griffith takes care to explain, "Wine was deemed a fit offering to God; the drinking of it a part of the Jewish religion.") *Intolerance* confirms Griffith's view of crowds as natural places for love when he portrays Christ disbanding the Pharisees who are about to stone the Woman Taken in Adultery. Even when love is adulterous, Griffith presents its persecution as a perversion of the proper inclination of a crowd.

With its powerful portrayal of love and fields of blooming flowers, the end of *Intolerance* emphasizes Griffith's vision of an idealized humanity as a peaceful, loving crowd. "Cannon and prison bars wrought in the fires of intolerance" are represented by the degraded, misused crowds of battling armies and pleading prisoners; both are transformed into a state of peace and joy by divine hosts. Prison walls dissolve through a descent of heavenly power and give way to "flowery fields" in which happy families socialize and play. The remarkably pacific apocalyptic vision in which "perfect love shall bring peace forever more" comprises not individuals in isolation but loving, inclusive crowds. Their restored Eden is populated by modern reincarnations not only of Adam and Eve but also of their progeny. On this vision of humankind as a natural crowd— one restored to humanity's original unity and innocence—*Intolerance* joyfully concludes.

Although some of the crowds of *Intolerance* are anything but amiable—I consider them below—the chief adversary to human happiness in Griffith's film appears in the form of power or, as it is usually called in the intertitles, "ambition." Power, as Canetti describes it, is fundamentally characterized by the desire to outlive other people. The kind of survival that distinguishes power has to do not just with staying alive, but with staying alive while others perish. Other people, especially those who are different or unknown, represent threats. They inspire the fear of an alien touch that Canetti identifies as the basic terror underlying the desire to form crowds. Expressed in a pathological form, that terror also underlies the desire for power. "In survival, each man is the enemy of every other" (227).

There exists a deep, logical connection between power and the destructive, often murderous, human inclination that provides the title of Griffith's film. By its very nature, power opposes egali-

Edenic crowds

tarian open crowds and the human talent for transformation that underlies sympathy and fellow feeling. It suppresses the capacity that connects people imaginatively with each other, with other living entities, and with the universe itself. It is hostile and profoundly alienated. The Catholic court in the French story separates itself both from the Huguenots and from the unifying, conciliatory crowd that celebrates the Huguenot-Catholic marriage. The principal enemies of Babylon are "ambitious Persians" with a treacherous ally in the High Priest of Bel, who "fears the loss of *his own great powers*" (emphasis in original). Like most seekers of power, the High Priest is driven to kill anyone who threatens his exclusivity. When the Mountain Girl defies his edict, he presumes to sentence her to death, a fate from which she is rescued by the providential appearance of Belshazzar.

In contrast to the High Priest's attempt to seize the "power of death," "Babylonian justice[,] according to the code of Hammurabi, protect[s] the weak from the strong." Given Griffith's contrasting portrayals of the masses of the meek and the secretive, isolate masters and warriors, the Babylonian code amounts to the protection of crowds from power. A sanctimonious Pharisee in the Christ story brings to a halt the productive activity of the marketplace when he offers a prayer of thanks for being "better than other men"; and the Pharisees later observe the wedding crowd's celebration with unfriendly suspicion. When three ambitious Uplifters seize the Dear One's baby and consign him to the pediatric equivalent of solitary confinement, Griffith intercuts as commentary an image of Christ surrounded by a crowd of children and mothers.

The outcome of power's desire for uniqueness must finally be isolation, both from enemies and, eventually, from whatever supporters the survivor may retain. The alienation of Miss Jenkins from the world of the young and merry at her ball is both a cause and a symptom of her readiness to shift her ambitions from love to power—in her case, to the cause of "reform." Equally ambitious, her brother is consistently shown set against the crowds of his workers. The most notable images of his separation occur during the strike sequence, when he sits in an enormous room almost empty of furniture and, save for him, empty of people. From that bleak setting he telephones the command for his private guards to fire upon the workers.

Power in *Intolerance* isolates both those who exercise it and its victims. Very much alone, the Boy approaches his execution. Nor

The isolation of power

do the other prisoners condense into a crowd. They lack all the qualities of a crowd, except, in their shared abjection, equality. A prison, the institution that most clearly expresses the intolerance and life-denying force of power, can hardly be a seedbed for a crowd, no matter how many people it lodges. In mass, the prisoners still remain individually separate: "And wondered if each one of us / Would end the self-same way." The revealingly named Friendless One, alone in the city, not only is the victim of power but becomes a killer herself in her jealous loneliness. The most pathetic victims of the French and Babylonian stories, Prosper and Brown Eyes and the Mountain Girl, live and love in the midst of crowds but die pretty much alone.

Love in *Intolerance* generally runs afoul of the crudest form of power, force—whether exercised by individuals or by hostile crowds. "The lowest form of survival," writes Canetti, "is killing" (227). The High Priest of Bel, jealously eager to preserve the unique place of his deity, schemes secretively against the festive crowds behind him. As Mr. Jenkins seizes the power of death, a power that the legitimate keepers of the peace, the militia, refuse to exercise, so the High Priest tries to usurp the same absolute command from the ruler of Babylon. King Charles in the French story, conspicuously isolated on his throne and eventually convinced that his life and that of his followers are at risk, also turns to killing for survival: "Kill them all! Let not one escape to upbraid me." In a form less extreme than killing, the opposition of power to love appears as sexual force or predation. The Dear One, the Friendless One, Brown Eyes, and the Mountain Girl are threatened with rape, sexual blackmail, or compelled marriage. The absolute incompatibility of love and force underlies the decision of the Princess in Babylon to commit suicide along with her maids after the triumph of Cyrus.

The chase sequences that climax the secular stories—the Dear One's frantic race with the Governor to prevent the Boy's execution, Prosper's struggle to cross Paris in order to save Brown Eyes and her family, and the Mountain Girl's chariot ride to warn Babylon of Cyrus's approaching army—all emblematize love's attempts to forestall murderous power. The Judean story stages the divine alternative: Christ's sacrifice will eventually banish forever the isolation, violence, and hatred into which humans have fallen throughout recorded history. For Christian cultures, that action remains the ultimate story of concord triumphing over enmity.

The climaxes of all four stories share another aspect: they represent the threats of homicidal crowds. In the case of the modern and Judean stories, the killing crowds are attached to state executions; in the other two narratives, war crowds are bent on the extermination of their foes. For all four plot lines, crowds constitute the locus of bloody power, a circumstance that clashes with Griffith's frequent presentation of crowds as amiable and power as isolated. It is worth repeating here that neither Griffith nor Canetti uncritically romanticizes crowds. Certain sorts of crowds, war and killing crowds in particular, are associated with the characteristic modalities of power: force, viewing opponents as subhuman, self-righteousness, and paranoia. As a consequence, even though Griffith's vision of love and charity tends to reproduce the dynamics of democratic masses, vicious crowds in *Intolerance* appear as allies of power. They attack benign groups and such icons of love as the Dear One and the Boy, Prosper and Brown Eyes, the Mountain Girl, the ruler of Babylon and his Princess, and Jesus.

The attraction and vitality of double crowds derives from the fact that they serve the desire of any crowd to persevere; with their powerful sense of direction, they also promote density and growth: "The surest, and often the only, way by which a crowd can preserve itself lies in the existence of a second crowd to which it is related. Whether the two crowds confront each other as rivals in a game, or as a serious threat to each other, the sight, or simply the powerful image of the second crowd, prevents the disintegration of the first" (63).

The appalling attraction nations have to wars and the difficulty of bringing them to an end can be to a considerable degree explained as a crowd phenomenon: while an opposing crowd threatens, its adversary must persist. In the French story, the Catholics seem intent upon inventing, or at least magnifying, the threat of the Huguenots in order to enlarge and strengthen their own crowd. The end of wars comes not so much with the manifest defeat of one of the contestants—wars continue, more often than not, long after the outcome is certain—but with the disintegration of one of the two opposing crowds. In extreme cases, Canetti writes, "people prefer to perish together with open eyes, rather than acknowledge defeat and thus experience the disintegration of their own crowd" (71).

War crowds dominate the French and Babylonian stories. Griffith's portrayal of the conflict between Catholics and Huguenots demonstrates the crowd dynamics that underlie the beginnings of war. Although a title introducing the French story announces that Paris of 1572 is "a hotbed of intolerance," the first images of the court are of Charles IX sitting in front of an apparently harmonious, homogeneous crowd of courtiers. More intertitles inform the audience of the rivalry between Catholic and Huguenot factions, but the personages themselves are indistinguishable as to their religious persuasions. The first major action we see in the French story, in fact, is a marriage with the politic aim of uniting the sectarian rivals. The approaching conflict, as Griffith's sequencing suggests, is neither natural nor inevitable. A pair of key utterances in the court, however, signal the crisis to come: Catherine de Medici, leader of the Catholics, and the Admiral Coligny, the Protestant leader, both express regret that the other side does not "think as we do." This is tantamount to wishing that one's own crowd could be larger, that of the opposite side smaller—a desire that fundamentally matches the aim of war: "The adversary in war is the growing number of one's neighbors. . . . In this rivalry between growing crowds lies an essential, and it may even be the prime, cause of wars" (68).

The formation of a belligerent crowd comes when "people decide that they are threatened. . . . They say, 'I can be killed,' and secretly add 'because I myself want to kill this or that man'" (72). The memory of the Protestant attack on Catholics in Nîmes is invoked to justify the St. Bartholomew's Day massacre of Huguenots; a flashback shows the Nîmois Protestants hard at work butchering men and women and destroying Catholic statuary. The two sides in the French narrative are not painted with moral black and white: each contributes to the process by which belligerent crowds are galvanized into "extreme prejudice," as the modern phrase aptly puts it. The Catholics convince themselves that "our very lives depend upon their extermination," and they persuade the king with similar logic: "We must destroy or be destroyed." The result of Charles's authorization of a surprise attack is not so much a war as a slaughter, "Intolerance burning and slaying." As in the modern story, one side in Paris has overwhelming force and the crowd of the other consequently breaks up in panic, with everyone attempting to save himself.

The struggle between the Babylonians and Cyrus's Medes and Persians also conforms in most of its features to Canetti's account of double crowds. The Babylonians, however, intermittently forget that they face an opposing war crowd. As a result, they function as part of the configuration of a double crowd only when actively doing battle. The rest of the time, the conflict between Cyrus's legions and Babylon may be better characterized as between a society devoted to war and one devoted to love and increase—that is to say, a war crowd versus a festival crowd. For Griffith, such a conflict amounts to intolerance versus love.

The crowds that fill the opening shots of Babylon are characterized by a title, "Merchants, farmers, East Indians, with trains of elephants, Egyptians, Numidians, and ambitious Persians spying upon the city." The word "ambitious" has already been associated with the Uplifters of the modern story and, through that association, with intrusive power—that is, with intolerance. The majority of the crowd in Babylon is devoted to love and increase, but the presence of the "ambitious Persians" brings into the midst of that festival crowd the representatives of another, the war crowd of Cyrus.

47

Paradoxically, the radical contrast between the Babylonian increase crowd and its belligerent opposite appears most clearly when they seem most similar, during the quarter-hour battle sequence that climaxes the first of *Intolerance*'s two sections. Babylon prevails, Griffith's complex sequence suggests, at least partly because of its powers of transmutation. Possessed of but a single purpose, Cyrus's war crowd worships only power: its leader "repeats the world-old prayer of intolerance, to kill, kill, kill—and to God be the glory, world without end, Amen." The increase crowd of Babylon, on the other hand, can change into a war crowd without losing its underlying identity. While Belshazzar, the Man of Valor, the Mountain Girl, and Babylon's army face the enemy in battle, the Princess Beloved and the priests and acolytes of Ishtar intensify their worship.

In the case of the struggle between the Persian-led legions of war and the more flexible, more deeply motivated civilization of Babylon, the power of social metamorphosis appears decisive. The most humanizing and efficacious capacity of homo sapiens, according to Canetti, is that of transformation; it bestows on the besieged city of Babylon both humanity and defensive strength. On the battlefield, monstrous machines of war and defensive walls and towers paint an image of two cities devoted to fire and destruction. The crowd symbols associated with the battle also liken the opposing sides: "Great timbers against the towers." The combatants each seek another crowd symbol, fire, as an ally on the battlefield and, on the Babylonian side, through the dragon-like engine that emerges to burn the Persian siege towers. But another civilization lies within Babylon, whereas Cyrus's army has no such core. In its rigidity, it is all surface; it exists only for power—"to kill, kill, kill." When the Persians finally prevail, only destruction follows their triumph. The Babylonians, after they win the first battle, transform again from a city of war and prayers for aid into one of celebration and thankful worship. Writing of "The Transmutation of Packs," Canetti describes a contrast between social metamorphosis and its absence that is precisely applicable to Griffith's portrayal of the Babylonians and the Persians: "The communal *hunt,* if successful, leads to distribution. . . . *Victories* degenerate into looting" (127).

Although the High Priest's betrayal figures critically in Babylon's eventual defeat, Griffith also suggests that the very strength of the city, the exuberance of its civilization, can divide its purposes and render it vulnerable to unalloyed power. "Babylon's last Bacchanal" is being celebrated at the very moment that the Medes and Persians and their barbarous allies march a second time. Griffith enforces the contrast with a high shot of the peaceful crowds of Babylon—a shot that suggests their vulnerability "down there"— set against an eye-level shot of the attacking army, a perspective that makes them appear especially formidable. Between the attacking army and the feast-crowds, and unable to resist the one or effectively warn the other, the Mountain Girl drives her desperate race.

Opposing crowds or packs appear less emphatically in the other stories. Those of the French story, as we have seen, are not very clearly defined as contesting crowds and quickly devolve into slaughterers and victims. In the modern story, opposing crowds also tend to disintegrate into attackers and victims, although the strikers and the guards of the Jenkins plant do wage war briefly.

Nonetheless, in the modern story, Griffith develops the growing mass of Uplifters along lines that largely duplicate Canetti's description of an evolving crowd. The initial three reformers function as crowd crystals: a small number of people who can lurk dormant or ineffective within the social fabric but about whom packs and crowds quickly form when conditions become favorable. (The "Meddlers then as now" of the Judean story serve as crowd crystals parallel to the "certain ambitious ladies" of the modern story.) The sense of exclusion that Miss Jenkins feels and the gift of her brother's money to the reformers effect such a change. A pack of Uplifters rapidly develops and soon becomes a crowd, with an immense office full of institutionalized busybodies. The Uplifters sponsor their own sedate ball, an occasion that at once parallels and contrasts with the workers' high-spirited dance. The growth in numbers and zeal of the reformers, however, is fueled by a sense of social difference and antagonism that eventually leads them to degenerate into a killing crowd. During the Boy's trial, an ironic intertitle emphasizes the point: "Universal justice, an eye for an eye, a tooth for a tooth, *a murder for a murder.*" Adding emphasis to the crowd dynamics, Griffith repeatedly turns the camera on the courtroom spectators.

The determined attack in the name of justice on the Boy; the murder of Prosper Latour, Brown Eyes, and her family; the destruction of Belshazzar's and his Beloved's Babylon; and the crucifixion of Jesus all appear to ultimately align crowds with power and to set them in opposition to loving individuals. Deeper consideration, however, leads to a different conclusion. The French and Babylonian stories, though they end in catastrophe, present loving crowds as not only possible but natural to human beings. Grief and outrage attach to death and destruction in sixteenth-century France and ancient Babylon. *Intolerance* denies that such horrific events and murderous crowds were—or are—inevitable. The modern story, as we have seen, ends with the sort of resolution described by Northrop Frye: "Domestic comedy is usually based on the Cinderella archetype, the kind of thing that happens when Pamela's virtue is rewarded, the incorporation of an individual very like the reader [or viewer] into the society aspired to by both."[15]

Most revealing of Griffith's determined optimism in the face of history's dismal record is his handling of the Judean story and his characterization of Christ. That story is more than moral seasoning on the main dishes of the other narratives; it effectively sums up both the lessons taught by the errors and malice of the other stories and the hope that underlies them. Griffith's retelling of the gospels confirms his democratic favoring of crowds and reconciles the love sited within masses with the love experienced and expressed by individuals.

To understand Christ's role in *Intolerance,* we must take literally Griffith's introductory label "the Man of Men, the greatest enemy of intolerance." The first phrase iterates Christ's humanity, that he is a man among men; at the same time, it identifies him as *the* Man, the only one since Adam conceived and born without sin. Traditional enough. But for Griffith's epic film, the phrase also suggests that Christ not only represents but incorporates humankind; he is, so to speak, an inclusive crowd in himself, a man composed of all men. As Walt Whitman provided the epigram attached to the image of Lillian Gish rocking the cradle, so Griffith's conception of Christ may be conceived through another famous Whitman phrase, "I contain multitudes."

Nevertheless, Griffith repeatedly emphasizes Christ's persecution by killing crowds. A killing crowd after his trial yells for crucifixion, and he carries the cross through a jeering mob. These scenes represent a tormented man among human tormentors. Because of the inclusive humanity that Christ carries within him, however, these sequences also represent conflict between a crowd at its most hateful and, in the person of Jesus, humanity in its divine plenitude of love and forgiveness. Griffith's high-contrast filming of the crucifixion confirms his understanding of the symbology of the

"Man of Men." It is filled with the flames and multitudes of a great battle, presumably between the armies of hatred and those of tolerance. Within *Intolerance,* it is most closely aligned visually with the great struggles at Babylon, the other epic battle between destructive power and love. The scene of the crucifixion moves without transition to the final sequence, in which armies lay down their weapons and joy pervades the world. Griffith imagines the apocalypse—in contrast to the *Revelation of Saint John*—as lovingly peaceful.

Like the endlessly rocking cradle, the self-sacrifice of Christ serves as "uniter of here and hereafter." Without effacing the pastness of the past, it brings ancient Babylon, Jesus' Judea, sixteenth-century France, and twentieth-century America into a unifying present. The cinematic art of *Intolerance* edits together both separate places and disparate times. Jesus as an individual struggling to awaken the forces of human love is echoed by the Mountain Girl, Prosper Latour, and the Dear One in their races against death. The Catholic priest who saves a Protestant child by hiding her in his robes represents at once another such individual and the proper legacy of tolerant Christianity.

The most pointed analog to Christ—were *Intolerance* in the Old Testament, he would be called a "type"—is Belshazzar. A man of love and an "apostle of tolerance," he anticipates Christ's rescue of the Woman Taken in Adultery by stopping the sanctimonious murder that the High Priest is about to inflict on the Mountain Girl. As Christ endorses a loving marriage through his miraculous transformation of water into wine, Belshazzar supports the connection of marriage with love by freeing the unwilling Mountain Girl from what threatens to become a state-sanctioned rape and sale into indentured servitude. Griffith numerically emphasizes the parallel between Belshazzar and Christ when the former, facing his death as did Jesus with his apostles, is left with "only twelve guards to defend his palace gates."

The three secular narratives of *Intolerance* portray the fundamental qualities of human nature manifested in both individuals and crowds. Humans change through time, but cultural alterations remain superficial. The outcomes of history may be mixed, but the contesting forces remain the same: love versus hate, toleration versus intolerance, life versus death. Fundamental transformation, for Griffith as for Canetti, comes imaginatively, from the power to feelingly become another being. "The talent for transformation which . . . everyone possesses is one of the great mysteries and few are

51

aware that to it they owe what is best in themselves" (337). *Intolerance* equates the people of Babylon, France, and modern America; in their diverse forms and fashions they can be seen as one. Jesus Christ, however, contains within him all human transformations. His story therefore ethically guides all others.

At the end of *Intolerance*, Griffith introduces a new camera set-up for the Woman with the cradle and the three Fates by changing to a lens of greater focal length. As a result, the scene is brought visually toward the audience and, at the same time, the figures of the Woman with the cradle and those behind her appear closer together. The camera also moves slightly to the right and the Fates therefore move toward the center of the frame. But the Woman and the endlessly rocking cradle retain precedence, just as life must precede death. On the cycle of life everything depends—the death that lurks behind the cradle as well as the life that the cradle, the love that creates the living universe, endlessly renews. *Intolerance* confronts the most dismal human behavior, from the attacking hordes of Cyrus and the St. Bartholomew Day Massacre, to the sexually repressed and love-denying Uplifters, to the death that shadows all life. In the face of such knowledge, Griffith's "Sun Play for the Ages" nonetheless embraces hope. Its ultimate faith extends from the humble geranium in the Dear One's austere flat, to the fecund resurrection of Tammuz in Babylon, to the Priest's instinctive mercy in the midst of slaughter, and finally to the triumph of light, peace, and human community that follows—at once directly and two millennia later—Christ's loving agony.

2

The Comedic Crowds of Preston Sturges

Few filmmakers have portrayed crowds or addressed the implied crowd of the audience as shrewdly as Preston Sturges. Nor have many understood so well the deep connection between crowds, love stories, and comic narratives. Even in *Unfaithfully Yours* (1948), a film largely concerned with its protagonist's paranoid fantasies (which Canetti identifies as a malady characteristic of power), Sir Alfred's (Rex Harrison) recovery at the end is confirmed when he embraces the crowd of common people that he has scorned throughout the film. For Canetti, interestingly, "There is no more obvious expression of power than the performance of a conductor. . . . The applause he receives is the ancient salute to the victor and the magnitude of his victory is measured by its volume" (394, 395). When Sir Alfred experiences the epiphany that sets him free of his jealousy, he simultaneously gives up his power and renounces his cultural elitism: "Will you put on your lowest cut, most vulgarly ostentatious dress, with the largest and vulgarest jewels that you possess, and then accompany me to the vulgarest, most ostentatious, loudest, and hardest-to-get-into establishment the city affords? . . . I want everyone to see." *The Great McGinty* (1940), Sturges's first film, and *Christmas in July* (1940) repeatedly invoke the masses and crowd symbols of thronged neighborhoods, building-crowded cityscapes, and the audiences of millions commanded by newspapers and radio. Behind Hopsie in *The Lady Eve* (1941) is a fortune continuously increased by the fact that every second of every day masses of people open fourteen bottles of "Pike's Pale, The Ale that Won for Yale." The one film Sturges wrote and directed that is not a comedy, *The Great Moment* (1944), repeatedly insists on the power of anesthesia to mitigate the suffering "of millions."

53

The populism of Sturges's movies has not gone unnoticed, but it has often been considered ironic—as if Sturges were an unrepentant Sir Alfred.[1] I am convinced, on the contrary, that Sturges's comedies work out as predominantly romantic rather than ironic or satiric—though there is certainly irony and satire in all his screenwriting—and that taking note of the pervasive role of crowds in his movies confirms that understanding. In particular, the celebratory crowds at (or just before) the conclusions of Sturges's comedies—often the first true crowds, from a Canettian understanding, to appear in the film—give emphatic imprimaturs to their happy endings. These concluding throngs both validate the resolution of whatever problems have vexed the protagonists and/or their communities and invite the audience in the theater to join the celebration. Such validations figure crucially in four of Sturges's most crowd-crowded movies, *Hail the Conquering Hero* (1944), *The Miracle of Morgan's Creek* (1944), *The Sin of Harold Diddlebock* (1947), and *Sullivan's Travels* (1941).

Hail the Conquering Hero:
"We want you very much!"

Numerous, often chaotic crowds throng *Hail the Conquering Hero* (1943). Sturges's wartime comedy moves from an opening in which the protagonist is miserably isolated to an ending that puts him at the center of an adulatory crowd, one that he has helped to create. Between the sharp contrasts of beginning and end, however, the treatment of crowds is complex and often ironic: they gather under circumstances both true and false; they are intricately related to actions of love and growing up, and to themes of war and politics.

As *Hail the Conquering Hero* begins, Woodrow Trusmith (Eddie Bracken) sits solitary and morose in a crowded club. A cantankerous group of marines, reduced to fifteen cents among them, orders what they can afford, a single beer. After Woodrow sends over more beer and sandwiches, they join him and we learn the reason for his gloom. The son of a marine who died in World War I, he enlisted in the marines himself, but washed out because of chronic hay fever. It turns out that the sergeant of the small group served with "Hinky-Dinky" Trusmith, Woodrow's father. This coincidence and the mother-fixation of one of the men, Bugsy (Freddie Steele), pushes off a series of actions that will end with the lonely hero engaged to his childhood sweetheart, his formerly divided town ready to "Win with Woodrow," the quarreling marines reunified, and, by emphatic implication, a confident United States gratefully celebrating its past and present defenders.

Woodrow's course to true love, homecoming, and an ecstatic crowd never did run smooth, in part because *Hail the Conquering Hero* is a story about attaining adulthood. The first words addressed to him come from the bartender, "Why don't you grab yourself off a skirt and have yourself a time?" Woodrow begins to respond sarcastically, then subsides; but the next shot appears to answer the question. In the adjoining room, a torchy singer (with four male waiters singing harmony) begins the chorus of a saccharine ballad, "Home to the Arms of Mother." As is often the case for protagonists of romantic comedies, Woodrow appears at the start of the story to be an overripe mamma's boy. Ashamed of his removal from the service, he's been deceiving his mother with fake letters. Also suggestive of his belated maturity is the circumstance that when his father was killed—about the time Woodrow was being born—he was younger than his son is now.

But Hinky-Dinky's offspring is not the only overage man-child in the movie. In the nightclub, balding men sniffle into their beer during the song and the four middle-aged waiters follow the womanly (if younger) singer like so many chicks clustered behind a mother hen. Bugsy is obsessed with mothers because, as the Sarge (William Demarest) explains, "He never had any" and "He's been shot up a little, nothing serious." Back in Oakridge, Woodrow's hometown, the young man who replaced Woodrow as his sweetheart's fiancé also remains belatedly under the sway of his parents and, like his predecessor, has been kept out of uniform by chronic hay fever.

Trying to escape his unexpected nomination for mayor, Woodrow proclaims, "I love my Mother very much." The crowd cheers and a local pol remarks, "He has a natural flare for politics." As the reluctant candidate goes on to say that he's delivered milk to the homes of his neighbors and watched their babies grow up, the same character can hardly contain his enthusiasm: "The milk and babies part is remarkable; after that, he could be President!" Childishness doesn't seem to diminish a candidate's voter appeal.

Innocently silly as they may be, crowds in *Hail the Conquering Hero* have a complex relation to its politics, with which they are both implicated and contrasted. As in most movies (and as Canetti argues), politics in *Hail the Conquering Hero* has more to do with power than crowds, which power may use but with which it is not congruent. The isolating paranoia of power must finally set it in opposition to the congenial trust of most crowds, even if they ultimately share the same originary motivation. The predominance of crowds, especially at its conclusion, confirms that *Hail the Conquering Hero* is unequivocally a comedy; equally revealing, its exemplars of power generally appear ridiculous and incongruous rather than threatening. Crowds and power in a movie like *Intolerance,* as we have seen, engage in truly dangerous struggles; and that generically conflicted work splits its episodes between happy and grim outcomes.[2] In the chapter on *North by Northwest,* we see that even in a comic romance, Hitchcock balances crowds and power precariously—proverbial "master of suspense" that he is.

One of the modes of power, as Canetti conceives it, is deceit; and politics in *Hail the Conquering Hero* is usually connected with falsehood and deception. When Woodrow protests that his nomination for mayor is based on lies, the Sarge reassures him, "Anyway, those ain't lies; those are campaign promises. They expect 'em." The beleaguered incumbent mayor's campaign manager, swimming alone against the tide of enthusiastic Oakridge citizens, supposes that their favorite son may not be what he appears; he wonders "if he really is a hero." A professional politician—equivalent in this film to a professional liar—he naturally suspects others of lying as well.

However much power may use crowds, and whether straightforwardly or deceitfully, it finally remains isolated from and distrustful of them. It assumes that all other people are rivals: "Everybody wants to be mayor. That's human nature." Power employs crowds only as long as they suit its purposes. Reflecting on the Oakridge citizens' embrace of Woodrow, the mayor draws a revealing conclusion, "There you see one of the fallacies of the democratic principle; they can vote for anybody they like."

Like the hero of *The Miracle of Morgan's Creek,* Woodrow's eventual greatness and his lies are mostly "thrust upon" him. As a result of the lies, however, his crowds of supporters assemble most of the time on the basis of false information. Not coincidentally, these throngs are chaotic and discordant. Bands repeatedly strike up at the wrong moment and are whistled into silence; speakers cannot make themselves heard; marchers bump into each other. As the Sarge says just before Sturges cuts to the huge crowd awaiting Woodrow at the train station, "Nobody's hep to nothin'." Only in the final sequence, when the town finally has the whole truth, do we see what Canetti would regard as a genuine crowd: dense and growing, and unified in its desire to forgive Woodrow and, we assume, to elect him mayor.

Before that happy ending, Woodrow's relation to the crowd is well summed up by the spectacle of his being dragged from his mother's home to face the mass of his would-be constituents. His terror is reasonable. As Canetti points out and Woodrow is only too aware, crowds can quickly change direction; the exuberant crowd calling for his nomination may soon be calling for his head if it learns the truth.

The ambiguous portrayal of crowds in *Hail the Conquering Hero* hints at an ambivalent attitude toward war. War, Canetti argues, consists of rival killing crowds, each of which wishes to increase while diminishing the other. Partisan representative politics is much the same, but with the crucial difference that killing is forbidden. The hysterical eagerness of the crowds to embrace Woodrow as a hero and to accept the preposterous tales the Sarge and others tell of him tints their patriotic enthusiasm with comic irony. There is general disapproval when Woodrow punches Bugsy; the supposed mass-killer of enemy soldiers should behave differently at home. Libby's aunt muses, "Either they take your man away and never send him back a'tall, or they send him back just to embarrass you." As the mayor remarks, "A hero's a fine thing—in its place." "Its" place, one gathers from a conclusion that sends the marines (however reverentially) back into battle, is not Oakridge. Sturges's script also suggests considerable sympathy for those "who also serve" in factories, making chairs for the army, and keeping democracy running.

The ironies, ambiguities, and falsehoods of *Hail the Conquering Hero*, however, are largely overwhelmed by the true crowds, true heroes, and true Trusmith of its conclusion. Woodrow's surname suggests not only his honesty and commitment to the Marine Corps motto "Semper Fidelis" but also his status as an ordinary everyman. He has little talent for deception: "I'm no good at lying." When he is at last free of the falsehoods into which he's been swept, his supporters simultaneously come into being as a fully realized "Canettian" crowd, untroubled by the chaos and conflicts of earlier versions. The only crowd assembled in good faith before the end of the film pays off and burns the mortgage on the house of Woodrow's mother—an action that benefits an entirely worthy and honest person.

"The coward," Woodrow announces as he begins his confession, "is at least cured of his fear." As he continues, Bugsy rejoins him and the other marines on the stage, a gesture that anticipates the crowd support that will result from Woodrow's courage and initiate "a vindication campaign." Alone for the last time in the film, Woodrow leaves the town hall, having apparently lost everything: the nomination, the respect of the once-adoring crowd, the pride of his mother and former sweetheart, and his beloved home. When he tells another small lie to exonerate the marines of their more-than-complicity in the deception, he takes on himself blame beyond his desserts. From the beginning, his motives, as here, have been basically unexceptional. "Not that I really wanted to fool any of you. I just wanted to come home."

While he walks away through the deserted town, his restoration is beginning in the assembly he has just left. As soon as he leaves and his mother and sweetheart Libby (Ella Raines) are escorted out of the hall, the Sarge pushes to the front of the stage. "I seen a lotta brave men in my life—that's my business—but what that kid did took real courage . . . now ya might as well hear the rest of it."

A complete reversal ensues. It establishes Woodrow as a true hero in ways that *Crowds and Power* clarifies. "The way of the hero," Canetti writes, "is towards the greatest danger and an ineluctable decision" (229). There are two ways that a crowd can inflict death, of which "the first is expulsion" (50). This penalty Woodrow assesses on himself and assumes the assembly will confirm. He has gone from hero to pariah, and his transformation back to hero seems all but impossible. Indeed, he says that he would be happy to be the town "dogcatcher," let alone its mayor. As Manny Farber wrote, Woodrow is one of a number of Sturges protagonists "haunted by . . . the great American nightmare that some monstrous error can drive individuals clean out of society into a forlorn no man's land, to be the lonely objects of an eternity of scorn, derision, and self-humiliation."[3] One more appeal to *Crowds and Power* is relevant here. Of transformations among classes—and Woodrow has just demoted himself to the lowest—Canetti writes, "The most important of all prohibitions on transformation are the social. . . . Often the candidate is thought of as dying in the lower class, to be brought back to life in the higher: death itself divides class from class" (380). Woodrow's restoration to the good graces of the crowd, as Sturges makes clear in his brilliant script, amounts to something like such a resurrection. Before his vindication, the last words Woodrow utters to the silent throng are, "I wish I was dead."

Woodrow's rebirth begins not with the crowd but with his mother and his sweetheart. Sturges takes pains to have them escorted from the hall before the Sarge's explanation to the assembly. The forgiveness of his mother and Libby's declaration of unswerving love need no excuses. "Oh, stupid! Stupid! Stupid!" Libby cries as she embraces the disgraced Woodrow, "I've never loved anybody but you and you've never loved anybody but me. You can't say it's because you're a hero that I'm running after you, can you?" With that embrace and the confession that preceded it, Woodrow gains a wife without losing a mother. He has grown up. He also undoes his last operative lie, the one he told Libby to keep her from waiting for him.

Woodrow's mother and restored fiancée implicitly answer the question he asks the crowd a little later: "You mean you still want me?" "We want you very much." Urging Woodrow to run for mayor, one of the party opposing the incumbent had declared, "There's something rotten in the town. . . . We need an honest man for mayor." Woodrow's confession, Doc Bissel (Harry Haden) proclaims, proves "beyond doubt that he [is] honest, courageous, and veracious." In its reluctant hero, Oakridge has just the mayor it needs. "What do we need a soldier for anyway?" exclaims a supporter. True love and an honest candidate finally come together in Woodrow Lafayette Pershing Trusmith. So does an undeceived, forgiving, and adoring crowd: "Politics is a very peculiar thing," Doc Bissel explains. "If they want you, they want you. They don't need reasons anymore; they find their own reasons. It's just like when a girl wants a man."

The Miracle of Morgan's Creek: "The Spots!"

The narrative of *The Miracle of Morgan's Creek* is framed by a rapidly growing crowd in the governor's office, a crowd that goes from puzzlement through incredulity to joyful hysteria. As the story unfolds, its crowds expand from the town of Morgan's Creek, through the governor's office to the state, the United States, and eventually the entire world. In Morgan's Creek and the United States, everyone is exultant. The flashbacks that occupy most of the movie develop themes and plot much as they do in Sturges's other wartime comedy, *Hail the Conquering Hero.* An isolated protagonist, unable for medical reasons to be a soldier, gets into trouble for which he is largely not responsible, is ostracized, and finally returns to claim a wife and the adulation of his hometown citizens. In doing so, as in *Hail the Conquering Hero,* he heals local conflicts, achieves a sort of rebirth, and bolsters the confidence of a nation at war.

As the first flashback begins, the screen is filled with crowds, principally made up of soldiers. Crossing the street, they disrupt traffic and pedestrians; a group enters a music store and invites Trudy (Betty Hutton) to their going-away dance. Sturges gives considerable screen time to the boisterous dancing and singing crowds of soldiers and local girls, the kind of crowd that Canetti calls a "*Festmasse.*" The next day, we watch the throngs of soldiers departing for the battlefield. In short, a war crowd dominates the opening of *The Miracle of Morgan's Creek,* although, as befits a comedy, it is in a festive mood.

Canetti remarks that each of two opposing nations at war "wants to constitute the larger crowd" (68). In its quirky way, that will also be the goal of *The Miracle of Morgan's Creek,* on behalf of its characters and, eventually, the allies in World War II. (Sturges carefully ignores the other goal of a war crowd, to pile up heaps of enemy dead—hardly an appropriate subject for this comic film.)

One of the largest conceivable crowds is the ever-increasing progeny that most societies have hoped for, and it is this crowd that *The Miracle of Morgan's Creek* ultimately invokes. Early in the film, Trudy's father (William Demarest) reads an alarming editorial about the danger of impulsive marriages "made in a moment" between impressionable girls and departing soldiers. During the farewell dance for those going off to battle, an intoxicated G.I. repeatedly says, "I got a wunnerful idea; let's all get married!" The chief threat to Morgan's Creek of these young men is not their capacity for killing but for procreating. That is also, *The Miracle of Morgan's Creek* will suggest, their promise. Just that promise is fulfilled at the end of the film when Trudy delivers "SIX! ALL BOYS! SIX!" an inspiring event that provokes a succession of newspaper headlines like "PLATOON BORN IN MIDWEST." As one of the characters says in *The Sin of Harold Diddlebock,* "Posterity is just around the corner."

Newspapers and their readers create an especially common and easy-to-recruit crowd. Filmmakers were quick to discover and embrace this combination as a mainstay "Hollywood montage," one that became a cliché by the 1930s. In *The Miracle of Morgan's Creek*, these montages of newspaper headlines and the readers they imply not only express the joy of the Allied war crowd but also convey the alarm of the leaders of the opposing one: "MUSSOLINI RESIGNS," "HITLER DEMANDS RECOUNT."

Soldiers-as-breeders call up an incongruously peaceful war crowd, yet one that is also—to use a word Sturges favors—natural. "NATURE ANSWERS TOTAL WAR," declares one of the headlines. Presiding over Norval's futile attempt to marry Trudy as "Ratziwatski," the justice of the peace advises them, "You'll want lots and lots of little babies. You know, for the patter of little footsie-wootsies." (In this comedy of multiplication, Sturges's writing favors doublets.) The night before the sextuplets arrive, the benignant Mr. Raffery (Julius Tannen) says, "Trudy, you're feeling good, huh? It's natural." Nature is on our side, it seems.

For all that love and marriage may be natural, however, *The Miracle of Morgan's Creek* often views them equivocally. In a film full of symbolic pratfalls, perhaps the most pointed comes when Norval spectacularly brings down porch railing, gutter, foliage, and himself immediately after Trudy maneuvers him into proposing. When she finds herself unable to continue deceiving him, her sister (Diana Lynn) protests, "But he's perfect; he could do the housework." The partly ironic view of marriage embedded in *The Miracle of Morgan's Creek* is well summed up by the titles of the triple-feature playing at the local cinema: *The Bride Wore Purple*, *The Road to Reno*, and *Are Husbands Necessary?*—the last of which anticipates *Are Snakes Necessary?* the book Hopsie reads in *The Lady Eve* (and alludes to Thurber's *Is Sex Necessary?* [1929]).

The eventual marriage of Trudy and Norval is redeemed from irony by Norval's declaration that he has loved Trudy since "you weren't hardly bigger than the firecrackers" at their first Fourth of July party. "It's always been for you and nobody but you." Similar formulations certify true love in *Hail the Conquering Hero* and *The Lady Eve*. Stanley Cavell has discussed such romantic configurations in *Pursuits of Happiness*. "Almost without exception these films [comedies of remarriage] allow the principal pair to express the wish to be children again, or perhaps to be children together. In part this is a wish . . . to be cared for first, and unconditionally."[4] *The Miracle of Morgan's Creek* is a particularly eccentric variation of a comedy of remarriage. Trudy's first husband, "Ratziwatski or Zitzskiwitski," never appears, has no real name or memorable identity, and for purposes of the film hardly exists at all. What's more, Norval attempts to marry Trudy under the name Ratziwatski, a marriage later validated retroactively by the governor of the state. Guided by Cavell, one might argue that the maturing necessary for the heroes of Sturges's films requires a return to childishness, a childishness sometimes abandoned prematurely, before it was concluded. Lacking a childhood—which we can consider a sort of crowd membership—these heroes lack the qualifications, as it were, to join the next developmental crowd, that of adults. Brian Henderson notes that "Norval has a job in a bank but he has no prospects, no self-confidence, and no sense of belonging anywhere."[5] Such protagonists must, as Cavell writes, "turn the tables on time, making marriage the arena and the discovery of innocence."[6] We see this most strikingly in *The Sin of Harold Diddlebock.*

For love to triumph in Morgan's Creek, it requires the aid of its near relative, the other part of the title, a miracle. Sturges, as I have argued elsewhere, often evokes Christian myths; and *The Miracle of Morgan's Creek* does so insistently.[7] The first religious allusion comes, appropriately, from Norval: "Remember what it says in the Bible, 'Sufficient unto the day is the evil thereof.'" The miraculous rebirth of hope and forgiveness in Morgan's Creek takes place on Christmas, which occurs in the dead of winter during a time of threat and rejection and which is the obvious Christian analog for what becomes of Trudy and Norval. The churchy sound of an organ being played by Trudy's sister introduces the scene on Christmas Eve. Trudy's father urges his discouraged daughter to have more faith in "the Almighty, or whatever it is that makes the wheels go round." As the sequence unfolds, the invocation of the Nativity is elaborated, with an old Jewish man (Mr. Raffery) bearing a gift, a cow appearing in the kitchen, and Trudy's father saying, "Remember where He was born."

We should notice another Christian analog, Norval's sublimated imitation of Christ. The strongest clue may be found in his repeatedly expressed desire to sacrifice himself for Trudy. At first, it appears that this desire achieves little more than the firing of Trudy's father from his job as a town policeman and the ostracism of Trudy's whole family. From a lonely beginning, Norval himself eventually falls to the status of pariah. He becomes the prey of baiting crowds of citizens and of cops who comically struggle for the privilege of arresting him, while from the townspeople comes a cry condemning the supposed deceiver, "Shame on you, Norval Jones!"

An everymanish Jones, just as the protagonist of *Hail the Conquering Hero* was a (Tru)Smith, Norval also faintly echoes the Son of Man in his mysterious parentage (he doesn't have any). Rejected and depised, he finds himself on Christmas Eve in jail again with his persecutors threatening to throw away the key to his cell.

As in *Hail the Conquering Hero,* the brilliant reversal that comes immediately after darkest night is compressed, complete, and attended by exuberant crowds. Newly uniformed and elevated to colonel in the State Guard by the governor, married "for always and always" to Trudy, Norval ascends to his wife's hospital room in a cheering crowd accompanied by a spirited rendition of "The Stars and Stripes Forever." "You're a papa," Trudy tells him. Norval, accepting his adult role, allows, "I feel like one, anyway."

At this point, we need to remember the affliction that kept Norval out of the armed forces, "the spots." Canetti identifies such symptoms as interior crowds, associated with mental illness and ailments like delirium tremens. Norval's anxiety-produced internal crowd prevents him from joining the external one of soldiers and, incidentally, from attracting the young women who follow them. When Norval discovers that he is now father and colonel to sextuplets, he crashes panic stricken back into Trudy's room. The uproar summons the throng in the hall, and Sturges brings together in a final moment the lovers and three important crowds: the previously bickering townspeople, the six infants (just down the hall), and—superimposed on the screen and now external to Norval, who is in the shot—"the spots." Norval will recover from his shock, accept the "greatness thrust upon" him, and "become increasingly happy." The crowd of anxious spots within that prevented him from joining the crowd of soldiers and, therefore, the other crowds of his community, has merged with them. Norval finds himself not just a soldier, the husband of the woman he has always loved, and "a papa," but also at the center of the crowds of his community, state, nation, and its worldwide allies.

The Sin of Harold Diddlebock

The Sin of Harold Diddlebock is another of Sturges's comic romances in which crowds figure as largely as the conventional fortune and bride-to-be-won. Harold's (Harold Lloyd) principal task is to regain the adulation of the crowd he won at the beginning of his adult life (as a college freshman), then lost during twenty years of anonymous, ill-paid drudgery. Sturges treats money in this film as much as a crowd symbol as currency; and the bride the hero claims at the end is the seventh Miss Otis (Frances Ramsden) of a succession of sisters with whom he has been in love—a small crowd there, too. Harold's summary of his amorous history with the Otis clan verifies their status as a crowd: "I've been in love with the same girl all my life, 'cept in different bodies." In a crowd, Canetti noted, "it is as though everything were happening in one and the same body" (16).

When *The Sin of Harold Diddlebock* begins after the opening credits, the audience learns, "The football game you are about to see was *actually photographed* in 1923 as part of Harold Lloyd's famous picture 'The Freshman': The story of a waterboy who thought he was a member of the team." Behind this text is an image of what Canetti identifies as an especially dense crowd, a packed stadium. During the roughly seven minutes that include footage from Lloyd's *The Freshman,* Sturges cuts back and forth between the football game (itself a crowd scene) and the alternately cheering and despairing crowd, with a long sequence of the exultant mass of spectators after the waterboy scores the winning touchdown. For the first seven and a half minutes of *The Sin of Harold Diddlebock,* we look at images of crowds most of the time.

The penultimate scenes of the movie are also dominated by crowd images, first as Harold tours the financial district with a docile lion named Jackie and then when his publicity stunt succeeds in bringing a host of buyers to bid on the circus he imprudently bought while under the influence. The first of these crowds, the "near riot . . . created when he appeared on Wall Street leading the lion," as one of the newspaper headlines in the Hollywood montage describes it, has an archetypal resonance. The original command, according to Canetti, results in flight and is "older than speech" (303). His example of such a command is a lion's roar. When animals living in large groups—gazelles, for example, or humans—hear that primitive command, they flee; and "the collective fear of a herd in flight is the oldest and perhaps the commonest example of a crowd state" (309). I consider predation and command in more depth during discussions of *North by Northwest, Killer of Sheep,* and *The Silence of the Lambs,* but for *The Sin of Harold Diddlebock* we should note, first, Sturges's instinct for turning out flight crowds with a prototypical lion; and, second, his ironic enlisting of this primal hunter against the financial predators called, in this movie, "bankers." That bankers are predators Sturges makes clear;

the first one we see is happily sending notice to a debtor that he intends "to take over your building." He is amused by a flight crowd that rushes through his office, followed a few moments later by Harold and Jackie—who amuse him much less. Similar scenes of panicked bankers are replayed when Harold and Jackie terrify a succession of these "despised" financiers.

Like the final crowds of *Hail the Conquering Hero* and *The Miracle of Morgan's Creek,* that of *The Sin of Harold Diddlebock* transforms into a *Festmasse,* a joyful group united by a happy occasion. In primitive societies, the occasion is often the feast in which the prey is divided following a successful hunt. In *The Sin of Harold Diddlebock* something of a hunting crowd remains in the bankers who are contesting for Harold's circus.

As often happens at the end of romantic narratives, the betrothed or newly wedded couple is removed from the madding crowd. It is also frequently the case that the happy couple is accompanied by crowd symbols and/or some sort of guiding spirit for the actual crowd of the audience. In *The Sin of Harold Diddlebock* both are present. The crowd symbol is money, the check for $175,000, a number Harold repeats again and again in wonderment. After his firing—his expulsion from the company that seems to have constituted his main (if meager) social place—Harold begins to create a new crowd around himself with the modest nest egg he has accumulated during two decades of accountancy. As this money multiplies, so do the crowd symbols and, predictably, the crowds. These include Harold wearing an outlandish suit of "the check within the check within the check" in crowded nightclubs surrounded by new friends and dancing, on one occasion, in a line of chorines. By the end of this delirious night, he has also acquired the enormous pack of hungry carnivores, hay eaters, and employees that come with a circus.

One of the last shots of the film is addressed to the audience in the movie theater. After Harold learns that he's married to Miss Otis, he offers to have the marriage annulled because of the difference in their ages. "I don't think that would be practical, Mr. Diddlebock," she replies demurely. He then offers a divorce, which brings an even more remarkable response: "I, I love you, Mr. Diddlebock." As the newlyweds embrace after this declaration, Sturges cuts to the starchy English driver of Harold's horse-drawn cab. He wipes a tear from his eye, this witness within the film cuing the audience in the theater with a self-conscious emotion and humor at once sincere and parodic. Precisely such multiple meanings, one might add, characterize the film as a whole and most of Sturges's other work as well.

Between the scarcely plausible triumphs of beginning and end, Harold's career follows the trajectory one would expect of a romantic hero: loss of position, descent into the underworld (a comic one in this slapstick comedy), harrowing adventures during a precarious ascent, personal maturing, and recovery of all that was lost with much more added.

Harold's decline begins when he shows up to claim the job promised him by an ecstatic alum, E. J. Waggleberry (Raymond Walburn), after his winning touchdown. His new boss no longer remembers him; Harold's bright young star has already started to dim. A few minutes of screen time and twenty-two years of plot time later, the tattered, tired, middle-aged man that he has become meets the boss in his office again, this time to be told, "You have become a bottleneck" and to be released from the company. As he leaves the office building, crowd and crowd symbols alike only emphasize his isolation. Passing pedestrians bump into him as if he weren't there and cause him to drop the stack of cards with uplifting slogans that he attached to the wall by his desk when he first put his bottom on the stool there (a shot that Sturges includes in close-up). Another close-up shows the feet of the passing crowd stepping on the card that was closest to Harold's desk, "Success is just around the corner." (Within his dismal exit interview, however, is buried another cliché to add to Harold's abundant collection, one that the rest of the film will confirm: "A man is as young as his ideas.")

As it happens, success does come literally from just around the corner in the person of Wormy (Jimmy Conlin), an out-of-luck-and-money player of horses. At the end of the duel of popular admonitions in which the two engage, this aptly named person leads Harold down into a basement bar and it appears that two of the other cards we see on Harold's wall will be more to the point, "An ounce of security is worth a pound of pipe dreams" and "A fool and his money are soon parted." Harold's fondness for such slogans, we should note, has at least two functions. First, they confirm his dearth of anything like independent thought, a dearth he shares with many of the other characters. Second, his partiality for such bromides marks him as one of the crowd of ordinary people, much as did the names of Trusmith and Jones in *Hail the Conquering Hero* and *The Miracle of Morgan's Creek*.

When a sympathetic bartender (Edgar Kennedy, in a memorable performance typical of the character actors in Sturges's films) learns that Harold is about to have his first alcoholic drink, he invents an infernally potent mix that he calls "The Diddlebock." A few hefty swallows transform Harold into an impulsive, howling creature that he himself seems partly unconscious of—a comic Dr. Jekyll and Mr. Hyde. So begin the underground adventures that will ultimatey lead back up to the glory of renewed crowds, rehiring with a promotion, and a beautiful wife. Harold's reascent has its ups and downs, the most precarious of which comes near the end of the film and has him dangling many stories above the street, his fall prevented only by a leash attached to Jackie. Escaping that fatal descent, he finds himself in jail—very much as Norval does just before the reversal of his fortunes.

Harold's alcoholic loss of himself is a plot device *The Sin of Harold Diddlebock* shares with the concussions of Trudy in *The Miracle of Morgan's Creek* and John Sullivan in *Sullivan's Travels*. The lie forced on Woodrow in *Hail the Conquering Hero* and the misleading detective's report that Sir Alfred has more or less forced upon him in *Unfaithfully Yours* lead to similar temporary losses of their true identities. The heroes of romantic comedies, like other seekers in other contexts, must lose themselves in order to find themselves.

In addition to losing his identity, and the crowds, job, and future he might have had with the last of the Miss Otises, Harold loses time—a point that Sturges takes some pains to emphasize. As the photos of the U.S. presidents change on a calendar above his desk, twenty-two years hurry by. While dismissing him, Waggleberry remarks that Harold has "gone backward" and "stopped thinking" in the years of his employment. The slogans on the wall by his desk leave white rectangles in the grime of two decades when Harold removes them (and himself) from his corner. Most important, he can remember nothing of the Wednesday between his Tuesday morning firing and his awakening on a living room sofa Thursday. "That must be what I was doing all day Wednesday!" he exclaims when he realizes that he spent the day marrying and consummating his marriage to Miss Otis. He then emits, for the last time, the unearthly cry that he first uttered unconsciously as The Diddlebock took effect. But this yowl signifies the redemption of the lost day and the lost years, his long-postponed adulthood and success, and his recovery of the embraces of the surrounding crowd that he first experienced as The Freshman.

Sullivan's Travels

"The most revolutionary emotion of the masses: their laughter."

WALTER BENJAMIN[8]

Sullivan's Travels embodies one of the theses of this study: movies are crowd machines. Its protagonist (Joel McCrea) looks and acts much like a standard-issue hero of a romantic comedy. Somewhat immature (his youth is emphasized in his early dispute with two studio executives), he nonetheless has a prestigious place in Hollywood that he will lose and, after harrowing adventures in a terrifying world far below the one he used to inhabit, regain. He also has a good deal of the innocence of his literary forebear, Swift's Gulliver. For all that, he is old enough to have a wife; and he does, but the wrong one. On the tax advice of his dishonest business manager, he married a woman he neither loves nor lives with, but whom legalities prevent him from divorcing. Updating only slightly a familiar fairy tale, Sturges will arrange for him to be rescued from this "dragon lady" by a poor maiden, noble in heart and lovely in person.

As in the majority of Sturges's comedies, the loss and recovery of a crowd is as important as the more standard goals of his romantic quest. Within this familiar (for Sturges) pattern, *Sullivan's Travels* portrays with particular complexity the textures and motives of its crowds, the relation of its hero to them, and the relation of both to Hollywood movies and the culture of which they are part.

Among the groups depicted in *Sullivan's Travels,* the smallest is the one to which Sullivan belongs as the story opens, the rich and glamorous and their servants and retainers. This group does not have the equality of a true crowd, and Sullivan spends most of the first hour of the movie trying to escape it—with little success and considerable slapstick comedy.

Although it appears that he is attempting to leave his privileged surroundings in order to join the crowd of depression poor, such is not exactly the case. He proposes his excursion into the world of the dispossessed because he wishes to stop making frothy comedies and become a serious, socially conscious filmmaker, "like

Capra." He wants to make the sort of thing invoked by the movie-within-the-movie that we see as *Sullivan's Travels* begins. When it ends after a few overwrought minutes, Sullivan enthusiastically declares it to be a morally significant allegory in which "capital and labor destroy each other." Describing the next film he aspires to make, *O Brother, Where Art Thou?* he unleashes a fusillade of earnest high-brow clichés: "social significance," "a commentary on modern conditions, stark realism, the problems that confront the average man," "a mirror up to life," "a true canvas of the suffering of humanity," "the potentialities of film as the sociological and artistic medium that it is." Though he is spouting a different set of slogans, Sullivan's pretentious oration contains no more real thinking than does Harold Diddlebock's collection of uplifting mottoes. It does, however, define the group that he would like to join, an elite group of serious, socially significant filmmakers.

Yet another group is implied during the opening sequences of *Sullivan's Travels*, the crowd of movie fans who have flocked to such Sullivan hits as *Hey! Hey! In the Hayloft* and *Ants in Your Pants of 1939*. From this vulgar crowd, as from the elite group around him in the studio, Sullivan also desires to flee.

To qualify himself to make his "picture of dignity," Sullivan decides to explore the ranks of the rootless poor by becoming a hobo. The homeless and transient that he joins are multitudinous, but from the perspective of *Crowds and Power* they do not make up a true crowd. The characteristics that all crowds share, to review, are the desire to grow, equality among members, density, and a clearly understood goal (direction). The masses of poor, as Sturges portrays them, have density and the undesired equality of impoverishment, but lack any urge to grow as a crowd or any shared goal beyond changing their situation. They are unified only under compulsion, as when the convicts march in chains or when the hungry sit through a sermon in order to get the free lunch that follows. Even were these poor to make up a crowd, moreover, Sullivan could not honestly join it. Like Woodrow during most of *Hail the Conquering Hero* or the title character in *The Great McGinty*, he is a fake—a point Sturges emphasizes by having a studio photographer surreptitiously take a publicity shot of Sullivan among the real hobos in his costume from the studio's wardrobe department.

When Sullivan tries on his new ragged outfit early in the movie, his butler (Robert Greig) warns him against his proposed excursion. The "filth, criminality, vice, and despair" of poverty, he declares, are "only a few of its symptoms. It is to be stayed away from, even for purposes of study. It is to be shunned." In a lighter vein, but expressing the same distaste for Sullivan's pretensions, The Girl (Veronica Lake) pushes him into his swimming pool "for making fun of a poor girl like me who only tried to help you."

Sturges underlines both the squalor of poverty and the fact that those afflicted with it do not constitute a crowd when he inserts a contrasting sequence into the story during Sullivan's third attempt to do his research. Accompanied this time by The Girl, Sullivan has spent two days and nights among filthy, sad, hungry people. Faced with the prospect of a third miserable night, he and The Girl take an evening stroll through small trees along a lake, under billowing clouds. Considered as part of their developing romance, this detour gives them a chance to be alone together, away from surrounding masses. Equally important, however, is the difference between the miserable, anomic human environment and a lovely natural setting made up of the woods, clouds, and water that Canetti identified as suggesting various aspects of crowds. Sturges's inserting of these natural crowd symbols here subtly sharpens our sense of the poor as hosts that, even in their mutual misery, are not coherent crowds.

Movie audiences, elsewhere the most unified crowds in *Sullivan's Travels*, appear to be as uninterested in portrayals of "the suffering of humanity" as Sullivan's butler and the studio executives. "Who wants to see that kind of stuff?" one of them says. "It gives me the creeps." During a triple-feature to which an unenthusiastic Sullivan has been hauled, cellophane rattles, a boy blows a whistle, a baby loudly fusses, a man hiccups while crunching popcorn, and the matron whose wood Sullivan has been chopping makes tentative advances. The titles of these unengaging pictures? *Beyond These Tears*, *The Valley of the Shadow*, and *The Buzzard of Berlin*. One suspects that most of the audience is there for the added attraction: "also *Swingo*."

The most serious warning the butler offers, "Such excursions can be extremely dangerous," comes to pass, ironically, when Sullivan dons his costume a last time to distribute five-dollar bills among the needy. One of them follows him and knocks him unconscious in order to rob him. We may remember again the interchange with the butler. "I'm doing it for the poor; don't you understand?" "I doubt if they would appreciate it, Sir," replies this man whose own study of poverty was undertaken "quite unwillingly."

As if to second the butler's reservations, circumstances keep returning Sullivan, usually against his will, to Hollywood. His travels among the poor are not especially interesting, nor does he elicit much sympathy while on them—except when his role becomes comic as, for example, during his clumsy struggle to hop a freight train ("amateurs," says one watching tramp to another), or during his encounters with an amorous widow, fleas, and the unpalatable food served in mess halls for the indigent. Those uncomfortable but harmless adventures imply through our experience of the film a point that *Sullivan's Travels* will eventually make explicit; Sullivan is both a member and a creator of an especially unified and happy crowd, those who laugh.

We first witness such a crowd during one of Sturges's most famous sequences, the movie screening attended by chain gang prisoners, including Sullivan, in a simple country church. The sequence begins with two appeals to egalitarian feeling—the ironies of which are broad—by the black pastor. He asks the congregation to make their guests welcome and not to look down upon them, reminding his listeners, "We's all equal in the sight of God," and leading them in singing "Go Down Moses" ("let my people go") as the shackled men shuffle in. Only when the Disney cartoon comes on, however, do the people in the church unite as a crowd. As Sullivan joins the laughter, he experiences the membership he has sought from the beginning in the wide crowd of humanity. Chained, among poor blacks and wretched convicts, he realizes the freedom and community of laughter.

As in *The Miracle of Morgan's Creek,* the religious dimensions of this scene are obvious. Like the heroes of *Miracle* and *The Sin of Harold Diddlebock,* Sullivan finds himself in the ultimate symbol of ostracism, a jail. In an underworld that includes a dog named Pluto, he is figuratively as dead as the rest of the world believes him to be literally. A bit like a comically inept Christ, he will be resurrected—albeit he must confess to his own murder for that to be accomplished.

When he returns from the dead (Sturges shows Sullivan's wife-widow by his gravestone), he also reclaims the crowd that he attempted to spurn, those who love such movies as *Hey! Hey!* and *Ants in Your Pants.* We see this heretofore implied crowd for the first time when he is welcomed back by a throng of photographers and well-wishers—including the truck driver who once gave him a lift, his Hollywood colleagues, and, of course, The Girl. The last is

71

The crowd spirit of laughter

now—thanks to his wife's remarriage to his business manager after his apparent death—his fiancée. His resurrection frees him of the illusion that he ought to make a socially significant film, of his snobbishness toward his true audience, and of "the dragon lady."

As *Sullivan's Travels* ends, its happier but wiser hero declares that he no longer wishes to make *O Brother, Where Art Thou?* (the Coen brothers have since done so), but to direct another comedy instead. Laughter, he has learned, is "all some people have . . . in this cockeyed caravan." Twenty seconds of crowd imagery ends the film, a montage of multiple printing that begins with a reprise of the laughter in the church, including Sullivan's, then goes to a hospital ward, and ends with an imagistic whirlpool of laughing people of all ages, sexes, and—as far as one can tell—classes. The last shot places Sullivan and The Girl in the center of swirling, smiling, laughing faces—as summary an image of a joyful society coalescing around a newly joined couple as may be found at the conclusion of any comedy.[9] "The End" rises through this mélange toward the surface of the screen, referring us back to the movie-in-a-movie with which *Sullivan's Travels* began. (The closing title of that melodramatic bit of filmmaking, at once similar to and radically different from the final title of *Sullivan's Travels*, arose out of the turbulent waters into which disappeared the doomed personifications labor and capital, gripped together in death.) If we are alert to the implications of what we have just watched, we will turn back yet another page, to the dedication immediately preceding the opening of the movie: "To the memory of those who made us laugh: the motley mountebanks, the clowns, the buffoons, in all times and in all nations, whose efforts have lightened our burden a little." Introducing *Sullivan's Travels*, the movie in which more than any other he reflected upon his own role in the world, Sturges invokes as great a crowd as possible, a crowd that John Sullivan, his silly pictures, and his audiences create and belong to—as do Preston Sturges, his movies, and "us."

3

The Deceitful Dead
and the Triumph of Nothing:
Kurosawa's *Throne of Blood*

For all the freedom it takes with its source, Kurosawa's stirring, austere transformation of *Macbeth* remains remarkably faithful to the
spirit of its original. As with Shakespeare's great work, Kurosawa's
offers apt, precise emblems for the kind of survival sought by
power, for crowds and their symbols, and for the human horror of
the dead. Washizu's (Toshiro Mifune) ascent and ruin, like Macbeth's, traces the vanity of humankind's ambitions beyond its spectacular manifestation as the fall of a great man back to its deeper
origins in the fundamental unknowability of the world. In his
story, we see not only the isolation and paranoia that attaches to
seekers of power but a more universal and deeper terror that, despite all our struggles, only dissolution awaits us.

Macbeth is one of Shakespeare's most ironic tragedies, and
Kurosawa fully retains that pervasive irony in his cinematic adaptation. Shakespeare's drama shifts its realities as unpredictably as
the branches of Birnam Wood. All understanding "is smothered in
surmise, and nothing is but what is not" (III.iii.140–41).[1] The more
one knows, the more perspectives multiply, and the more confused
and self-contradictory become one's conclusions. "Welcome and
unwelcome things at once / 'Tis hard to reconcile" (IV.iii.138–39).
The radically ironic modality of both play and film has the effect of
making truth inconstant and point of view paramount in human
perception of the world.

The indeterminacy of knowledge in *Macbeth*—"Fair is foul and
foul is fair"—is specifically focused in Kurosawa's equally ambigu-

75

ous film on the traditional uncertainty of human enterprises and the reversals of pride and violent ambition. Kurosawa's addition of a moralizing chorus invokes both Western and Japanese classical and neoclassical tragedies thematically centered on the falls of overreachers and on the vanity of human wishes. As Macbeth comes to understand that "all our yesterdays have lighted fools / The way to dusty death" (V.v.22–23), so the chorus of *Throne of Blood* declares, "Death will reign; man dies in vain." But what appears to be the chorus' melancholy resignation to the inevitable end of human aspiration actually contains a surprisingly large measure of triumphant celebration.

Ernest Becker argues in *Escape from Evil* that human behavior—especially the violence that we do to each other—is fundamentally motivated by the fear of death and "the inevitable urge to deny mortality."[2] Summarizing his argument, he writes, "In this book I attempt to show that man's natural and inevitable urge to deny mortality and achieve a heroic self-image are the root causes of human evil."[3] To a considerable degree, *Throne of Blood* may be seen as embodying Becker's view of human behavior and consciousness. It portrays the archetypal heroic struggle as occurring between life and death, with the victory invariably going to the latter.

The antagonists in Kurosawa's film, however, are not simply an ambitious man versus his fate, but a mortal against what is identified in *Crowds and Power* as half of one of three archetypal human "double crowds," the double crowd comprised of the living and the dead. (The others are "war crowds" and the opposing crowds of women and men.) The fear of the dead, Canetti writes, is "universal," for people everywhere attribute to the dead a hostility "to life itself" (262). "In the eyes of those who are still alive, everyone who is dead has suffered a defeat, which consists in *having been survived.* The dead cannot resign themselves to this injury which was inflicted on them, and so it is natural that they should want to inflict it on others" (263). Freud takes a similar view in his oft-cited essay on "The 'Uncanny'" (1919): "Most likely our fear still contains the old belief that the deceased becomes the enemy of his survivor and wants to carry him off to share his new life with him."[4] In *Throne of Blood,* the dead have already outlived the (formerly) living of whom the narrative tells. Such an outcome, from the points of view of both classical tragedy and *Crowds and Power,* is inescapable; for in the "age-old antagonism between the living and the dead," the weight of numbers is on the side of the latter, and "dying is thus a fight, a fight between two enemies of unequal strength" (66–67). Nonetheless, the living continue their "rear-guard action" and the living and dead form an embattled "double crowd, whose component parts continually interact" (67).

(In special cases, however, notably in the ancestor worship of some Chinese and when the quest for fame is aimed at succeeding generations, the relation between the living and the dead can be mutually nourishing.[5] Much more commonly, however, the dead are seen as dangerous to and resentful of the living. Such is the case in *Throne of Blood*. A more benign relationship between living and dead, as we shall see, is portrayed in one important aspect of *The Silence of the Lambs*.)

The ongoing struggle between the ambitions of the living and the malice of the dead often takes the form, in *Throne of Blood*, of a counterpointing of images and themes of crowds set against those of lethal power. In Kurosawa's filmic tragedy, the struggle is indeed unequal; power, associated with death, must emerge ascendant. The alternative to power as a mode of survival, the crowd, is ultimately either enlisted by the forces of the dead or relegated to ineffectuality. The ghostly spirits of *Throne of Blood*, the equivalent of *Macbeth*'s witches, serve as delegates of death. They are a deceitful nexus between the living and those who have died, between crowds and power. In Kurosawa's film, paradoxically, only the hosts of the dead survive.

Dissolution and death begin and conclude *Throne of Blood*. The forlorn sound of wind accompanies the opening images of fog and receding mountain ranges, while the chorus sings of "a proud warrior murdered by ambition." The fortress that will condense from the mists of time as the principal emblem of power in the historical present appears in the narrative present as no more than a few foundation stones. This scene, and many of the same words, end the picture. The spirit of the once-commanding warrior is "walking still," but now as a member of the legions of the dead.

Between these desolate bookends, memento mori recur. After the Spirit of the Cobweb Forest vanishes, Washizu and Miki find themselves among heaps of helmeted skeletal warriors, an army of perished soldiers. When Washizu later returns to receive the Spirit's misleading reassurances, he finds the ghostly figure once more among heaps of skulls, long bones, and armor. The ineradicable bloodstain of the self-murdered traitor Fujimaki serves as backdrop to the assassination of the lord of the Cobweb Castle. Subsequently,

Memento mori early in *Throne of Blood*

only "his Lordship's coffin" will have the power to persuade the defenders of the castle to open its gates. Miki's ghost attends Washizu's ceremonial banquet. The shot of the drugged guards outside the lord's castle—not so much a *tableau vivant* as a *tableau mort*—shows death invading the living and reminds one that, as Lady Macbeth asserts, "The sleeping and the dead / Are but as pictures" (II.ii.52–53).

Reversing her longed-for role as queen mother, Asaji becomes literally a bearer of death. In a disturbing pair of shots, she disappears into the darkness of a mysterious doorway from which she reemerges bearing drugged wine—a brief, parodic death and rebirth, a disappearance into and return from the underworld.[6] When she announces her pregnancy to Washizu, she effectively forces him to arrange the assassination of Miki and his son, an action only half successful. She is quick, however, not with life but with death. Her child is "born dead; it had been dead within her."

Near the end of the film, the dying Washizu collapses onto the fog-wreathed ground in front of his awe-stricken soldiers. A few minutes before, he strode across the screen powerful, confident, and sure of his forces. When the fatal arrow strikes through his throat, he has already begun his descent, his body bristling with the arrows of his own troops. Peter Donaldson notes that "Washizu is killed by . . . a perfectly horizontal shot . . . not merely unexpected, then, but [one which] hints at a supernatural retribution."[7] Like everyone else in *Throne of Blood,* the trajectory of his living ascent is ultimately reversed by the messengers of mortality.

The impulse to form crowds contrasts with movement toward isolation, which characterizes power. Both impulses originate in the desire to survive by avoiding a potentially lethal seizure. (The common use of "seizure" to describe a dire physiological event seems apropos here.) Crowds, of course, are not necessarily benign nor need power be always or wholly malignant. As a deviation of the desire to survive, however, which is tantamount to a deviation of the desire to form crowds, power must finally be malign.

The relatively few (though spectacular) actual crowds in *Throne of Blood* are multiplied symbolically by pervasive crowd symbols. The density of these mostly natural symbols replaces visually the verbal richness of *Macbeth.* Of the dozen examples of crowd symbols Canetti offers, more than half occur repeatedly in *Throne of Blood:* fire, rain, rivers, forest, grain, wind, the heap. Add the fog, tangles of vines and brush, and the invisible but audible crowd of the chorus, and the importance of crowd dynamics—however symbolically sublimated—is unmistakable.

Crowd symbols and most actual crowds ultimately enlist in *Throne of Blood* on the side of the powerful army of the dead. In a work more balanced between irony and the redemption of romance, one could expect to find crowds and their symbols opposing the isolated individualism of power. Such is the case, as I have argued, in most comedies and in cinematic epics like *Intolerance.* In *Throne of Blood,* on the contrary, there is little comedy to balance tragedy; few redemptive notes sweeten what Wallace Stevens called "death's ironic scraping."

Of the witches in *Macbeth,* Banquo remarks, "The earth hath bubbles as the water has And these are of them" (I.iii.79–80). The misty landscapes of *Throne of Blood* bring to the film a similar sense of natural dissolution and the ephemeral. After the foggy opening images, the mists rise like curtains on the stage of the past. The morning of the last day of the action dawns with the stage again shrouded. Symmetrically, the same misty curtain falls on Washizu's death and the end of the tragedy.

Throughout the narrative, crowd symbols of rain, fog, and storm are associated with threat, bafflement, and the contrasting isolation of the protagonists. They are also associated with the ghostly spirits of the Cobweb Forest and, eventually, with death. Lost in a forest they usually know well, Washizu and Miki gallop bewilderedly for a full two minutes of screen time before confronting the Spirit responsible for their confusion. After hearing her prophecy, they wander errant on-screen for another three minutes. These five minutes of disoriented riding in a tightly paced and edited film emphasize not only the amazement and loss of bearings that befall Washizu and Miki, but also the association of tempest, fog, and setting with the deceptive agent of death, the Spirit of the Cobweb Forest.

Stylized images of wind-blown clouds, the heraldic device of the lord of the Cobweb Castle, decorate the walls behind the elevated mats of the Ruler and his Lady. The design recalls the fog and clouds elsewhere in the film, and the representation here is again associated with the isolation of the protagonists. That connection becomes clear when Kurosawa cuts contrastively between Miki's son and the senior general at the head of their army to a shot of Washizu and Asaji sitting alone in front of the cloud mural. *Crowds and Power* helps clarify the interpretation of this imagery. Clouds and rain are ambivalent crowd symbols: "Rain is the crowd in the moment of discharge, and stands also for its disintegration. The clouds whence it comes dissolve into rain; the drops fall because they can keep together no longer, and it is not clear whether, or when, they can coalesce again" (82). This description accords with the equivocal imagery of fog and downpour in *Throne of Blood*. At once a symbol of crowds and of their dissolution, the mist and rain suggest simultaneously both masses (often dangerous ones, as I have argued) and the mortal solitude that precedes absorption into the host of those who have passed into the eternity of death.

Another of the predominant images of *Throne of Blood*, the forest, stands as a complex, resonant crowd symbol. Dense and compelling awe, it "is *higher* than man. It may be enclosed and overgrown with all kinds of scrub; it may be hard to penetrate, and still

Army merging into its symbol

harder to traverse" (84). *Throne of Blood* portrays the forest very much as *Crowds and Power* describes it. Canetti develops his discussion further, to make a point equally illuminating for Kurosawa's film: "Another, and no less important, aspect of the forest is its multiple immovability. . . . Its resistance is absolute. . . . And thus the forest has become the symbol of the *army,* an army which has taken up a position" (84). The irony of Washizu's dependence upon the forest's archetypal immobility is obvious; the deep cultural power of that irony (as in Shakespeare's original) can be understood in light of Canetti's insights into the forest's symbolic martial steadfastness. If the reassurance of the forest is illusory then, by extension, human hope for security may be equally fleeting.

As *Throne of Blood* unfolds, the forest transforms from an image of an army into the army itself. Two shots of the soldiers advancing to attack Washizu in the castle make explicit the conjunction between the forest and the army. In the first—which Kurosawa

81

holds for a full forty seconds without any camera movement—a line of soldiers at the top of the screen advances toward the trees at the bottom. In the second, the camera tracks the soldiers as they stream into the vegetation. By the next morning, after a night full of the sound of axes in dark woods, the army and the trees have literally become one: "The forest has begun to move this way!" The boughs of the Cobweb Forest, concealing the soldiers who bear them, advance toward the castle; and in that startling sight, Washizu and his troops see the certainty of their defeat by a natural crowd, the mobility of which had been unimaginable. In this sequence, it might be added, we see again the power of the cinema to morph the symbol of a crowd into the crowd itself.

Immediately preceding this image, another crowd merged with its symbol. What sounds at first like a downpour turns out to be the noise of the armor of hundreds of soldiers, Washizu's defenders, fleeing panic-stricken before the moving forest. Rain again signifies at once a crowd and the moment of its dissolution. As Washizu lies dead before his army—which stands immobile as forests and armies are supposed to—two of the crowd symbols that dominate *Throne of Blood* flow together; fog swirls around the corpse while the branches of the conquering army advance.[8]

Let us detour briefly from Kurosawa's film into one whose similarities become evident when viewed from a Canettian perspective. Like *Throne of Blood*, Stanley Kubrick's *The Shining* (1980) has a central figure whom the dead deceive into an assault on the living that is ultimately fatal to himself. The hosts of the dead and their symbolic equivalents bear a striking resemblance in both substance and function to the spirits and central crowd symbols (the forest and the rain and fog, particularly) of *Throne of Blood*.

The first three minutes of *The Shining*, which encompass spectacular aerial shots during the credit sequence, are dense with images of forest and mountains similar to those in the opening of *Throne of Blood*. The alpine snowfields of *The Shining* occupy the place of rain in *Throne of Blood*. When Jack (Jack Nicholson) returns with his family to the Overlook Hotel, the imagery is repeated, with the addition of clouds and fog wreathing the snowy mountains. This imagery will become more conspicuous when the family returns to take up residence on closing day in the fall. The snow intensifies as *The Shining* moves toward an ending in which, as in *Throne of Blood*, the protagonist joins the hosts of the dead. As the blizzard begins, we see for the first time that Jack has become man-

ifestly unbalanced and isolated from his family. His craziness intensifies as the storm intensifies; simultaneously, the crowd of the
dead appears more insistently and numerously in the hotel. The
second time Jack is at the bar, the ballroom is filled with celebrants
in 1920s dress and Jack is baited into attacking ("correcting") his
wife and child by the long-dead axe-murderer Grady. (On this occasion, the equally long-dead Lloyd and Grady function much as
do the witches/spirits in *Macbeth* and *Throne of Blood*.)

By the closing sequences of *The Shining*, the snow has become
a dominant presence outside the hotel while the ghosts of its violent, dissolute past dominate the inside, ultimately shedding their
living identities for dead ones, skeletons covered with dust and
cobwebs. As the dead terrorize Jack's wife (Shelly Duvall) within,
Jack pursues his son with an axe in the storm outside.

Like Macbeth and Washizu, Jack is transformed into one of
the dead. His final metamorphosis is analogous to a cinematic
crowd symbol that blends into the actual crowd itself. We first see
Jack's dead, unblinking face in the snow; he has become physically
a part of the frozen world. Kubrick then cuts to the inside of the
hotel, and a tracking shot takes us to a group photo hanging on the
wall, evidently memorializing a grand occasion in the Overlook's
past. Prominent in the front of the pictured crowd is Jack. Two dissolves bring an extreme close-up of his grinning face, then the camera tilts down to reveal the date and occasion of the photo: "Overlook Hotel, July 4th Ball, 1921." Outside, Jack has been incorporated into the blizzard; inside, he has somehow been added to the
crowd of long dead hotel guests and employees.[9]

Forests—another crowd symbol *The Shining* shares with *Throne
of Blood*—recur as the hedge of the maze adjacent to the hotel,
which we first see densely green and later covered with snow. Between those images, the maze appears as a drawing and as a model
that changes into a three-dimensional abstraction with a particularly crowdlike aspect. When it reveals the tiny speaking figures of
the wife and child, it seems to collaborate (in retrospect) with the
wicked dead of the hotel in isolating them from Jack. Even more
than the labyrinthine Cobweb Forest in which Washizu and Miki
go astray, the maze of *The Shining* fits quite literally Canetti's description of the forest-as-crowd-symbol; it is tall, enclosed, and
dense, "hard to penetrate, and still harder to traverse." And it ultimately traps and kills the protagonist of *The Shining*, as the Cobweb
Forest does Washizu.

The point of this digression is not to claim that *Throne of Blood* influenced *The Shining*. Rather, the fact that the crowd symbols of the earlier film recur in similar contexts in the later one demonstrates how akin such symbols can be in movies of quite different genres, times and places of production, and literary pedigrees.

To return to *Throne of Blood,* imagery of signifying animals—frequently flocks of them—reaches its aural and visual climax during the closing moments of Kurosawa's film. When Washizu's soldiers flee like sheets of rain, flocks of terrified pigeons and screaming crows, birds of ill omen, fly from the castle. The birds, and elsewhere horses, transport from Shakespeare's play pervasive animal imagery: croaking ravens, shrieking owls, steeds become cannibals. As Asaji spells out her plan to murder the lord, crows scream outside; they call again as she puts a spear into her husband's irresolute hand. Earlier, when she first broached the idea of his taking over the castle, a horse whinnied, recalling his and Miki's terrified mounts when they were lost in the forest. Like Banquo's horses in *Macbeth,* Miki's suddenly turns wild, refusing to allow grooms to put on its saddle. When it comes back without its noble rider, the servants call it "possessed." Chorus-like, Washizu's soldiers and servants talk later of rats deserting the castle's rotten foundations.

The horses, crows, and other animals of *Throne of Blood* function as yet another set of crowd symbols. Like all the symbolic crowds of this intensely ironic work, they join the spirit of death that subtends its world. The linking of the animals, the forest, and the primal crowd symbols of fog, wind, and rainstorm suggest that underlying life lurk powers of dissolution. The crowds and crowd symbols in *Throne of Blood* either serve the armies of death or are absorbed into them. So too will those individuals whose power gives them, for a season, command. The picture of the world in *Throne of Blood* supports a cosmic understanding like that in Freud's *Beyond the Pleasure Principle.* Within life itself the elemental forces of death lie in wait, forces that neither living crowds nor mortal power can long resist.

Murder, traps, weapons, and deceit—the means of power in *Throne of Blood*—all turn against those who wield them. Killing saturates the culture of power; Washizu and Asaji are not its sole purveyors. We first witness political execution when the Lord of the Forest, refusing to accept the rebel leader Fujimaki's apology, orders his senior commander to put him to death for his treachery. The lord, we later learn, achieved his station by killing his predecessor;

and Miki will assume command of the castle after Washizu's troops slaughter him. Like the suicide's blood and like the imagined blood that Asaji cannot wash from her hands, the stain of killing is indelibly fixed in the politics of power.

Advocating the murder of the lord, Asaji makes arguments that illustrate quite specifically Canetti's description of how wars begin: "People decide that they are threatened with physical destruction. . . . They say 'I can be killed,' and secretly add 'because I myself want to kill this or that man'" (71). There can be no peace, Asaji tells her husband, because the lord will attack him if Miki reveals the prophecy. He has "only two choices," to await destruction or to kill his lord. Her argument ends with a concise abstract of the inherent paranoia of power: "In this world you must strike first if you do not want to be killed." All killing, then, becomes self-defense.

Even for those who accept this rationale for murder, however, outliving "carries with it considerable uneasiness for the survivors" (269). Asaji cries, "The blood, will it never come off?" Washizu's suspicion of his generals drives two of them to kill themselves and he murders the assassin he employed to kill Miki and his son. These actions reflect the restless anxiety of those who survive through power. The Spirit, and the three others who assemble for the final prophecy, carry the ethos of power to its logical extremes. "If you would walk with demons," urges the Second Spirit, "do so only in the most cruel, hideous way." "I will kill everyone!" shouts Washizu. The Third Spirit urges him to build a mountain of bodies that reaches the sky, and the Fourth tells him to let blood flow like a river.

Although it has notable minutes of violent action, *Throne of Blood* more frequently settles into an intensely charged stasis. When the lord is murdered, we hear no cry, see no rapid movement. Immediately afterward, Washizu sits panting and motionless. Like the long periods of stillness or indecisive movement punctuated by occasional episodes of energetic action that characterize *Throne of Blood,* the exercise of power "begins with the active and deliberate secrecy of lying in wait and ends as something unknown and involuntary in the secret recesses of the body. Only the intervening moment of seizure flashes out, like lightning illuminating its own brief passage" (290).

In accordance with this secretive, lurking sense of power, images that suggest traps reappear throughout *Throne of Blood.* As

One of the snares of the dead in *Throne of Blood*

Washizu and Miki gallop in circles, the tracking camera views them through natural snares of vines, brush, and branches. Similar shots accompany Washizu when he returns alone. The Forest Spirit becomes visible at the end of these tangled journeys in a hut that looks like a trap or cage. Before they pierce him, the volleys of arrows aimed at Washizu by his forces, recalling the stick-walls of the Spirit's dwelling, restrain his flight.

The arrows fired at him by Washizu's own archers underline the tendency of weapons in *Throne of Blood*—when they are not simply useless—to recoil against those who wield them. The first attempt to use weapons, Washizu's bowshots and Miki's spear thrusts against the unseen Forest Spirit, yields only derisive laughter. Later Washizu will draw his sword and slash at the air above Miki's empty seat at the banquet, making obvious again the helplessness of weapons against the spirits of the dead. When he returns after murdering the lord, one feels that the blood on Washizu's spear will

The anxiety of command

stick ineradicably to him and Asaji, that, indeed, the blood will prove to be theirs as well as their victim's.

Washizu's armor, bejeweling his powerful calves and massive body, serves him as ineffectually as his weapons. A low-angle shot makes his shoulder guards look like wings; but he will fall rather than soar, and the gorgeous plates of his mail do not stop the arrows that finally kill him. Against the most powerful weapon of his foes, the humble axes whose strokes free the boughs of the forest, neither Washizu's armor nor his armies avail.

When he slides down the stairs of the castle and totters across the ground toward his men, he bristles with fletched shafts. His death recalls Canetti's understanding of command: "The *arrow* [is] the exact image of the original, non-domesticated command" (318), that is, of the command in which the death threat remains overt. Obeyed, a command sinks into a person like a sting or an arrowhead. Those who carry such stings must always long to extract them by turning them back onto someone else. If they can be attacked safely, the issuers of commands are the most desirable targets. In *Throne of Blood,* Washizu's troops turn his commands back on him. The primitive, irresistible order, "You must die," with which he has afflicted foe and ally alike, rebounds to stick literally in his own flesh.

Washizu's perishing summarizes the underlying logic of all tragedies that center on the fall of a great and powerful protagonist. Surrounding those who have given many commands are those who have obeyed them, who carry their stings. "A command which threatens death and then does not kill leaves the memory of the threat" (308). Anyone who has suffered this threat, who has carried out or fled from a command, "will invariably revenge himself when the moment comes" (308). "The anxiety of command is strongest in the mightiest . . . , one who creates orders and receives them from no-one above him" (309). The tragic fall of a great man is the realization of the anxiety of command; and the immediate agents of his fall are likely to be the crowds that he once commanded. However loyal they may have been, they have suffered his commands and the death threat behind them. When Washizu falls to the arrows of his own soldiers, he may be said to be the victim of a vengeful crowd that has at the end rejected his usurpation of power.

The audience to such a tragedy will at once identify with the great hero and at the same time desire to see enacted the inevitable outcome of his power. Identifying with him, they will feel pity; but as those who carry the stings of commands, they will also fear the mighty protagonist. An understanding of command may thus be seen to underlie Aristotle's famously enigmatic observation that tragedy at once raises and casts out pity and fear.

As Washizu grows in power, his anxiety and his vulnerability increase. The fear of him also grows, as Kurosawa is careful to show; messengers tremble to face him and the generals who commit suicide carry out the underlying threat of the commands they are suspected of resisting. Although Washizu murders some of his subordinates and drives others to suicide, most remain alive either as his servants and soldiers or as those who have fled his power, the enemies who will return and whom those under his orders will join in revenge.

Power trades in deceit. As secrecy is a fundamental mode of power, so dissimulation is one of its most important means. Force flashes out at key moments in *Throne of Blood,* but for most of the time power conceals its hostility behind a friendly false-face. All the powerful and the power-seekers employ deception. Upon hearing the Spirit's initial prophecy, Washizu instinctively tries to conceal his excitement. The Spirit, a dealer in power herself, is not fooled: "You mortals! . . . You want something and then you act as if you do not want it." The Spirit's line comes transformed from Shakespeare's play. There, however, it is Banquo's; and since Banquo lacks Macbeth's urge toward power, he is genuinely puzzled.

Because they know their own concealed hostility, the powerful assume the existence of similar deceit in other people. The lord of the Forest Castle conceals his plan to strike back at his enemy behind an apparent hunting expedition, but Asaji assumes that his ruse conceals a deeper plot to attack Washizu. Elsewhere, Asaji tirelessly dissimulates. At the banquet ostensibly given to announce the naming of Miki's son as Washizu's heir, she convincingly performs the roles of cordial hostess and concerned, reassuring wife. Her private interchanges with her husband almost always involve an element of manipulative playacting.

The master of deceit, however, remains the Forest Spirit, about whom—as about the witches in *Macbeth*—we wonder whether she causes the events, only predicts them, or achieves a bit of both. In any case, her deceptions put into practice Hecate's aphorism in *Macbeth:* "security / Is mortal's chiefest enemy" (III.v.32–33). Such an understanding of life, in its global paranoia, can stand as a motto for those who seek survival through power.

Although she sings of the vanity of ambition, the Spirit baits her traps with appeals to it. She also serves as a screen onto which Washizu may project the ambition that he attempts to conceal. The weird woman and her prophecies may have been a dream, Washizu and Miki agree; but "we dream of what we want." Echoing Miki, Asaji asks her husband, "What samurai does not want to be the lord of a castle?" Miki's son declares his father to be bewitched and to be making the prophecy come true through his own actions. Like the Spirit, Washizu himself may be seen to function as a locus for the projection of other characters. James Goodwin argues that "not once does he voice his inner drives. The spinner-prophet and Lady Asaji dictate to him the urgings of ambition that *they* attribute to his own desires."[10] Such an interpretation, however, does not necessarily rule out Washizu's own ambition, to which the chorus and his actions testify.

Throne of Blood favors a mixture equally compounded of uncertainty and the supposition that the Spirit is partially prophetic
and partially an incitement. The first prophecy comes to pass without intervention from Washizu or Miki. Yet it may be, as Banquo
warns in *Macbeth*, that "to win us to our harm, the instruments of
darkness tell us truths / Win us with honest trifles" (I.iii.123–25).

Whatever the reality of the Spirit—prophet, fate, projection,
tempter, or all of these—the ethical lessons of *Throne of Blood* remain unchanged. The chorus reads the same moral at the beginning and the end. Death rules. Ambition leads to violence, which
sooner or later—usually sooner—turns against those who employ
it. The dancer at the banquet, who resembles the Spirit, offends
Washizu with his song of an arrogant, ambitious man who could
not escape his just punishment. Ambition brings murders, and
command shortens survival. As Toshiro Mifune at the end of *Yo-
jimbo* remarks to a young peasant who has been tempted by the
dangerous ways of power, "A long life eating rice is best."

In Kurosawa's redaction and transformation of *Macbeth*, the
motives of power—that is, both its incentives and the images associated with it—appear as ambition in the first sense and as isolation
in the second. But irony always shackles ambition. *Throne of Blood*
makes clear that the goal of ambition is ultimately to outlive other
people. It seeks power not to impress—for from those whom it does
not kill it receives fear and hatred—but to perpetuate itself. Always
to no avail, however, for "this false fame falls. Death will reign:
man dies in vain." So sings the Spirit, spinning thread in her
ghostly hut like one of the Fates.

In contrast to an ordinary existence among crowds of ordinary people, the powerful live, and soon die, in relative isolation.
Chiefly through editing and mise-en-scène, *Throne of Blood* depicts
the growing loneliness of those who rise from the ranks of the commanded to the solitude of commander. The movement of power
away from other people begins early in *Throne of Blood*. After they
hear the Spirit's prophecy, Washizu and Miki talk about it, but they
are seated as far apart as the width of the screen will allow. A little
later, they advance side by side to receive praise and rewards for
their loyalty and valor from the lord; but the sequence ends with
them alone in possession of their dangerous knowledge of the now
partly fulfilled prediction. Again, they occupy opposite sides of the
screen. Kurosawa uses the same shot at the banquet for Washizu

The fellowship of secrecy

and Asaji, who share not only the same dangerous secret of the prophecy—now fully realized—but of the assassination plot against Miki and his son. A few minutes later, they are shown even more isolated, each centered alone in the frame. When they appear together again, they have turned away from each other, facing in opposite directions.

Secrecy means concealing from other people the words containing the secret. It requires more and more silence and, as it grows quieter and more restricted, isolation intensifies. Washizu and his wife are increasingly removed from the society they aspire to rule. Following Washizu's elevation to commander of the North Fort, we see communal peasants peacefully harvesting grain. Within the fort, however, the room in which Asaji is trying to persuade her husband to murder is isolated and empty of other people. Through a window, the bright day and fertile land are visible; but as Asaji continues her argument, the camera moves to largely exclude the window. The image of the conspirators becomes increasingly self-contained, absent of reference to anything beyond the place of dangerous secrets. As they plot the last details in the blood-stained room, their isolation is underlined when the lights of passing guards startle Washizu—an effect reminding him, and us, that people beyond the pair of conspirators are also deeply interested in the lord's welfare. (This moment functions rather as does the celebrated "knocking at the gate" in *Macbeth*.) During the assassination, the samurai and his wife are usually separated from each other and accompanied only by the unconscious guards—pictures, as we have observed, of death. After the murder, Washizu seems utterly alone, unconscious of Asaji's presence even as she pries the spear from his insensate hands.

Following Washizu's elevation as the lord's successor, Kurosawa inserts a sequence of communal contentment parallel to that which opened the action at the North Castle. Again the editing emphasizes the isolation of Washizu and Asaji, who is now urging the elimination of Miki and his son. The next time we see Washizu's soldiers, after Miki's murder, they are speaking of the desertion of some of Washizu's subjects and the avoidance of him by most of the rest. The trembling hand of the woman who opens the door on a monumentally solitary Washizu in order to tell him of his wife's illness and delivery of a dead child dramatizes the soldiers' words. When he goes to Asaji, scattering on the way her fleeing ladies-in-waiting, Washizu finds her talking to herself and washing her hands in the air, as unconscious of her husband as he was of her after murdering Lord Tsuzuki. That is the last we see of her. If she dies, she does so unwitnessed and unmourned, without the lamenting crowd who wept for her predecessor. Her madness and disappearance from the screen leave her husband entirely alone.

Writing about a characteristically tragic film genre, the gangster movie, Robert Warshow describes a plot logic that aptly summarizes the fate of the hero of *Throne of Blood:* "No convention of the gangster film is more strongly established than this: it is dangerous to be alone. And yet the very conditions of success make it impossible not to be alone, for success is always the establishment of an *individual* pre-eminence that must be imposed on others, in whom it automatically arouses hatred; the successful man is an outlaw."[11] Very much the same could be said of many of the central figures of westerns, the other Hollywood genre that deeply influenced Kurosawa's filmmaking.

Probing Washizu's fall a little more deeply, we may conclude that it stems not only from his isolation but also, somewhat paradoxically, from his inability to escape the crowd of his society that he, like all people, has internalized. (The same internalized crowd similarly afflicts Macbeth.) Whether we identify that socialized part of the psyche as conscience or something else, it has the potential, as Hamlet says, to "make cowards of us all"—for those who seek power, to arouse guilt and invite hesitation. The hero who seeks to survive through power is caught between the mixed safety and dangers of solitude and the compelling influence of the undistorted human instinct toward survival, the crowd, which persists within the paranoia of power.

The triumph of power—and therefore of death—in *Throne of Blood* is advanced and celebrated by three principal agencies: the spirit world, the chorus, and an active, collaborating cinematography. As we have seen, the Spirit of the Cobweb Forest and her companions are associated with and facilitate death. Ostensibly a mediator between the dead and the living, between fate and volition, the Spirit deceitfully separates Washizu, Miki, and Asaji from the crowds of the living, isolates them, and entices them to their doom.

Her tactics resemble the role of the deceitful dead in the story Canetti recounts as "The Self-Destruction of Xosas." In 1856, a young Xosa girl and her uncle encountered "strange men" who promised to help drive their white enemies from the land. Kreli, the chief of the tribe and, in retrospect, the suspected author of the scheme, greeted the emissaries from the spirit world with joy, even though they demanded that the Xosas destroy all their domestic animals and granaries. In addition to driving the English from their land, the spirits promised the Xosas the return, many times over, of their cattle and millet, the banishment of sickness and sorrow, and the resurrection of the tribe's ancient heroes. When the day of triumph arrived, however, no cattle, grain, or liberating armies appeared. In the next year, 68,000 of 105,000 Xosas starved. From the point of view of the Xosas, Canetti observes, "they had indeed been deceived by their dead," who were finally concerned "simply with their own aggrandizement. . . . In the end, it was they who were left the *largest crowd*" (198–99).

The treachery of the Xosas' ancestors parallels that of the Forest Spirit in *Throne of Blood*. Their tactics, the source of their authority, and the baits they dangle practically duplicate the temptations offered to Washizu and his wife. Canetti concludes the Xosas' history by remarking,

> The command to kill comes from the dead themselves, as though they were the final authority. . . . One cannot escape the impression that death has increased their power. The fact that, through the prophet [in *Throne of Blood*, the Spirit] they can make themselves heard, that they appear at all, and speak to him, adds to their former natural authority a supernatural one; they have cheated death and are still impressively active. To circumvent death, to evade it, is one of the oldest and strongest desires of rulers. (200)

Throne of Blood concludes similarly, if more succinctly: "Murderous ambition will pursue / Beyond the grave to give its due."

The chorus, as I suggested earlier, celebrates the victory of the dead. It does not simply present us with prudential platitudes like "All ends as dust," but declares the irresistible gravity of mortality. It claims as one of the host of the deceased the "proud warrior . . . his spirit walking still." Presumably, he has been humbled, for "pride dies first within the grave." The dancer at the banquet, who recalls both the chorus and the Spirit, tells the same story. As fog overwhelms the historical present and returns us to the narrative present at the end of the film, the chorus underlines the ascendancy of dissolution. All that remains of "a mighty fortress" and its mighty warrior, the voices intone, is "this desolate place." Under the treble of regret sounds the primary melody of triumph.

A movie camera may photograph the action of a film in a relatively inconspicuous manner, drawing little attention to its presence by unusual angles, lighting, lenses, and so on. It may, on the other hand, approach the status of an active participant in the narrative. Conspicuous pans and zooms, complex tracking shots, and other signals of the camera's presence draw attention to its capacity to respond to and perhaps even affect the narrative. Most of the time in *Throne of Blood*, Kurosawa's camera stands back and more or less inconspicuously records what passes before it. At several critical junctures, however, it enters the action more assertively. When it does, it too appears to be party to the deceit and destruction associated with the chorus and the Forest Spirit.

An example of the camera's autonomy occurs just before the murder of Lord Tsuzuki. The brief sequence begins with what appears to be a point-of-view shot of the lord's drugged, unconscious guards. The gaze then moves toward the door behind which the lord sleeps. But who originates this look, this approach? For Asaji now enters the frame from the right rear and a cut shows the thought-tormented Washizu sitting in the bloodstained room. Does the camera represent the sudden appearance of the Spirit, unseen but overseeing, joining its motive presence to that of the visible plotters? Or has the camera itself become one of the conspirators? We cannot definitively answer these questions—indeed, other hypotheses are possible—but we can say that the active, independent camera appears to be moving in synchrony with those who have plotted and will shortly achieve the lord's death.

More conventionally rhetorical, the camera on the night before Washizu's overthrow looks up at him from a series of extreme low-angle shots—unique in *Throne of Blood*. By doing so, it underscores the main theme of the chorus, the fall of "proud ambition." Washizu laughs as he goes to address his soldiers; and the upward-looking shots—only partly identified with his audience—give him an appearance of almost grotesque power as he boasts of the prophecy that he assumes guarantees his victory. The camera thus anticipates the central primitive irony that the chorus insists upon. No one, however powerful, can cheat death; attempts to do so, moreover, will only speed it. Towering above his men and the camera, Washizu stands at his most imposing before his fall. His soldiers raise their weapons and shout their trust in the leader whom tomorrow they will kill.

The behavior—it can accurately be called that—of the camera also helps to create the most expressive emblem in *Throne of Blood* for the dangerously equivocal spirit world. During the banquet after Washizu's elevation to Lord of the Forest Castle, Kurosawa adapts to the cinema one of the most famous scenes in *Macbeth*. It begins with the camera behind Miki's empty mat—empty, we know, because he has been intercepted by Washizu's assassin. The camera dollies in for a medium close-up of Washizu, who stares past it in fright and amazement. Retracing its path, it tracks back to its position behind Miki's mat, now occupied by his ghost. Chalk-white, the ghost resembles the Forest Spirit; and he evidently appears only to Washizu. As the apparition disappears, Asaji explains to the distressed assembly that her husband has had too much to drink and that the death of Lord Tsuzuki "is still hanging heavy on his mind"—which is probably true, but not in the sense that Asaji intends to convey. The ghostly Miki reappears and again Washizu scuttles backward in terror, ending his retreat literally cornered. Drawing his sword, he advances as the camera follows, once again viewing him from behind Miki's place, which is now vacant to us but still seems to hold a figure for Washizu. He approaches the seat and slashes at the air above it, an action that recalls the arrows and spear thrusts that he and Miki directed against the invisible, derisive Forest Spirit. With hurried apologies, Asaji dismisses the guests. All the action from the second appearance of Miki's ghost to the departure of the guests takes place in a single shot that lasts more than a minute, panning and dollying repeatedly.

How does this complex choreography of camera and characters affect our comprehension of the action? Most obviously, it renders much of what we see, and of what we have seen before, ambiguous, "smothered in surmise." Is Miki's spirit present? If it is present, is it visible only to his murderer? Or perhaps also to his wife? Asaji's reproach of Washizu for being afraid of a ghost suggests that she too might have seen it, and the camera does focus on her for the last twenty seconds of this shot. In any case, why does Miki's ghost appear to the camera and therefore to us? Are we somehow implicated in Washizu's lethal ambition? Alternatively, we might suppose that Miki's ghost is a hallucination of the guilty Washizu, whose crimes have overwhelmed his capacity to rationalize them. In that case, we take the camera as showing us the first two appearances of the ghost to Washizu's addled consciousness. The third shot of Washizu attacking empty air would then confirm that the earlier shots were records of his hallucination, not of a real exterior presence.

If we adopt the last interpretation, however, the appearances of the Spirit are brought into question, for the resemblance between it and the shade of the murdered Miki is pointed. We are then left to account for Miki's sharing of the first hallucination and accuracy of its prophecy. Are we and the camera perhaps hallucinating along with Washizu, rather as the audience does with Dorothy in *The Wizard of Oz*? Since we see the ghost twice and fail to see it once, no conclusion about our culpability or delusiveness would appear to be decisive.

The activity of the camera throughout the entire banquet sequence and especially in the last shot gives it the quality of another participant, or at least of an active judge. It raises yet another set of questions having to do with the conventions of representation throughout the film—including the (fictional) "reality" of the entire story from the dissolve back into history until the return to the fictional present. Who is this camera? Or who might be behind it? Does the camera figure forth the same gloomy-but-honest moral position that the unseen chorus appears to espouse? Or does it, like the Spirit, serve as an instrument of the malignant dead, giving us a few "honest trifles" to lure us to our doom? Might it, perhaps like the chorus, like the Spirit, like *Throne of Blood* itself, like the feigning of all art, exist only as substanceless illusion, the outcome of a vain attempt to mold some solid reality from a viscous world?

Remarkably, Kurosawa's camera renders as images the profound ambiguities of *Macbeth*. Shakespeare's radical irony is transferred from the early seventeenth-century English stage to the modern Japanese movie screen. The ironies of both the film and the play hold in suspension a series of questions that cannot be answered, because they ask about the nature of truth itself. Epistemologically, Kurosawa's first adaptation of Shakespeare is at least as complex, sophisticated, and equivocal as his earlier, more famous exploration of such themes in *Rashomon*. The tragedy of *Throne of Blood*, like that of *Macbeth*, extends beyond the fall of an excessively ambitious man whose acts overrun his capacity to tolerate the guilt they bring. It sinks downward from the human ambition for power, for survival, to a deeper ambition that proves even more terrifyingly unattainable: the vain hope of ascertaining who one is; whether other people and a world beyond oneself exist; and, if they do exist, what their intentions may be. *Throne of Blood* ultimately raises the profoundest doubts and fears of the power-seeker. Kurosawa's film asks, first, if one can ever be safely alone, given the ubiquitous, voracious spirits of the dead that inhabit all spaces. Perhaps still more horrifyingly, it suggests that the dead may be interior to all of us, that we ourselves may be the domain of all-consuming, moribund hosts. Finally, most hopelessly, *Throne of Blood* persistently raises the possibility that we are already fundamentally alone, cut off from an unknowable reality by illusion, deceit, or self-deception. In that case, survival could have no meaning and the only crowd would be the host of the dead. In any case, like Shakespeare's *Macbeth, Throne of Blood* refuses to answer "the question that is most intimate to our heart—what men have always yearned to know, namely, What is possible?"[12]

Crowds, Isolation, and Transformation in Welles's *Citizen Kane*

With *Citizen Kane* we turn to the most researched, interpreted, and annotated film in cinema's brief history. Yet even for this picture, attending to crowds, power, and transformation illuminates some generally neglected issues. More strikingly, such ideas allow one to simplify and streamline much of the commentary that already exists; that is to say, to achieve elegance and economy in the interpretation of its central images and themes. In the thousands of pages that have been published on Orson Welles's first picture, some of what I observe has already been noted, but a Canettian perspective clarifies the internal logic of the film and relates its central themes and its celebrated style to each other with a directness that has been elusive.[1]

Let us examine a sequence that exemplifies many of the issues and techniques of *Citizen Kane* as a whole. At the apogee of his life and career, Charles Foster Kane (Welles) addresses a boisterous, confident rally of his political supporters, a rally attended also by his newspaper associates, his wife (Ruth Warrick), and his young son. The sequence begins with a close-up of an election poster featuring a likeness of Kane. As the camera tilts down to the speechifying man himself, it reveals that the image behind him is immense, twenty or thirty feet tall. Kane, in front of a dozen or so seated dignitaries, is standing on a stage. Welles then cuts to a long view—an establishing shot characteristically for this film placed in second position in the sequence. We see an enormous amphitheater, its main floor and balconies packed with people listening to Kane's words. A series of medium and medium-close shots and reverse shots of the speaker and his listeners follow. The sequence ends with another long shot, the camera next to a lone man high

Kane ascendant

above—a spectator whom the film will soon reveal to be the object of Kane's execrations, "Boss" Jim W. Gettys (Ray Collins).

Under "Aspects of Power" Canetti includes a discussion that precisely articulates the significance of the disposition of figures in this scene: "If there is a space between the standing man and those around him the effect he makes is enhanced. Particularly impressive is a man who stands isolated by himself, facing many others, but somehow detached from them. It is as though he, in his single person, *stood for* them all" (388). These insights describe both Kane's effect and his intentions. Significantly, the only spectator standing above Kane, Gettys, is also the only one capable of threatening him.

This three-minute sequence displays the oversized, overconfident tragic hero in his moment of greatest exultation, hubris, and—in accord with conventional tragic logic—vulnerability. Kane's pronouncements express clearly his paradoxical combination of self-aggrandizement and sympathy for the underprivileged and underregarded. Stylistically, the vigor, assurance, and theatricality of camera work and acting typify *Citizen Kane*. The political festival portrayed in the sequence is bracketed, also typically, by private actions; it is preceded by Kane's first encounter with Susan Alexander (Dorothy Comingore) and followed by the confrontation in her apartment among her, him, his wife, and Gettys. The election rally sequence and its context highlight the theme of power and the characterization of Kane as a man often among but rarely a part of crowds and unable to sustain private relationships. Stylistically, the rally employs the conspicuous artifice with which the film draws our attention to its status as an artwork creating life through a fiction rather than revealing it by cutting a slice from factual history—the sort of slice that *Citizen Kane* imitates in its own fictional creation of the newsreel.

Power has been widely recognized as a central theme of Welles's film, as has Kane's isolation. Less noticed has been the importance of crowds and crowd symbols. There are crucial connections, however, among crowds and crowd symbols, power, and the characterization of the hero. The apparent paradoxes of Kane's loneliness, his desire to form and manipulate crowds, his need for love and his inability to offer it, his attraction to "decent, ordinary citizens" from whom he remains profoundly isolated by circumstance and temperament, and his love of power—all derive from the natural anxieties that lead humans to desire to join crowds or to accumulate power. The amassing of power, as Canetti emphasizes, arises as a disease or corruption of the motives that impel crowd formation. Those motives underlie the best and worst qualities of Charles Foster Kane. Understanding the most difficult interpretative problem of *Citizen Kane*, the relation between its dominant themes and its ostentatious artifice, is facilitated through a conception central to Canetti's meditations on power, the complex idea of transformation.

Crowd Symbols and Crowds

Citizen Kane is turgid with crowd symbols. After the camera penetrates the fence around Xanadu in the opening shot, the screen fills with a succession of landscapes that appear to be adjacent and yet are characteristic of widely separated parts of the globe. This mysterious opening suggests the world-collecting at which Kane excelled, an interpretation soon confirmed by "News! On the March!" the fictional newsreel that follows the enigmatic opening sequence.

101

Kane's city of treasure

Kane, nameless during the first several minutes of both the news-reel and *Citizen Kane* itself, is identified initially only as "XANADU'S LANDLORD." What follows as much concerns what he owned as what he did. The catalogue of his possessions includes many crowd symbols: "a private mountain" with 100,000 trees, "the loot of the world . . . the fowl of the air, the fish of the sea, the beast of the field and jungle . . . a collection of everything, so big it can never be cataloged or appraised." Shots of formal gardens, elaborate facades, gardens and bowers—more crowd symbols—are succeeded by an actual crowd, the attendees at Kane's funeral, and then by the most important of the many crowd symbols that reappear throughout *Citizen Kane*, newspapers. These crowd symbols and others—grocery stores, paper mills, apartment buildings, factories, forests, mines, radio stations—are interspersed with shots of actual crowds, a montage that implies their equivalence.

Enormous piles of boxes and goods end the narrative of *Citizen Kane* much as the images that began it. The crated treasures of the world recall the caged animals of the newsreel and resemble at the same time the buildings of a city. The engraved trophy that survives from Kane's early newspaper days emblematizes the interchangeability of his possessions and the crowds they evoke: "WELCOME HOME MR. KANE from 467 EMPLOYEES of the NEW YORK INQUIRER." In the last shots of Xanadu's interior, as in much of the montage, a crowd of reporters and workmen are interspersed with the crowd symbols of Kane's uncountable masses of goods.

The flames consuming these goods and the smoke ascending darkly from Xanadu's chimney represent yet another crowd symbol, for Canetti a particularly comprehensive one: "Fire is the same wherever it breaks out: it spreads rapidly; it is contagious and insatiable; it can break out anywhere, and with great suddenness; it is multiple; it is destructive; it has an enemy; it dies; it acts as though it were alive, and is so treated. All this is true of the crowd. . . . These likenesses between fire and the crowd have led to the close assimilation of their images" (77). Like the crowds that turn on or abandon Kane, the flames devouring his "junk" erase the concrete signs of his power and, indeed, the central symbols of Kane himself. The most individual and personal of those symbols, the "Rosebud" sled, has the most prominent place. Shots of it amidst the flames call to mind a funeral pyre; the rose and "Rosebud" lettering resemble tattoos on a torso. (Indeed, given that the long-lost toy partly symbolizes Kane's stolen childhood, the word being consumed by the flames might almost be imagined to read, more traditionally, "Mother.")

"The greatest newspaper tycoon of this or any other generation," Kane ruled an empire that amassed millions of readers. An image of bales of newspapers follows young Kane's "Declaration of Principles" and visually rhymes with shots of his stacked goods at the end of the film. The tracking shot of a train-car full of commuters with copies of the *Inquirer* headlined "TRACTION TRUST EXPOSED" explicitly equates the newspaper with its crowd of readers (and reiterates the paradox of Kane as at once capitalist and muckraker). The Hollywood montage that compresses Susan Alexander Kane's opera career into a series of *Inquirer* front pages from various cities double- and triple-exposed with the singer and her audiences similarly identifies crowds with their journalistic representations.

For Canetti, as in *Citizen Kane*, newspaper readers are a dangerous, easily manipulated crowd. "The baiting crowd is preserved in the newspaper reading public, in a milder form it is true, but, because of its distance from events, a more irresponsible one. One is tempted to say that it is the most despicable and, at the same time, most stable form of such a crowd. Since it does not even have to assemble, it escapes disintegration" (52). We may recall a relevant bon mot of Kane's at the *Inquirer* when Bernstein (Everett Sloane) reads him a cable from his reporter in Havana: "Dear Wheeler, you provide the prose poems, I'll provide the war." The publisher understands clearly enough his readers' enthusiasm for "collective, well-publicized killing."

Among the most volatile of crowds are "reversal crowds," masses that turn against former leaders and allies. Such a crowd develops when Kane the candidate is discovered in his "love nest" with Susan Alexander and loses the election for governor. The disastrous public revelation appears via a precise lap-dissolve from the front door of Susan's apartment building to a photo of it on the front page of a rival newspaper. The *Inquirer*, symbol of Kane's fled or slaughtered army, languishes in the gutter along with piles of election confetti and posters, now debris, the empty husks of his once mighty crowd of supporters. In the newsreel, imagery of disappearing crowd symbols follows directly after the story of his election loss, as a graphic removes one by one from a map of the United States Kane's failed newspaper and radio holdings.

The episode that leads to Kane's electoral defeat, his liaison with Susan Alexander, features crowds as much as romantic love. Not only is Susan associated with various crowd symbols, she is herself a crowd symbol. For Kane, Leland (Joseph Cotten) says, Susan was "a cross-section of the American public." He meets her on a set that is empty of people but full of objects: brick pavers gleaming from recent rain and a drugstore window crammed with merchandise. (When the reporter first goes to interview her, the camera tracks into the nightclub through rain, but across a conspicuously empty set. By choice, she is no longer part of any crowd.) Kane tells her that he "knows too many people. I guess we're both lonely." He undertakes his relationship with Susan after we see a more ordinary marital loneliness enter his life, the scene in which his wife deserts Kane's most cherished crowd by reading a rival newspaper. Later, the stencils of animals in Susan's bedroom at Xanadu and, more emphatically, her enormous jigsaw puzzles associate her further with crowd symbols. Solitary in the cavernous, empty space of the great room in Kane's castle, she longs for the teeming nightlife of

New York—the puzzle with its multiple pieces suggesting the yearned-for after-theater crowds.

Like many films, *Citizen Kane* sets crowds in opposition to romantic love. Kane begins both his marriages with conventional devotion; later, however, his intense desire to create and control crowds destroys his relationships with his wives. Leland articulates a similar interpretation of Kane with regard to friendship: "Seems we weren't enough. He wanted all the voters to love him, too." In Kane's second marriage, ironically, when the aging public man appears ready to retire and devote himself to domestic pleasures—however grandiose—he comes into conflict with his young wife's attachments to the crowds of cities and show business.

The direct juxtaposition of Susan Alexander Kane's printed reviews with the crowds at her performances optically fuses actual crowds and crowd symbols. Her most stinging pain is inflicted on her through derisive crowds represented by newspaper notices of her performances. The worst appears in the *Chicago Inquirer* when her husband, unknown to her, finishes Leland's column in the contemptuous spirit with which his former friend began it. Kane's destruction of her room after she leaves him suggests not only her equivalence with possessions in her husband's mind but, since his possessions are so frequently crowd symbols, her equivalence with the crowds of Americans whom Kane also controlled for a time, then lost.

Images of crowds themselves, as in the newsreel, are interspersed throughout the film. The most emphatic of such images appear at the election rally, but their conspicuous artificiality, as we shall see, complicates their interpretation. We also see Kane in front of crowds during the celebration party at the *Inquirer*—the feast of a "distribution crowd," an event that typically takes place after a successful hunt, in this case the successful recruitment of the best reporters from the rival *Chronicle*.

As Kane proves through painful experience, crowds can be changeable, hard to control, and prone to dissipate and disappear. Perhaps for those reasons, he generally prefers the crowds-at-a-distance that his mass media empire provides him and the crowd symbols that wealth at once buys and constitutes.

Power and Distance

The first and last words within the narrative of *Citizen Kane* are "NO TRESPASSING." Power consolidates itself at a distance, as the touch-

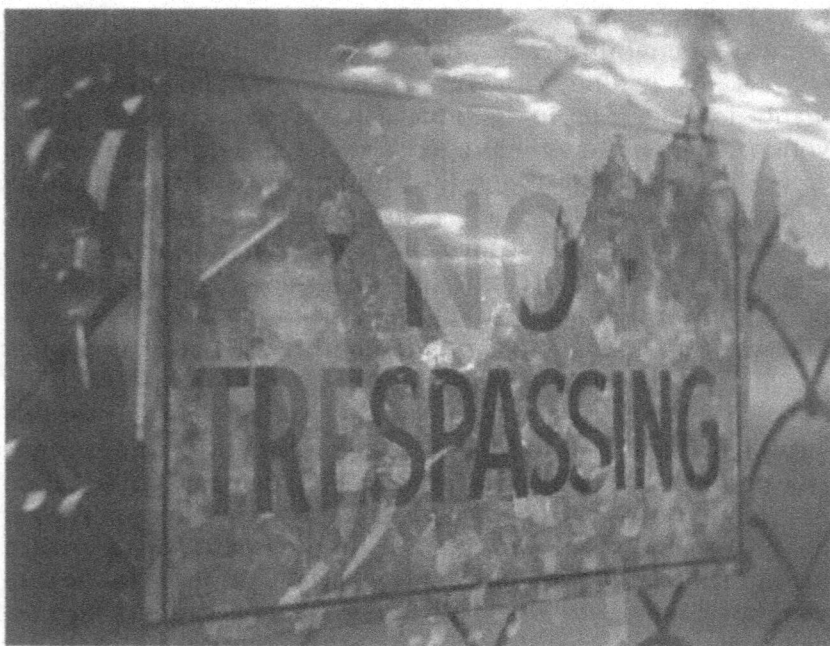

The fortress/prison of Xanadu

me-not sign on the fence surrounding Xanadu signifies. The camera's slow tilt up the wire rectangles and triangles to the circled letter "K" on the fence suggests the cohesive, traditionally tragic logic of the story to follow—"an iron mesh, links / of consequence."[2] Two monkeys sitting enigmatically on a cage labeled "Bengal Tiger" suggest a fortress that at once defends and entraps those within. Among the enormous piles of Kane's possessions at the end of the film, multitudinous crates recall the caged animals and people implied by the images of Xanadu at the beginning.

The newsreel's voice-over characterizes Kane as "alone . . . aloof." An early reviewer noted the connection between Kane's isolation and his name, "chosen, I am sure, from that Bible character, the black son of Adam, who was not his brother's keeper."[3] Similarly, within the film, Leland calls him a man who "never gave himself away." As Canetti notes, "Secrecy lies at the very core of power. . . . The man who has it . . . must be more reticent than anyone; no-one must know his opinions or intentions" (290, 292). Direct images of Kane frequently confirm such characterizations: we see him in splendid, dismal isolation in his private palace; at the *Inquirer* celebration, he is exultant but nonetheless generally standing (or dancing) aside from the rest of the party. Unmoving in the midst of the politely applauding audience at Susan's first performance, Kane illustrates negatively Canetti's understanding of the crowd formed in theaters: "The strength of the applause is the only clue to the extent to which they have become a crowd" (36). Only when the audience ceases its applause does Kane begin to clap—still alone in the masses, still trying to mold them into *his* crowd. Images like these ultimately return us to Kane as a solitary boy playing in the snow; they resonate forlornly with his mother's implausible reassurance, "You won't be lonely." More plausibly, they confirm Leland's assertion that Kane may never have had a friend, that he was a man who believed only in himself.

"Disappointed in the world"—to continue with Leland's analysis—Kane "built one of his own, an absolute monarchy." The cliché about the loneliness of power requires modification in the case of Kane, for whom power not only produces loneliness but is also partly a response to it. We recognize Kane in Canetti's description of the paranoid ruler and his demesne: "The enlargement of the royal enclosure and the construction of bigger rooms within it serve to establish distance as well as to protect him. Uniqueness, isolation, distance and preciousness thus form an important group of attributes which can be recognized at sight" (416). The famous shots of Kane tottering out of Susan's room, past his servants, and before multiple images of himself in the mirrored hallway of Xanadu reflect not just the crowds around and within him, but his alienation from both. In their suggestion of simultaneous isolation and entrapment, they further recall the opening images of the film.

Kane's isolation is not an ironic contrast to his power, his control of people and crowds, but an essential part of it. The apparent contraindications—his off-and-on control of crowds, his desire for love and inability to feel it, his attraction to "common, decent" masses—all seem less paradoxical when we understand that they arise from the same threats and injuries that motivate his drives for power. To a degree, Kane is the isolated victim of a position that was thrust upon him; but at the same time, power seeks such isolation for the same reasons that less powerful (and less paranoid) humans form crowds.

The power of Thatcher

Kane's desire to help "the underprivileged" originates in his ability to identify with them as the victims of the rich and powerful. But the expression of Kane's populist ideals represents also the disguise of the predator, the wolf in sheep's clothing. As he puts it concretely to his sometime guardian, Thatcher (George Coulouris), "Trouble is, you don't realize you're talking to two people": both the robber and the protector of those whom the robber robs.

As his own predator, Kane consumes himself and threatens to reduce himself to nothing much at all, like the tigers who run themselves into butter for pancakes in "Little Black Sambo." When he tangles with Gettys, he goes against a man who is "not a gentleman," who "doesn't even know what a gentleman is." He takes on, in short, one of the "common, ordinary citizens" whom he patronizes. In doing so, he is himself exposed as neither a gentleman nor a common man. Without either identity, he is crushed.

The emptiness produced by self-canceling identities is not long tolerable, and it is Kane's fate or sickness to resolve the con-

flict within himself chiefly on the side of power. "People will think
. . ." begins his first wife, Emily, "what I tell them to think!" inter-
rupts her husband. Leland understands both Kane's attitude toward
the ordinary man and the fear that underlies it: "You talk about
'the people' as though you own them." When they rise up, Leland
predicts, Kane will "sail away to a desert island, probably, and lord
it over the monkeys"—or over Bengal tigers transformed into monkeys.

The other center of power in *Citizen Kane* is Walter Parks
Thatcher. Despite the lifelong animosity between him and Kane,
despite their fundamentally opposed ideologies, backgrounds, and
personal styles, they share the truly significant indicators of power:
uniqueness, isolation, distance, preciousness. The severe opulence
of the Thatcher Memorial Library reflects a style of power different
from Kane's ostentation, but it equally creates space around the
possessor. Even in death, Thatcher announces his importance and
singularity and displays his wealth. For Thatcher and Kane alike—
however little they understand each other—wealth is power. Kane
uses money "to buy things," especially the crowds and crowd symbols of his newspapers and radio stations. Thatcher uses it, we
gather, chiefly to make more money, the ultimate crowd symbol in
a capitalist society. Testifying before Congress, Thatcher, too, is
amidst but not part of the mass of onlookers and its hubbub. He
controls the proceedings, reading a prepared statement, then refusing to receive any questions. Thatcher knows the ways and means
of power and seizes them for his own. Every question entertained,
every question answered "is an act of submission. Personal freedom
consists largely in having a defense against questions" (285).

The first clear indication that Leland has begun to resist
Kane's power comes when he separates himself from the festive
crowd at the *Inquirer* party and asks a series of tendentious questions of Bernstein, his boss's lackey. His boss himself, as we see
when he confronts Susan's voice coach, cannot be persuaded of
anything. So Leland withdraws almost entirely from Kane's sphere
of influence by transferring to the *Chicago Inquirer* and by breaking
all communications with him. When contact is resumed, it leads
immediately to a fatal exercise of power. "I thought we weren't
speaking," says Leland. "Sure we are," returns Kane. "You're fired."
Leland asserts his own power, in the end, by refusing to answer a
letter from his now old and abandoned former boss and friend.
Susan understands her power relationship with her husband in

similar terms: "Everything was his idea—except my leavin' 'im." When Welles shows her departure, he puts a doll in the left foreground of the set. Like the "underprivileged" that Kane treated as his possessions, the doll that he thought he owned rises against him.

Kane's seizing of the world and his exercise of power, as well as his experience of isolation that power both achieves and suffers, connect directly to the most famous image and conundrum in *Citizen Kane*, Rosebud. Recall the beginning of the story of Kane's life as we see it: his removal from playing with the Rosebud sled and his transfer into the hands of Walter Thatcher. Then recall the first sentences of the opening two paragraphs of *Crowds and Power*: "There is nothing that man fears more than the touch of the unknown. . . . All the distances which men create round themselves are dictated by this fear" (15). Juxtaposing these two beginnings adds resonance to Bernstein's speculation, "Rosebud . . . maybe that was something he lost." In addition to the obvious losses of his mother and father, his familiar life in Colorado, and his sled, the young Kane lost whatever sense of security he may have had; and he lost it, from his point of view, to the "touch of the unknown."

When he encounters Susan Alexander for the first time, he tells her that he "was on my way to the Western Manhattan Warehouse, in search of my youth." Perhaps he recovers some youth in the company of the much younger woman; perhaps he also finds again familiar safety in feminine affection. The young Charles Kane is seized and dragged away, rather like a snowbound, masculine Persephone, both from the earth he knows and, if not the spring flowers that she picks, from his Rosebud and the spring of his life. (As Robert Herrick famously wrote, "Gather ye rosebuds while ye may.") Unlike Persephone's parent, Kane's mother will not search for him; indeed, it is she who directs his abduction. The scene of young Charles's removal also alludes to another cultural archetype of loss. Kane is expelled from the innocent wilderness of Colorado; thereafter the bank, an especially concentrated locale of fallen materialistic civilization, becomes (as his father tells him) his "gar-dee-an." From garden to guardian.

Associated with the sled is the glass paperweight and its cabin and snow scene. We first see it during the sequence of Kane's death that precedes the newsreel; but in the unfolding of his life it initially appears in Susan's room during the tempestuous scene in which she quits her husband. At once geriatric and juvenile, he comes upon the paperweight during his destruction of the room and its furnishings. It not only escapes smashing, but it calms Kane, turns his rage into quiet, tearful grief. It elicits from him the famous name of his sled.

Why? The snowy scene of the paperweight circumscribes and immures in something at once fluid and fixed the long ago scene from which the youthful Charles Kane was removed. The answer to the editor's histrionic challenge, "Rosebud, dead or alive!" is nearly the same as the question itself: Rosebud, dead *and* alive. When Kane dies, the frozen cabin in the snowstorm is at last freed of its glass prison, as Kane is freed of his nearly lifelong prison of glass, his existence in the public eye. The snow too escapes the paperweight to cover the entire screen. We may see in the snow a final crowd symbol—perhaps as James Joyce and John Huston saw it in their versions of "The Dead"—a symbol of the largest crowd of all, that of everyone who dies. At the end of his life, Kane returns to its beginning, gives up what power he still has, and at last truly enters a crowd. It is a consummation, however common, devoutly to be desired, a consummation in accordance with the newsreel's sententious proclamation, "As it must to all men, death came to Charles Foster Kane."

Transformations

The newsreel, the brilliant re-creation of a practice that itself re-creates life in a highly conventionalized form, establishes at once the persuasiveness of the stories we tell ourselves and their inadequacy to fully comprehend human complexity and mystery. In doing so, it anticipates the ultimate modesty both of the reporter and of *Citizen Kane* as a whole. "I don't think any word can explain a man's life." Rosebud is just a piece of a jigsaw puzzle—another way to reassemble a picture of reality, or simply a picture. Yet solving such a puzzle, if it does not explain everything, means something. A puzzle or a newsreel or the more compendious art of a feature film are among the only entries we have into even fragments of each other's lives. *Citizen Kane* insists on the fragmentary, limited qualities of its own art while at the same time showing that such reconstructions achieve at least some understanding.[4]

"From beginning to end," writes James Naremore, "*Kane* casts doubt on its own conclusions. Moreover, Welles's brilliant manipulation of cinematic technique keeps reminding us that we are watching a movie, an exceedingly clever and entertaining manipulation of reality, rather than reality itself."[5] These reminders extend from the simple, neon-like main title to the old-fashioned cameo actor credits after the end of the story. Naremore's observation returns us to a crucial question for this discussion of *Citizen Kane*: What has the pervasively conspicuous artifice of Welles's first film to do with its main themes and with the psychology of its hero?

To answer that question, we are aided by one of the most subtly shaded concepts of *Crowds and Power*, transformation. *Citizen Kane* manifests transformation in two broad areas. The first is the life of Charles Foster Kane, in which we see transformations chiefly as failed, faked, arrested, or repressed—exemplified, in short, by negation. The second arena consists of the entirety of the film itself, in which conspicuous artifice has enormous thematic significance, especially with respect to transformation.

Transformation and crowds are closely related: "As we learn about transformation we find that we are learning just as much about crowds" (359). The isolated Kane is obsessed with crowds but unable to participate in them; analogously, his impulses toward the radical empathy and psychic flexibility of transformation lead instead toward separation and rigidity. The expansive force of transformation to connect "this" with "that" reverses in Kane, as in all hoarders of power, into a contraction of self that creates only unbridgeable gulfs.

As Kane ages, he retreats into his power and becomes more rigid. His face becomes less expressive, his body stiffer. Most frequently, we see him sitting, and he increasingly comes to resemble the seated statue of his late guardian and adversary, Thatcher. When he does move—during his destruction of Susan's room at Xanadu, notably—his face remains largely immobile and the movements of his body have the abruptness of an out-of-control robot. In part, these changes in Kane have to do with his age and with the heavy makeup the young Orson Welles required to play his elderly character. But only in part. They also have to do with Kane's gradual assumption of what Canetti calls a mask. "The *mask* is distinguished from all the other end-states of transformation by its rigidity. In place of the varying and continuous movements of the face it presents the exact opposite: a perfect fixity and sameness" (374).

Like the power that forestalls the clutch of an unperceived claw, the mask "above all . . . separates" (375). It is "a limit set to transformation" and its wearer, like the possessor of other modalities of power, "is bound to fear for it. . . . It must never be dropped and must never open" (377). Kane's masks and his money are equally instruments of his power. Both conceal and separate him from other people. To quote Leland's resonant pun about his former friend and boss, and the intricate connection between Kane's secrecy and his money: "He never gave himself away. He never gave anything away." At the same time, however, Kane cannot but reveal himself, at least partly: "He just left you a tip"—that is, both a gratuity and a clue. As Diane Arbus showed in her photography of people assuming other identities, nothing reveals us better than our lies, and nothing exposes our shame more clearly than the costumes with which we cover it.

Kane's mask, like other aspects of his power, is imposed on him as well as adopted; as it gives him the secrecy of power it simultaneously traps him. Like a command, his mask remains "something external . . . foreign, something which never wholly becomes part of himself; it hinders and constricts him" (377). It keeps Kane in his place, august as that may be. The transformation forced upon the young Charles Kane cannot be what Canetti calls "clean. . . . The individual identity is preserved . . . in the transformation" (341). Only in death can Kane return to what he was before he was seized. No wonder, then, that he muses to Thatcher that he might have been a really great man, had he not been so terribly wealthy.

Possessors of power may transform others, but to them "all *self*-transformation is forbidden" (382). Thatcher can transform a boy into a rich man, but he fails strikingly to transform himself into a child who could understand what has befallen his young ward. When Kane proclaims, "We're gonna be an opera star!" the "we" signifies ownership of his wife, not identification with her. He does turn her into an opera star, however ill received and miserable; but he remains, as he must, untouched by her sorry metamorphosis. Kane can transform employees of the *Chronicle* into employees of the *Inquirer*, but he cannot himself become an employee of the *Chronicle*. He can transform Leland from a present into a former critic for the *Inquirer*, but only the enormously powerful Thatcher, in combination with a world depression, can demote Kane from full ownership and control of his media empire.

As in many self-reflexive narratives, the genuine transformations of art stand in sharp contrast to the lies of bad faith, fake art, and masks. Pseudo-transformations have to do exclusively with externals. Enforced by her husband, Susan Alexander's transformation is pathetically lifeless. Apart from him, she is able to succeed, albeit modestly, as a singer. The only writing we ever see Kane do in his own name, his "Declaration of Principles," is eventually recognized as a mask by Leland, who rejects it along with another fundamental instrument of Kane's power: his money, the guilty "tip" of an enormous severance check.

We do see Kane attempt a genuine transformation at least once, perhaps only once. It occurs at the beginning of the film, before the newsreel, when he dies. We hear for the first time what he says for the last time, "Rosebud." We sense that he is straining to become someone else or to be somewhere else. Does he recover in the instant before death the identity bound, gagged, and mummified by wealth during his life? That is hard to know; but if we take the escape of the snow from the paperweight as reflecting Kane's consciousness, we might suppose that he does. In any event, the opening sequence of Kane lying supine as he dies gives him for the audience a lasting sympathy that his worst "brutal things" cannot fully erase. As Canetti remarked, "If you have seen a person sleeping, you can never hate him again."[6] Surely this insight applies even more emphatically to someone seen dying in his bed.

With greater certainty we can describe the sequence of his death as fraught with meaning, ostentatiously artful, and implicitly setting forth encompassing truth claims within the total story of the film. The first three minutes of *Citizen Kane* present mystery combined with concentrated significance, a bewildering fragmentation and sense of the partial, and a self-conscious virtuosity that recalls the conventional openings of nineteenth- and twentieth-century mystery novels. (So, of course, do innumerable other filmic derivatives of that genre, before and after *Citizen Kane*.) Between the light in the castle window to the beginning of the newsreel a minute later, the director uses at least fifteen shots, including several dissolves, fades, and double exposures, a match-dissolve that violates the "180 degree rule," tracking shots, and wide-angle shots with severe, attention-getting, barrel distortion.[7] Indeed, the minute of screen time devoted to Kane's death serves as a fair catalogue of the technical resources then available to imaginative cinematographers and editors.

The sequence of Kane's death strongly associates conspicuous artifice with intensified significance, with truth. The artistic elaborations of the scene envelop another work of art, however unpretentious, the glass paperweight. Like the artifice of the filmic setting, the paperweight and the scene that it represents implicitly lay claim to an import at once mysterious and potentially central to explaining the enigma that an experienced reader or viewer of mystery fictions expects. The cryptic opening of *Citizen Kane* promises, ornately and quite conventionally, that the truth will out.

When we return to the scene of the political rally with which this chapter began, the textures of the representation appear quite different. Most notably, the camera work and editing are straightforward—especially for *Citizen Kane*—and the set, although spectacular, is much less elegant than most of the other sets. Indeed, at least one shot in this sequence seems strikingly uncharacteristic: the cheap-looking, patently artificial setting of painted crowds on a painted backdrop. In a film that assembles the sets and properties that we see at Xanadu or during the opera sequences, the crudely portrayed ocean of heads appears incongruous. Despite budget reductions, sets were elsewhere ingeniously managed to look luxurious, even on a fiscal shoestring.[8] How could Perry Ferguson, the effective art director, or Van Nest Polglase, the scrupulous, imaginative chief of the art department not only for *Citizen Kane* but for numerous other extravagantly decorated RKO features, let such a sorry moment find its way into the movie's otherwise gorgeous, credibly incredible world? The answer has in part to do with masks and transformations, in part with an inaccurate assumption concealed in the question: to wit, that the obvious fakery may be dismissed as deficient production values caused by budgetary constraints or some other circumstance.

Let us ask instead what meanings the undisguised fakery of this set contributes to *Citizen Kane* and how they affect our understanding of its main themes. I need at this point to make a simple distinction between what we may call "internal" and "external" artifice. By internal artifice, I mean art (broadly conceived) that exists or is enacted within the containing fiction; examples of internal artifice in *Citizen Kane* include the ornate decor of Xanadu, the singing at the picnic excursion, an artifact as humble as the paperweight, or one as elaborate as the newsreel. External artifice refers to the cinematic representation of the action, characters, and world of the entire fiction. It may be primitive or sophisticated, coarse or delicate, ostentatious or self-effacing; but it is the vehicle of what is represented and is not itself part of the fiction. The complexity, elegance, and subtlety with which Kane's death is shown concern the external artifice of *Citizen Kane*; so do the obviously painted crowd backdrops during his political speech. The speech itself and the enormous poster of Kane behind the stage, on the other hand, are elements of internal artifice.

Like symbols, the meaning of either internal or external artifice in any particular work is context bound, tied to both its immediate setting and patterns throughout the work as a whole. In romantic fictions, however, external artifice of especially striking richness, neatness, or implausibility tends to be associated with essential thematic and characterological truth. This association exists because romantic fictions implicitly set out to reveal fundamental realities behind the apparent chaos of life's contingent detail. For ironic fictions—the opposite of romantic ones—ornate or elegant settings and tidy resolutions of complicated action tend to signal falsehood because such fictions accept the disorderly surface of the world as its whole reality, or at least as all that we can ever know. Time does not reveal hidden truths or circle back toward renewal; it consists only of pointless strings of

> Tomorrow, and tomorrow, and tomorrow . . .
> . . . a tale
> Told by an idiot, full of sound and fury,
> Signifying nothing.
> (*Macbeth*, V.v.19–28)

To judge by Rosebud or, less directly, by the history of the reception of *Citizen Kane*, Welles's first film balances between the poles of irony and romance.

Art may be seen as a socially developed form of transformation. As there exists a sort of false transformation that serves power and that Canetti calls "simulation," so does there exist a sort of false art that we may call lying. Poetry, as Philip Sidney famously argued, does not lie because it does not present itself as true; it purports only to model general truths through the representation of specific details. Lies have to do with what philosophers call truth claims. Making art and lying, respectively, are roughly analogous to transformation and simulation; the latter includes both ordinary dissimulation and the adoption of masks. In contrast to masks— fixed, false, and hiding a dangerous reality—transformations unify multiplicity without effacing individualities. Art does the same. It is, as Dante asserted and as modern theorists have reiterated through a variety of later jargons, "polysemous," the bearer of

116

many meanings. The paradoxical carrier of truth through "feigning" (to return to Sidney), art allows "this" to be "that."

Kane dwells behind masks. The performances he authors—including his statement of principles, political speech, drama review in Jed Leland's name, and attempt to persuade Susan to stay with him—are all suspect. Because his pseudo-transformations serve power, they amount to dissimulation. The internal artifice created by Kane, his "art," equates finally to lying.

How do we understand the *external* artifice of *Citizen Kane*, either in its totality or piece by piece in such sequences as the death of Kane or his political rally? Transformation, the performance in this case of the entire film, allows "this" to be "that." Thus Rosebud can be a crucial clue to Kane's character and motives, and, at the same time, only one of innumerable pieces of a puzzle impossible to complete. Given that fundamental transformation occurs when "one body is equated with another" (as Canetti asserts), the most obvious arts of transformation are the dramatic ones: theater, opera, movies, and so on. Although Kane's acting deceives, Welles's tells truths.

The mysterious, concentrated cinematic artifice of the minute during which Kane dies claims for itself the truth of myth. Differences between inside and outside—whether we mean between Kane's consciousness and the world around him or between one side of the lighted window and the other—are effaced. The veils of quotidian detail part as they are transformed to reveal significance, truth. If the "facts" of "News! On the March!" prove to be hopelessly uninformative about who Kane "really was," the representations of *Citizen Kane* stand as corrective, both in their richness and in their capacity to reflect on themselves and acknowledge their own inadequacy—an inadequacy that becomes in its very acknowledgment a further enrichment of understanding. The transparent falseness of the scene of Kane's campaign rally at once certifies the truth and openness of the external art of its representation and echoes the falseness of the internal art of Kane, the mask of virtue that he has assumed.

If Kane is finally redeemed in some sense, the film itself does the redeeming. (I take redemption here to mean sympathetic understanding and forgiveness, as of a debt.) Welles's and his collaborators' transformations accomplish that understanding. "You know, all the same, I feel kinda sorry for Mr. Kane," muses the reporter near the end of his journalistic quest. "Don't cha think I do?" Susan replies. In its entirety, the movie also pities Kane, a commiseration that its creators achieve through their transformation into him and their simultaneous retention of their separateness.

Citizen Kane creates and re-creates, understands empathetically, and celebrates a life that is at once fictional and inspired by an actual human being (William Randolph Hearst). It sets forth the universal truths of a person who is both unique and an especially revealing model of all human beings in their potential relations to crowds, to power, and to transformation. It fashions its model from the inside, through its own practice of transformation. In doing so, in going inside its subject, *Citizen Kane* models transformation itself. Its understanding of its protagonist's losses and isolation restores what he lost and reconnects him first to his identity, then to the crowds of "common, ordinary, decent citizens" with whom he can otherwise only simulate fraternity. Finally, it connects him to the crowds of movie audiences, themselves transformed into Kane and transported into his world while retaining their own identities.

Those fixated on power, the paranoid and the despot, are virtually identical in constitution, if not in circumstances. Both desire above all to survive, a desire that means not simply to live but to *outlive* their fellow creatures. The power they strive to grasp creates neurotic feedback; the sense of isolation and vulnerability increases and that, in turn, increases further the appetite for power and the distrust of other people. (Note in *Citizen Kane* the connection of Kane with Hitler, the latter the model par excellence of a modern paranoid despot.) Only through transformation can people finally bridge the gulf that separates them from each other and from the world; only transformation can remove the "un" from the unknown whose clasp fills us with terror. Transformation achieves knowledge and equality. It offers the only possible true survival in joining the one who transforms with other people, with other creatures, with the universe itself. Kane may or may not understand himself and his plight in the last moments of his life. *Citizen Kane*, however, the film of his life, leads us to an understanding of both the particular and the broadly human dilemmas that it figures forth. It joins us to Kane. We witness and empathize with him; we become one with each other as the united, egalitarian audience of the film of his life. Through him we better understand terrified, striving humankind, however unkind it may sometimes be. Guided by Canetti's thinking about crowds, power, and transformation, we better understand both Welles's understanding and our own.

PART II

PREDATION
VERSUS
TRANSFORMATION

5

Packs, Predators, and Love in Hitchcock's *North by Northwest*

North by Northwest, Alfred Hitchcock's 1959 comedy-thriller, has enjoyed enduring favor for more than forty years among both popular and academic audiences. The latter, indeed, have made it one of the more explicated works of the director who is by far the most analyzed and written about auteur in the history of cinema. (*Vertigo*, the film preceding *North by Northwest*, seems to be its maker's *Hamlet*; everyone has something to say about that picture.) Even though *North by Northwest* has achieved an elevated place in the consciousness of movie fans and critics, however, some aspects of it have gone unremarked, from single shots through configurations of images and themes. Giving attention to issues of crowds, power, and predation allows us to focus on aspects of Hitchcock's much-studied movie that have hitherto been only thinly understood: the significance of the threat to individuals of the predators that pursue them and the potential shelter of the crowds that they seek to rejoin.

Hunters and Prey

"There is nothing that man fears more," writes Canetti at the beginning of *Crowds and Power*, "than the touch of the unknown. He wants to *see* what is reaching toward him, and to be able to recognize or at least classify it. . . . It is only in a crowd that man can become free of this fear of being touched" (15). But Roger Thornhill (Cary Grant), abducted at the beginning of *North by Northwest*, cannot flee back into the crowds from which he has been plucked. (Thornhill may have exposed himself to his fate, as I observed in the introduction, by leaving the crowd to grab a taxi not rightfully his.) However much he may wish to attend the Wintergarden The-

121

The touch of the unknown

ater as he had planned, the safety of masses of people will not be his again until he regains the freedom that he has lost to "the touch of the unknown."

Human horror at the touch of the unknown derives from our biological heritage of hunting and of suffering predation, whether by other species or our own. "The design of one body on the other becomes concrete from the moment of touching. Even at the lowest levels of life this moment has something decisive about it. It contains the oldest terrors; we dream of it, we imagine it, and civilized life is nothing but a sustained effort to avoid it" (204). Many of Hitchcock's films vividly illustrate Canetti's assertion. In particular, *North by Northwest*—however comic its frights may be—consistently develops actions that suggest flight from a predator.

Thornhill is first touched, seized, and stuffed into a waiting car by two thugs of Philip Vandamm (James Mason) when he separates himself from acquaintances to send a telegram. One of the thugs will later stalk him with a knife in the United Nations building and later still will lurk in ambush to pounce on him at the Mount Rushmore monument. Police and park rangers—intermittently benign, but ultimately associated with the violence of both the espionage and counterespionage forces—substantially duplicate Thornhill's first abduction by jailing him after his drunken ride down the coast road, grabbing and forcing him into a patrol car after an auction, loading him into an ambulance as part of a faked cafeteria shooting, and knocking him out and incarcerating him in a hospital afterward. Eve (Eva Marie Saint), the American counterespionage agent, is also seized: at the auction, we see a close-up of Vandamm's hand holding the back of her neck; later she enters the Mount Rushmore cafeteria in his grip. After the staged shooting, we are indirectly reminded of Vandamm and his control over Eve through the prominence of the pearl choker around her throat—a detail continued from the cafeteria and one which dramatizes that she is still in Vandamm's grasp.

Such seizings lead symbolically toward their primitive continuation, tearing and ingesting. The interiors of automobiles, ambulances, and jails suggest the armored maw of the predator. From a Canettian viewpoint, the knives and guns of the kidnappers and assassins repeat the smoothness and power of a predator's teeth; the cramped spaces into which they thrust their captives and prey recall mouths: "The teeth are the armed guardians of the mouth and the mouth is indeed a strait place, the prototype of all prisons" (209).

The gloves and weapons of Thornhill's (and eventually Eve's) pursuers evoke the crushing grip and the cutting teeth of the predator. Vandamm's hit man is equipped with both glove and knife at the United Nations and he attacks with another knife on the monument. The menacing teeth of Thornhill's stalkers flash in the hotel elevator that he unhappily shares with them. "In laughing," remarks Canetti, "the mouth is opened wide and the teeth are shown. Originally laughter contained a feeling of pleasure in prey or food which seemed certain" (223). The falsely amiable baring of teeth of Vandamm's thugs comes in response to the naïve question of Thornhill's mother (Jessie Royce Landis), "You gentlemen aren't really trying to kill my son, are you?" Their toothy smiles reveal the menace behind their laughter. Other occupants of the elevator join in the hilarity and fill the crowded space with their exposed teeth. Alone among the passengers, Thornhill, the prey who knows how lethal his pursuers are, stands unamused, keeping his mouth closed.

The name of another of Thornhill's pursuers, Leonard (Martin Landau), the man Vandamm calls his "right arm," suggests a feline predator. An avian predator, the raptor-like crop-dusting plane, stoops to attack Thornhill at Prairie Stop. Earlier, he sees himself as

Predators and prey

an insect pursued by Eve, who "uses sex like some people use a fly swatter." The venerable presidents seem ready to devour or throw him down in the penultimate sequence. As James Naremore reports, the scene as originally envisioned by Hitchcock would have been even more suggestive of ingestion or predation by the sculptured figures: "When the U.S. Park Service refused him permission to depict characters suspended from the presidential faces, he reluctantly moved all the action to the rocks between them."[1]

Sex is associated in *North by Northwest* with intimations of stalking, killing, and eating. In the dining car, Eve declares, "I never discuss love on an empty stomach," and when she advises Thornhill, "I wouldn't order any dessert if I were you," he takes her (wrongly) to be promising herself in its place. In her Pullman compartment the motif intensifies. The love-chatter that accompanies the protagonists' sophisticated necking includes a good deal of sexual double entendre based on murder and ingestion. In an essay on "Hitchcock and the Art of the Kiss," Sidney Gottlieb offers observations congenial to my analysis. "For Hitchcock," he writes, "kissing is frequently associated with a continuum of dominance, aggression, violence, and murder. That is to say, the lips often work for the teeth. . . . The larger expression of the kiss is the embrace, and frequently the embrace is barely distinguishable from an assault."[2] Thornhill's and Eve's amorous hands on each other's heads and necks—a more threatening gesture when it is Vandamm's at the auction—are associated, however playfully, with violence. Eve murmurs, "Maybe you're planning to murder me right here, tonight." "Shall I?" responds Thornhill. "Please do." A little later, Thornhill tells her, "I like your flavor." At a symbolic level, these amorous interchanges dramatize something approaching mutual cannibalism. As Maggie Kilgour writes, "Most acts of incorporation are extremely ambivalent, taking place between two extremes whose meeting seems very dangerous: a desire for the most intimate possible identification with another and a desire for total autonomy and control over others who are treated therefore as food, so that all exchanges are reduced to the alternatives of 'eat or be eaten.'"[3]

Attempting to evade the grasp of his predators even when chasing them, Thornhill comes to be associated with (and sometimes appears to consider himself as) food. Confined in the closed upper bunk on the train, he calls for the olive oil appropriate to a tinned sardine; Eve continues the metaphor when she frees him with the porter's key, which she calls a "can opener." In her hotel room, she tells him, "You belong in a stockyard, looking like this." To the Professor (Leo G. Carroll) he protests, "I'm an advertising man, not a red herring!" In the grasp of his predators, Thornhill is held down by Vandamm's two assassins while Leonard, like a spider ready to inject its prey, prepares an overwhelming dose of bourbon for him. After suffering this violation, Thornhill is again dragged into an automobile, rather like a piece of half-pickled meat.

The human terror of being consumed is connected, according to Canetti, with traditional tales of adventure: "The narrow gorge through which everything has to pass is, for the few who live so long, the ultimate terror. Man's imagination has been continually occupied by the several stages of incorporation. The gaping jaws of the large beasts which threatened him have pursued him even into his dreams and myths. Voyages of discovery down these jaws were no less important to him than those over the sea, and certainly as dangerous" (209).

Writing about the dragon-killing theme of romance, Northrop Frye offers observations that resemble Canetti's. He notes how frequently we encounter heroes who descend and return from the gullets of monsters, the importance of the anthropophagus leviathan and behemoth in biblical iconography, and the portrayal of hell as the "toothed gullet of an aged shark."[4]

The gullets into which Thornhill is propelled are cars, jails, elevators, and an ambulance. He enters the film being disgorged from an elevator. The inhuman monsters that ingest or expel people in *North by Northwest* are mostly architectural, their images sometimes verging on the abstract. Typical patterns are established by the geometric Saul Bass credit sequence design that dissolves out of white lines on a green background into the colors of the real world and one of its buildings. Captured in reflection is the traffic of a busy street and visible inside the cross-hatching of vertical and horizontal lines are some of the people that the structure has swallowed and that it will regurgitate at the end of the working day. The parallel lines of the throatlike hallway of the railway car into which Thornhill first flees on the Twentieth-Century Limited repeat the lines of the opening images.

Chromatic associations in Hitchcock's color films have a tendency to replicate the conventions of traffic lights: green often indicates safety, yellow and orange suggest caution, and red signals danger. For *North by Northwest*, Hitchcock's usual color symbolism mostly obtains; given the pattern of threatened predation, we might reasonably suppose that the alarm associated with red has something to do with the red of the predator's mouth and the prey's blood. (More generally, we might also suppose that the red of our traffic lights, stop signs, and other warnings hearken back to such associations.) The usual explanation of the symbolism of the U.S. flag, an insistent visual leitmotif in *North by Northwest,* is explicit about the blood signified by its red stripes.

Repeated flashes of red punctuate *North by Northwest.* A woman in a red dress leads the exodus from the elevator that introduces Thornhill; another in a red coat passes as he enters the airport in Chicago; and a third in a red sweater gives a conspicuous scarlet accent to the scene in the Mount Rushmore cafeteria. Elsewhere, numerous women with red hats, blouses, handbags, and skirts insert bright sparks into sets teeming with neutrally dressed people. The red interior of the red and orange cab that Thornhill appropriates with his secretary is as lushly crimson as the inside of a panther's mouth. Two red-tipped electric candles shine on the wall behind him just before he is abducted. When Thornhill is bundled into the posh blue-gray interior of a Cadillac, Hitchcock takes care to show briefly behind him a blood-red school bus. Among travelers in the stations of New York and Chicago, redcaps flicker like flames.

Thornhill's bizarre mother and the sister of Vandamm who plays a motherly Mrs. Townsend are both redheads, as are a number of extras, predominantly female.[5] Although neither Thornhill's mother nor any other feminine character shows the ferocity of the male predators, their association with menacing crimson marks them as more dangerous than they at first appear.[6] The men themselves—Thornhill and his cocktail companions in the hotel lounge; Vandamm, Leonard, and their thugs; the Professor and his colleagues—are generally attired in suits of conservative blue or blue-gray. Their surprisingly neutral coloration does not dissociate them from the cycles of predator and prey that they enact; rather it conceals them with a kind of protective camouflage as they stalk and attempt to evade each other—simultaneously the hunters and the hunted.

The ruby collar and burgundy floral gown Eve wears to the auction embody a particularly complex instance of the red motif in *North by Northwest.* At once bloody in color and rejuvenating in its explosion of flowers, the gown suggests both Eve's demonstrated dangerousness and her potential for bringing Thornhill back to life by helping him to regain the identity he lost when he was mistakenly seized as—and in a sense became—Kaplan. At the same time, the collar marks her as victim; and it anticipates the pearl choker later associated with Vandamm's restraining grasp.

The insistent red accents of the film, Eve's light platinum-blond hair, her white blouse and pajamas, and Thornhill's glowing white shirt when he arrives to rescue her combine with the repeated appearance of blue-suited men and blue-decorated spaces to create a color scale in *North by Northwest* approximating that of the U.S. flag. While red suggests bloody predators and prey, white promises something like purity or salvation (recall the florescent white halo over Eve's head in the penultimate shot of the movie), and blue is persistently associated with the men who are potential objects of either predation or salvation—or, most emphatically in Thornhill's case, both.

Crowds and Crowd Symbols

Hitchcock was fascinated by and ambivalent about crowds. His movies are full of them, and if they are sometimes menacing, they also often provide his heroes and heroines escape and shelter. Canetti's understanding of the genesis of human crowds begins with their relation to the terror of an unknown touch. "It is only in a crowd that man can become free of this fear of being touched. That is the only situation in which the fear changes into its opposite. . . . The more fiercely people press together, the more certain they feel that they do not fear each other" (15–16). Freud's view of the matter is somewhat different: "From the first there were two kinds of psychologies, that of the individual members of the group and that of the father, chief, or leader."[7]

Hitchcock portrays Thornhill as at once a member of crowds and their master—a conception of his character with elements of both Canetti's and Freud's views. In each role, Thornhill depends upon crowds for much of his identity. Among them he is comfortable, commanding, and safe. When he is threatened with assassination at the auction, he engineers his escape by joining and then manipulating the gathered crowd of bidders.

Crowds appear in *North by Northwest* almost continuously. Even in such isolated settings as Prairie Stop and the top of the Mount Rushmore monument they are present by proxy. The credit sequence dissolves from Saul Bass's graphic virtuosity to people emerging from a building and blending into crowds passing on the sidewalk. It cuts to more people flowing like water into a subway entrance, to crowds surging across the street, then to others streaming downstairs. For a moment we watch two women struggling for a cab as walkers pass by, then the image returns to more crowds crossing a street. The credits end, famously, with the first shot emphasizing a single individual, the director himself failing to catch the bus, excluded from the crowd. Then back to the front of the building and inside for the introduction, in a particularly compressed small crowd, of the film's hero. Of the first eleven shots, seven are principally of crowds and in none are crowds absent.

For Canetti, a crowd is not simply a mass of people, but a group that has density and direction, that is determined to grow, and that is characterized by a feeling of equality among its constituents (29). The crowds at the beginning of *North by Northwest* display three of these four attributes: density, growth, and direction—as they swell and flow downstairs, across streets, and into subway entrances. Robin Wood's characterization of the opening as conveying "a sense of apparently aimless and chaotic bustle and movement" is inaccurate and obscures the conformity to Canetti's description of these images of crowds.[8] The rather uniform appearance of those who make up the crowds implies the fourth fundamental crowd attribute, equality. Other masses of people around and within the United Nations building, in the train stations of New York and Chicago, at the auction, and in the cafeteria reproduce the crowd motif so emphatic in the first minutes of the film.

In addition to actual crowds, *North by Northwest* is saturated with crowd symbols. Canetti describes such symbols as "collective units which do not consist of men, but which are still felt to be crowds. Corn and forest, rain, wind, sand, fire and the sea are such units. Every one of these phenomena comprehends some of the essential attributes of the crowd. Although they do not consist of men, each of them recalls the crowd and stands as symbol for it in myth, dream, speech and song" (75). Siegfried Kracauer articulates a similar perception when he writes, specifically about film,

> Along with the familiar photographic leitmotif of the leaves, such kindred subjects as undulating waves, moving clouds, and changing facial expressions ranked high in early prophecies [concerning appropriate subjects for moving pictures]. All of them conveyed the longing for an instrument which would capture the slightest inci-

dents of the world about us—scenes that often would involve crowds, whose incalculable movements resemble, somehow, those of waves or leaves.[9]

The beginning of the credit sequence introduces the first crowd symbol of *North by Northwest,* the hivelike structure in which Thornhill works, with its architecture of parallel lines. Similar lines will be repeated in the extreme high shot that looks down the facade of the United Nations building at a fleeing Thornhill, in the hall of the Pullman car, in the telephone booths at the Chicago train station, and in Vandamm's modernist South Dakota residence. The crowd symbol of a pine forest is prominent when Eve and Thornhill meet among its multitudinous stems after the faked shooting, when Thornhill comes to Vandamm's home after escaping the hospital, and again when he and Eve flee.

The Mount Rushmore monument is another sort of crowd symbol, an example of what Canetti calls "stone heaps." It is, moreover, a literal transformation of the mountain into a group of giant human heads. Further emphasizing its connection with crowds, the parallel carving lines in the "rock" of Hitchcock's elaborate set rhyme visually with the lines of architectural forms elsewhere.[10] Partaking of both architectural crowd symbols and mountains, the sculptures of the American presidents represent a whole nation of people and much of its history. Here we see again the tendency of the cinema to underline the significance of its crowd symbols by returning them through transformation to literal representations of the people they symbolically represent.

Among further details that one might identify as crowd symbols are the shelves of books in the Townsend home library and in the meeting room of the U.S. intelligence organization, the rows of benches at the police station, and the newspapers with their accusatory headlines and incriminating photo of Thornhill. "The baiting crowd [one intent on "collective killing"] is preserved in the newspaper reading public" (52).

The contrast between the desolation of Prairie Stop and the bustling scenes elsewhere in *North by Northwest* has been widely noticed; but viewing this sequence with an eye to its crowd symbols also brings into focus its harmony with other actions and enriches our understanding of its underlying logic. The regular geometry of fields and fence posts echoes the architectural lines already associated with crowds. When the attacking airplane descends on Thornhill like a giant hawk, how does this man of crowds respond? He flees into a field of standing corn, hoping to lose himself among the massed stalks. Driven out, he turns to the road where he is saved both by what is for Canetti the most compelling of crowd symbols, fire, and by the distraction of a small pack of spectators drawn to the conflagration. "Fire is one of the most important and malleable of the crowd symbols. . . . The crowd which used to run from fire now feels strongly attracted by it" (77). Hitchcock's film practically duplicates Canetti's description of this sequence of events, as Thornhill and the drivers of the burning oil truck first flee; then the drivers and the locals edge toward the fire as Thornhill makes his escape. Even more illustrative of fire as a crowd symbol is the spectacular opening sequence of another Hitchcock movie, one that has strong affinities with *North by Northwest, Saboteur* (1942). In the opening of that film, arson and firefighters in a West Coast factory symbolize the conflict between Fifth Column fascism and the nascent armies of American democratic values.

Michael Wilding (as detective "Ordinary" Smith) in still another Hitchcock movie, *Stage Fright* (1950), remarks that the police are "inclined to accept the obvious as being obvious." This is a principle that interpreters of movies would do well to keep in mind also. Thus I am far from arguing that the isolation of the Prairie Stop sequence can be explained away by invoking ideas of crowd symbols. Thornhill clearly *is* isolated from the crowds and civilized shelters among which he spends most of the film, and that contrast accounts for much that is striking and meaningful in the sequence. Simultaneously, however, the predatory biplane that harries Thornhill and the graphic similarity of fence, field, and highway to the linear geometry of cityscapes echo and repeat actions of predation elsewhere in the film and the crowds and crowd symbols among which they take place. The visual dissonance of the empty landscape of Prairie Stop, in short, is enriched by underlying, if muted, visual and diegetic harmonies. Although Canetti allows for crowd symbols that are entirely natural—the sea and mountains, for example—a landscape unaltered by human industry hardly exists in *North by Northwest*. The patterns traced by masses of human beings recur in city and country alike, as do the dramas of predators stalking and prey attempting to escape into the safe anonymity of crowds and their analogs.

Like the images of Prairie Stop, the last shots of *North by Northwest* contrast with most of the rest of the film; but again *Crowds and*

Power suggests an underlying consonance. "The slow crowd," for Canetti, "has the form of a train" (39). Such a crowd "is characterized by the remoteness of its goal. . . . The road is long, the obstacles unknown and dangers threaten . . . from all sides. No discharge is permitted before the goal has been reached" (39). The association with crowds of the passenger train that carries Thornhill and Eve west and back east is strengthened by its bracketing between the crowds of Grand Central Station in New York—shot from a high camera that emphasizes the teeming masses below—and the swarms of travelers and redcaps in the Chicago terminal.

Train and tunnel, then, are not simply a self-consciously crude comic allegory for the sexual consummation of a marriage but also an emblem of a quest accomplished and of reunification with the crowds from which Thornhill was torn at the beginning and from which Eve has perhaps been estranged all her life. The Twentieth-Century Limited receives considerable visual emphasis; three times Hitchcock pans from or to its exterior as it winds along a great river (the Hudson?). With gradually increasing volume and leisurely progress to the sea, rivers are also emblems of slow crowds (40). During the train trip west, the sound track is paced by the metronomic clacking of steel wheels, a noise that is omnipresent and especially insistent during the exterior shots. This drumming of the wheels further associates the train with what Canetti calls "the *rhythmic* or *throbbing* crowd" (31). The final shot of the train entering the tunnel, in addition to its mock-salacious joke, suggests the long postponed true membership in the slow, rhythmic crowd that Eve and Thornhill joined under different false pretenses when they first boarded the train and to which they now belong legitimately as their quest, their relationship, and their story achieve resolution.

Marriage confers social acknowledgment and standing on a private relationship; and the culminating imagery of train, tracks, and mountainside summarizes social as well as personal themes. The hero and heroine of the film have managed to become themselves individually, as a pair, and as part of the crowds with which the film began. Individually, neither is forced any longer to live the lie of a false identity. As a pair, they are also perhaps metonymic for one of the great, potentially antagonistic double crowds that Canetti identifies, that of women and men. Their coming together signifies not just their joining but the reconciliation possible between men and women when, as Eve says, they "believe in marriage."

Packs, Power, and Transformation

The identification of Thornhill-the-isolated with Hitchcock-the-excluded associates the director with a hero whom he appears to set in literal and symbolic opposition to crowds. In other films, furthermore, Hitchcock usually characterizes crowds as impediments to the longed-for love and self-realization of the central figures. In *North by Northwest*, both opposed bands of agents are manifestly inimical to Thornhill's hopes for a future with Eve. From the point of view of *Crowds and Power*, however, Thornhill is not struggling with crowds but with packs: the originary units of crowds, but distinguishable from them in their size and the constraints upon their growth. The contrasting war packs of espionage and counterespionage agents, unlike the crowds among which they operate, are fundamentally undemocratic; and it is partly for this reason that the ethical tenor of the film is so ill disposed toward both Vandamm's pack and the Professor's.

Of the four functions of packs that Canetti identifies, those which give their names to hunting and war packs are exemplified by the contesting sides in *North by Northwest*. "The two decisive factors" in the formation of a hunting pack "are the *sighting* and the *killing* of the prey" (98). With notable economy, *North by Northwest* establishes the hunting pack that misidentifies Thornhill and captures him for elimination. But all packs change fluidly from one form into another. In Hitchcock's film, Vandamm's agents function as a hunting pack in pursuit of Thornhill and as a war pack with respect to the Professor's group. "The factor determining the shape of the war pack is that there are *two* packs, both of them out to do exactly the same thing to each other. The duplication of the pack is unquestioned, and the cleavage between the two remains absolute so long as a state of war exists" (99). As Canetti makes explicit here, such absolute "cleavage" is based not on dissimilarity but on functional duplications that oppose each other like an object and its mirror reflection. The fundamental identity of opposing war packs—whether of contesting agents or of the police and criminals—may be perceived at the center of many of Hitchcock's films. In such movies, the abiding conflict is not between cops and criminals or patriots and subversives, but between lovers and the war/hunting packs that threaten both their existence and that of love itself. When the Professor eventually appears nearly forty minutes into *North by Northwest*, the audience discovers that the hunting pack in pursuit of Thornhill is primarily a war pack in conflict with some "alphabet soup" agency in Washington. On the runway in Chicago, Thornhill belatedly makes the same discovery.

The Professor's self-satisfied declaration that "war is hell, Mr. Thornhill, even when it's a cold one," incorporates a brutal worldview that Hitchcock characteristically portrays with horror, the notion that societies must embrace a quasi-permanent state of war and the amorality it justifies. *Notorious* embodies perhaps the best-known indictment of such an outlook, but Hitchcock's hatred for that attitude is expressed in all his films that have overt political content, from the first *The Man Who Knew Too Much* (1934) to *Topaz* (1969).

For most of the film, Thornhill is separated from the crowds to which he securely belongs as *North by Northwest* begins. The name attached to the estate to which he is abducted, "Townsend" (town's end), emphasizes this separation. He must learn to escape capture and assassination on his own. He develops, as he tells a skeptical Vandamm, a deep interest in "the art of survival." Canetti notes that heroes survive by killing, but survivors need not be heroes. They can run away, hide, or otherwise outlast their enemies. Thornhill is the latter sort of survivor, as befits the protagonist of a comic film that is antipathetic toward those who assume the power to kill. His instinctive physical and rhetorical attempts to maintain distance between himself and his captors in the Townsend library are characteristic of Thornhill's reaction to his bewildering, desperate situation. The high camera that diminishes him as his captors "get down to business" both emphasizes his helplessness and optically pushes him down for the first of many times before he achieves a secure station in the upper berth on the train home. With that final ascent, Thornhill triumphantly asserts the most meaningful power, the power to survive.

Secrets and questions prove to be the principal forms through which power is expressed in *North by Northwest*. "Secrecy lies at the very core of power. The act of lying in wait for prey is essentially secret" (290). When Thornhill asks the Professor what Vandamm does, he replies (somewhat obscurely, himself) that he is "a sort of importer-exporter . . . of government secrets, perhaps." As an advertising man, Thornhill professes a diametrically opposite mode, assertive publicity. Like the meek who shall inherit the earth, he may be expected to prevail if he can extricate himself from Vandamm's sphere. For "in the long run," Canetti writes, "all secrets which are confined to one faction, or, still more, to one man must bring disaster" (295).

Equally apposite to Vandamm's exercise of power is Canetti's discussion of questions. "All questioning is a forcible intrusion. When used as an instrument of power it is like a knife cutting into the flesh of the victim. The questioner knows what there is to find, but he wants actually to touch it and bring it to light" (284–85). These words make sense of some important moments in *North by Northwest*—why Vandamm subjects Thornhill to a trenchant interrogation, for example, when he already knows, or thinks he knows, most of what he wants Thornhill to reveal. Fleeing, Thornhill hides behind sunglasses. "Something wrong with your eyes, Mister?" a ticket agent asks provocatively. "Yes, they're sensitive to questions." An interrogatory dynamic governs as long as Eve and Thornhill remain antagonists; they interact chiefly by asking each other questions and by evading answering. When Leonard wishes to assert his power over Vandamm and to expose Eve, he operates in a similar mode: he asks his companion in espionage leading questions and he keeps Eve's gun with its blank cartridges his own secret until the last moment.

The most obvious instrument of power, the command, is little used in *North by Northwest*, but it does arise revealingly on two occasions. The first occurs when Thornhill encounters Eve in her hotel room after surviving Prairie Stop. To her demand that he leave and never see her again, he responds with ingenuous questions, which he follows by an outright refusal. Taking Eve's part in the pinewoods, he flatly contradicts the Professor's assertion that "she has to" go with Vandamm: "Nobody has to do anything."

For *North by Northwest*, one of the conclusions that Canetti reaches about commands has particular importance: "the 'free' man is not the man who rids himself of commands after he has received them, but the man who knows how to evade them in the first place" (306). Thornhill's evasion of questions, his flight from seizure whether by Vandamm's crew or the authorities, and his refusal of commands altogether secure his freedom of action and self-determination. In a violent world determined to convince him that "he has to," he preserves himself by audacious escapes, evasions, and—when nothing else avails—defiance.

But given the death threat connected, for example, to Vandamm's demand that Thornhill "cooperate," assertive noncooperation is seldom an option. Thornhill's elusiveness is essential to both his avoidance of commands and his survival. His deftness in a profession that acknowledges no lies, only "the expedient exaggeration," serves him in good stead. So does the professionally associated (in contemporary popular mythology) toleration for alcohol that enables him to escape his captors after they have poured most of a bottle of bourbon into him.

To elude his pursuers, Thornhill repeatedly turns to what Canetti calls transformations. His transformations are part of a pervasive theme of acting and theatricality that numerous critics (I among them) have identified in *North by Northwest,* but a Canettian perspective is more inclusive and takes us, I believe, a bit deeper.[11] "Transformation for flight, that is, in order to escape an enemy, is universal, being found in myths and fairy stories all over the world" (342). Canetti goes on to identify linear and circular forms of transformations. The linear form applies to Thornhill chiefly as prey, the circular one as a hunter—for, like many Hitchcock protagonists, he is at once fleeing and pursuing most of the time.

Canetti illustrates linear transformations by recounting a Georgian tale, "The Master and His Apprentice," in which the Devil attempts to imprison his rebellious apprentice in a dark stable. (We may recall the quiet threat expressed by Vandamm's drawing the library curtains.) In the retelling, the imprisoned youth

> changes himself into a mouse and slips out through the crack. His master notices that he is gone, changes himself into a cat and runs after the mouse. . . . The cat opens its jaws in order to kill the mouse, but the mouse turns into a fish and jumps into water. Instantly the master turns into a net, and swims after the fish. He has almost caught it when it changes into a pheasant. This the master chases as a falcon. His claws are already on its body when the pheasant turns into a red-cheeked apple which drops straight into the king's lap. The master turns into a knife in the king's hand.

The story continues via more paired metamorphoses until the apprentice finally turns into a needle through the eye of which the Devil puts himself as a thread. "The needle bursts into flame and the thread is burnt up. The master is dead. The needle changes back into the boy, who goes home to his father" (343–44). We should recall that fire is an archetypal crowd symbol; the prey has triumphed over the predator by becoming, in a sense, a crowd.

Thornhill's extended flight from and pursuit of Vandamm and his cutthroats strongly recall the shape of such folktales, although his attempts to escape through transformations are displaced onto the more realistic forms of a narrative film. Whether attempting to evade or to capture Vandamm, Thornhill ultimately seeks to reclaim his identity. He becomes Kaplan (a role forced on him at first, then expediently assumed in the hotel room and at the United Nations building), "the outraged Madison Avenue man," an apparently helpless inebriate, "the fugitive from justice" and "the peevish lover" (transformations that Thornhill feels to have been coerced but that Vandamm identifies as play-acting), a redcap, a shaving traveler, a visitor whom "Miss Eve Kendall is expecting," an obstreperous disrupter of an auction, a "mad killer" in police custody, a critically wounded federal employee, "a cooperator" with the Professor, and finally a suitor proposing marriage. In all but the last of these incarnations, Thornhill achieves concealment that is at least temporarily efficacious; when he escapes in the Chicago train station as a redcap and then hides behind a mask of shaving lather, for example, police detectives repeatedly look at him—and evidently through him—without recognition.

At Prairie Stop, transformations educe mythic resonances with less displacement. Thornhill appears to become invisible in the corn into which he dives and from which, like an insect, he is flushed by a cloud of pesticide. He allows himself to be run over and shielded by a gasoline tanker, then turns to a comic refrigerator-carrying pickup truck, in which (and visually as which) we see him flee the scene.

The circular form of transformation reverses the role of Vandamm from pursuer to pursued. Canetti illustrates this form with the story from the *Odyssey* of Proteus, who unsuccessfully attempts to escape the clutches of Menelaus by a series of metamorphoses. In *North by Northwest,* Vandamm also attempts evasive transmutations; first he becomes Townsend, then an art collector, next a devoted lover, and subsequently a vengeful one. But like Proteus, he is unable to escape the grasp of those who seek knowledge from him.

Vandamm's transformations are more limited and less benign than Thornhill's. They illustrate in some respects Canetti's distinction between transformation and what he calls "imitation" or dissimulation: "Imitation and transformation might seem to be the same but it is advisable to keep the two apart, for they mean different things. . . . Imitation relates to externals" (369). Although Thornhill and Eve practice some dissimulation, they also undergo genuine transformations; that is, they become something other and more without losing their original identities. Vandamm's simulations have the quality and purpose of what Canetti calls a mask, which "is distinguished from all the other end-states of transformation by its rigidity. . . . To fixity of form is added fixity of distance. . . . A mask expresses much, but hides even more. Above all, it *separates*" (374, 375).

Simulation is related to the secrecy of power. The constant accusations of play-acting that Vandamm directs toward Thornhill reflect his understanding of himself and, by paranoid projection, of the world. The brittle figurine in which Vandamm conceals his secrets makes an apt emblem for the man himself. When the Professor orders Leonard shot, Vandamm dryly observes, "Not very sporting, using real bullets." He thereby registers his perception—accurate with respect to the Professor but less so with respect to Eve and Thornhill—that with this fatal command the real face of his enemy has emerged from behind a mask like his own.

Guilt, Individuality, Nations

Within packs or crowds, the sacrifice of innocents represents an action of social expiation (145). Feeling like prey, according to Canetti, lies at the root of feelings of guilt; a sacrifice transfers that feeling of guilt from the crowd to a single victim. A person "like us" (that is, neither exceptionally gifted nor contemptible) plucked accidentally from among the Madison Avenue crowds, Thornhill admirably fills many requirements for a sacrificial victim. He carries only venial burdens of guilt: twice divorced, he is cavalier and dishonest with other people, something of a Sybarite, and a manifestly overripe mother's boy. As I have noted elsewhere, "Vandamm, Eve, and Thornhill retain some qualities of the devil, the biblical Eve, and the savior who wore a crown of thorns and was crucified on a hill."[12] In Hitchcock's comic romance, Thornhill is thrust down into a shadowy underworld where he loses his identity if not his life. After horrific, incredible adventures, he struggles back up with renewed innocence and an integrity that he could not have claimed before. Like Preston Sturges's everyman heroes, he is an ordinary man who could have been anyone. Thornhill undergoes his trials both as an individual with rather pedestrian crimes and failings and on behalf of the rest of the guilty crowd. His per-ils are comic because of their outcomes and, more fundamentally, because the mode of the film assures us that nothing too awful is likely to happen. But his exclusion from the crowd and his ordeals nonetheless recall those of a sacrificial scapegoat.[13]

With a few exceptions, analyses of *North by Northwest* concentrate on the story of Thornhill and the characters with whom he collides; they relegate to background or secondary status the profuse, emphatic social contexts that the movie invokes.[14] But the saturation of Hitchcock's picture with images and symbols of crowds argues for its preoccupation with collective as well as individual identity, and with the complicated, ambivalent relations between them. The hero and the crowd are often in conflict in *North by Northwest*. Canetti noted that everyone who belongs to a crowd "carries within him a small traitor who wants to eat, drink, make love and be left alone" (23). This "small traitor" is observable in Thornhill from his casual amatory arrangements and meeting for drinks at the start of the film to his proposition near the end that he and Eve get together for "a lot of apologizing to each other, in private."

The United Nations with its varied flags suggests an emphasis on national identity; repeated appearances of the U.S. flag particularize the national identity to which Hitchcock especially attends. The climactic chase across the heads of the presidents and the red, white, and blue patterning of colors throughout the film reinforce this emphasis.

Having traversed *North by Northwest* from starting points other than mine, Stanley Cavell arrives at the conclusion that "while America, or any discovered world, can no longer ratify marriage, the achievement of true marriage might ratify something called America as a place in which to seek it."[15] The ending of *North by Northwest*, with its recourse to park rangers and the U.S. agency answering Thornhill's "Help me," and with its crowd symbols of train and mountain, leads toward a similar conclusion. Persons and couples on the one hand, crowds and nations on the other, achieve at least a momentary reconciliation. *North by Northwest* may be seen as illustrating what Canetti wrote in the second volume of his autobiography: "I realized that there is such a thing as a crowd instinct, which is always in conflict with the personality instinct, and that the struggle between the two of them can explain the course of human history."[16]

Although Canetti does not analyze this conflict extensively in *Crowds and Power,* it is implied in some descriptions of the crowd, notably that "all are equal there; no distinctions count, not even that of sex" (15). Such radical equality would seem to be inimical to romantic heterosexual love, which depends not only on the distinction of sex but also, commonly, on an affinity between lovers that is partly based on their shared difference from other people around them. When films present romantic love as a principal solution to human dilemmas, the crowd tends to be cast as a foe and the films therefore exhibit a recurrent demophobia. In contrast, a picture like Fritz Lang's *Metropolis* (1926), despite its love story, favors the masses. It deemphasizes the development of the couple and gives most of its attention—as does *Potemkin*—to the formation of the crowd. At the same time, however, the combined mother-lover role of Maria in Lang's film suggests that the heterosexual pair is an ur-pack, the beginning of the most open of all increasing crowds, that of progeny. In John Huston's *The African Queen* (1951) and in his less-renowned meditation upon similar themes, *Heaven Knows, Mr. Allison* (1957), the combination of natural crowd symbols with variations on the myth of Adam and Eve hints at the procreative connection between the heterosexual couple and the potential growth of a crowd. With comic overstatement, Sturges invokes the same logic in *The Miracle of Morgan's Creek.*

In many of Hitchcock's pictures, conflict between crowds and lovers is pervasive. Most resolve the struggle between crowd and couple in favor of the lovers, but in some—*The Birds* (1963) or *Topaz,* for instance—the crowd largely prevails and the lovers are partly or wholly defeated. At the end of *Strangers on a Train* (1951), Guy and Ann, like Eve and Thornhill, are alone on a train. Their refusal even to speak with so safe a person as a clergyman represents an extreme apprehension of the threat posed by other people. *North by Northwest,* with its similar final setting, would seem to lean toward a similar conclusion.

But despite the sexual and romantic cadences with which *North by Northwest* closes, the continuing prominence of crowd symbols suggests that elements of both the crowd and the "small traitor" retain vitality. Furthermore, although one might argue that the action of *North by Northwest* leads to the usual cinematic formation of a heterosexual couple, such a conclusion would not accord with Canetti's thought, which in other respects is consonant with

Hitchcock's practice. In an uncharacteristically moralistic aside, Canetti indicates that the couple offers no solution to conflicting human instincts: "The 'family' of two is man's most contemptible creation" (222). There is little reason to conclude that Thornhill and Eve are about to merge into an exclusionary "family of two." The writing and photography of the final shots portray them as attaining full individual identities at the very moment of symbolic coupling, which is also symbolically the moment of their reabsorption by society, as they are propelled by one crowd symbol, the train, into another, the mountain.

Canetti and Hitchcock belonged to a generation of European thinkers and artists who came to maturity during the fragile, dangerous years after the Great War and before a greater, still more appalling eruption. Hitchcock's films of the thirties give ample evidence of the dread with which the director watched the next conflagration approach. The first *The Man Who Knew Too Much, The Thirty-Nine Steps* (1935), *Secret Agent* (1936), *Sabotage* (1936), and *The Lady Vanishes* (1938) all warn against virulent national suspicion and hatred, against organizations with bellicose inclinations, and against the dangers of ignoring the threats that such cultures and people pose to human peace, happiness, and (especially) love. All of Hitchcock's political movies are full of images of crowds and power like those that Canetti experienced in postwar Vienna and to which he then devoted three and a half decades of thought, study, and writing.

When the cold war developed, Hitchcock watched with disgust and alarm as the horrifying dynamics of opposed crowds and of political power persisted. The films that he made on political themes after the defeat of the Axis powers—*Notorious* (1946), the second *The Man Who Knew Too Much* (1956), *North by Northwest, Torn Curtain* (1966), and *Topaz*—all inflect the actions of crowds and power very much as do his political thrillers of the thirties.

Images and themes like those in *North by Northwest* repeatedly arise in Hitchcock's other films and in movies from other creators, countries, continents, and eras. As volatile, fluid, and hard as the metamorphoses of water, the complex textures and transformations of crowds and the serpentine affliction of power together comprehend many of the central issues of how humans become what they are. Throughout the brief but abundant history of the cinema, in its pictures and stories and its manifold visions of human life, movies have figured forth images of crowds and power. Along with love, crowds and power constitute not just the central subject of *North by Northwest* but of cinema itself.

"Boundaries, Burdens, and Stings":
Living as Prey in Burnett's *Killer of Sheep*

> What a strange thing meat is in the history of mankind. The leap from the flesh of prey to one's own flesh is the enigma of all enigmas. Compassion begins with it, arising from a feeling for one's own flesh. Today, the butchers' shops futilely recall one's own flesh.
>
> CANETTI, *The Human Province* (249)

Despite enjoying a considerable reputation among those who know it, Charles Burnett's first feature-length film has been little seen by movie audiences and has achieved only modest repute among film scholars and critics. This state of affairs is not surprising; *Killer of Sheep* (1977) has never been commercially distributed.[1] But it is regrettable; for along with the resonant, fluent *To Sleep with Anger* (1990), the underrated *The Glass Shield* (1995), and two surprisingly complex made-for-TV films (*NightJohn*, 1997, and *The Wedding*, 1999), *Killer of Sheep* marks Burnett as a gifted, original writer-director. The recognition achieved by *Killer of Sheep*, if not unprecedented for a first film, certainly signaled the debut of a major talent. It won the Critics' Prize at the Berlin International Film Festival in 1981 and in 1990 it was among the second group of twenty-five films selected for inclusion in The National Film Registry, a Library of Congress archive of U.S. films regarded as "culturally, historically or aesthetically significant." Burnett himself was acknowledged in 1988 with a MacArthur Foundation "genius grant."

Episodic in construction, *Killer of Sheep* runs approximately eighty minutes and consists of about thirty-five sequences, varying from as brief as fifteen seconds to more than seven minutes.[2] (Different viewers will make different counts, depending upon whether they consider some closely related actions to be one or more than one sequence.) Lacking a plot with a beginning, middle, and end, it portrays a series of events that occur among the members of its central family and their neighbors. Its episodes appear to succeed one another more or less randomly; they look to be all scrambled "middle."

Killer of Sheep is organized not as a sequence of actions but of imagistic and thematic equivalencies, variations, and contrasts. Its sequential development consists of images, incidents, words, and music that progressively elaborate such themes as the relations between children and adults, humans and sheep, men and women. More abstract issues arise simultaneously: predator and prey, for example, and play and work. The development of its ideas—which *does* have a beginning, middle, and end—arises as much through unfolding visual and aural patterns of imagery as through the sum of characters and their actions.

The opening episode of *Killer of Sheep* (following the imageless sound of children singing) evokes a dense, anxious set of emotions and ideas. Subsequently, the film consists largely of incidents involving the family of Stan, who works at a slaughterhouse. These incidents enlarge upon themes derived from the initial episode (which does not involve Stan's family). The concluding sequence of Stan killing sheep, hoisting their twitching bodies, and driving more of them into the slaughterhouse summarizes much of the film, both in its imagery and its music. At the thematic center of Burnett's film are actions and images of packs, predation, and transformation.

Since *Killer of Sheep* is not frequently shown and is currently unavailable on video, some description may be useful. It opens with an extreme close-up of a twelve- or thirteen-year-old boy being upbraided by his father for not coming to the aid of his brother in a fight. The boy is then slapped by a pregnant woman, evidently his young mother. After the film title and the director credit, Burnett cuts to a group of early adolescent boys having a dirt-fight by railroad tracks. In the next sequence, they chase and throw stones at a passing freight train, hang out along the right-of-way, and futilely try to push a single boxcar over a boy who lies with his head on the tracks. Stan Jr., the son of the title character, leaves to fetch his BB gun. Approaching his home through the alley, he witnesses two young men stealing a television. There follows a long sequence of Stan and several friends in the kitchen, then one of him at the slaughterhouse, followed by a transition to his wife and daughter at home. These sequences account for roughly the first quarter of the movie. Following sequences include such actions as preparations at the slaughterhouse, Stan talking with friends, a comic interlude of adults drinking beer in an immobile auto, kids playing on rooftops to the accompaniment of "Shake a Hand" on the sound track, sheep being butchered, Friday night family dinner in the kitchen, two goats at the slaughterhouse, a dice game, and an aborted trip to the racetrack.

Such descriptions indicate actions but give little sense of the film's richness of texture and variety of tone. Its quotidian images are packed with expressive detail; and its tone varies from neutral documentarism to ironic grimness, from the elegiac to the menacing or comic. The cinematography and writing portray urban poverty or semipoverty: the defeats, the sense of powerlessness, the antagonism among people, the normality of violence, and the frequency of predation that make up much of daily experience. There are also episodes of tenderness, comedy, and mutuality; but the images and words of daily life in this part of what appears to be Los Angeles are predominantly bleak. The accompanying music track—of collected recordings rather than music composed for the movie—variously enriches the imagery: by making it more emphatic, by implicit contrast, by adding ironic commentary, or by enlarging its implications. Formally, the recordings often delimit sequences or provide linkage between them.

Killer of Sheep has a powerful concreteness. Fundamentally metaphoric in structure, the images of the film, like the vehicles of all figurative rhetoric, exist first as vivid phenomena. Themes of predation and attack, for example, originate in fights, petty theft, slaughterhouse butchering, and so on. Their metaphorical tenor expands chiefly through what Eisenstein called "collisions" among images or sequences.

Metaphoric conceptions ripple outward from the particular, and the meanings of *Killer of Sheep* radiate to encompass a broad apprehension of life. To take an example, the children in Burnett's film have a relation to adults analogous to that which the sheep have to human beings; both children and sheep are at once de-

pendents and victims. When we observe that Stan is in a similar relation to the company for which he works, similar implications are
easily drawn—say, that people are in general the trusting, ovine victims of the society they create and inhabit. Such an enlarging of
meanings depends in part on textual signals and in part on the
imaginative, empathetic capacities of the audience that the picture
implicitly addresses.

Packs, Traps, and Predation

Following a black screen with a sound track of children and a
woman singing an unaccompanied lullaby, the precredit sequence
opens on a tight close-up of the slightly sullen face of a young
teenage boy. We hear an angry man's voice: "You let anyone jump
on your brother again. And you just stand and watch. Boy, I'll beat
you to death!" The camera begins to draw back, then Burnett cuts
to a two-shot over the man's shoulder toward the boy, who is lean-
ing away. "I don't care who started what, or whether he was win-
nin' or losin.' You get a stick or or a goddamn brick and you
knock the shit out of whoever's fightin' your brother 'cause if anything was to happen to me or your mother you ain't got nobody
except your brother." The man coughs and moves away; Burnett
cuts to a medium close-up of a pregnant woman with her hands
protectively around the neck of a child, perhaps the brother whom
the boy failed to defend. The man returns: "You are not a child anymore; you soon will be a goddamn man. Now, start learnin' what
life is about now, son." Burnett cuts to another young man of perhaps eighteen or twenty in the same room, reading a newspaper—
also learning, one gathers, about life. Then back to the woman,
who walks over with a faint smile that retrospectively seems punitive when she slaps the face of the boy. Yet more instruction. The
sequence ends as it began, with the camera close to the boy's face.
He remains stolidly silent.

The screen goes to black for the director credit, "A film by
Charles Burnett." Paul Robeson is heard singing the song the children sang:

> All the stars to play with,
> Or the moon to run away with,
> They'll come if you don't cry.

This exhortation to an implied child in a comforting bedtime ritual resonates with ironic dissonance against the images we have just seen. The sound track and words fade out, then fade in to the next sequence, which begins with a close-up of another boy peeking out from behind a large wooden panel as clods of dirt hit it or sail past.

The terrifying threat of a hostile touch that Canetti sees behind all commands are practically explicit in the father's menacing reproaches and the mother's slap. Related themes appear in the opening sequence: the equivocal relations, at once hostile and nurturing, between adults and children; similarly equivocal relations between males and females; the persistent anxiety of many of the characters.

After the angry first sequence, Burnett begins the next with another close-up of another boy, who dodges behind a plywood shield as he plays with a group of companions. When one boy is slightly hurt, the mock-battle stops while his friend attends him. Burnett's sequencing implies that a child can better find affection and safety among his pals than in a family that demands his loyalty while simultaneously attacking him. At the same time, however, the boys are attacking each other, forming themselves instinctively if playfully into war packs.

Indeed, throughout *Killer of Sheep* children play at fighting. Those who soar between rooftops during the "Shake a Hand" sequence, for example, quickly transform themselves into two groups throwing gravel at each other. These actions suggest that the human instinct to seek strength and protection in crowds or packs is likely to be only partly successful; for such groups introduce their own hazards, either because they are defined by hostile opposition to other groups or because they are likely to split into antagonistic pairs.

When a train passes at the beginning of the third sequence, the boys who were fighting each other leave their dirt piles and pursue it, hurling stones as the boxcars lumber by. We can turn to Canetti for a useful gloss on their transformation: "The war pack . . . has much in common with the hunting pack and is, indeed, connected with it by many transitional states" (95). After the train passes, Stan Jr. leaves to fetch his BB gun, presumably to add it to the pack's arsenal. On his way home, he encounters a smaller, more dangerous hunting pack, two young men stealing a television. "What you lookin' at punk?" says one of them to a middle-aged man watering his lawn. "I cut your heart out!" Despite the imperious command Stan Jr. receives from one of the thieves—"You ain't seen nothin'!"—he sides with the younger men, reporting to them when the middle-aged man drops his hose to go call the police. The antagonism between son and parents in the first sequence characterizes Stan Jr.'s relations with his family and may account for his choice of allies and his betrayal of the man who witnesses the theft.

Motives of hunting and murder are indistinguishable when a pair of rascals arrive at Stan's home and attempt to recruit him for what may be the assassination of a witness in an impending court case. Their proposition disgusts Stan's wife. "Why d'you always wanna hurt somebody?" she demands indignantly. Equally indignant, one of the pair responds, "Who, me? That's the way nature is. I mean the animal has his teeth and the man has his fists. That's the way I was brought up, God damn me." Like Burnett, Gaston Bachelard, in his study of Lautréamont, emphasizes the common inheritance of an impulse to violence shared by men and animals: "We have arrived at the conclusion that the will to lacerate, claw, nip and squeeze nervously in the fingers is fundamental. This is the principle of juvenile cruelty. The primal consciousness of the will is a clenched fist."[3] His remark seems especially apt for this moment in *Killer of Sheep,* because of its association of such behavior with juvenility; for the men who approach Stan, although clearly adults, act and dress like late-adolescent hoodlums. Earlier in the same book, Bachelard offers an insight closely related to Canetti's understanding of the motives of those who seek power, *"die Überlebenden"*: "For Lautréamont . . . animalized life is . . . the excess of a will-to-live that distorts beings."[4]

In the odd oath, "God damn me," that ends the man's reply to Stan's wife, we may hear an echo of the father of the opening sequence, telling his son that he will soon be "a goddamn man" and that he must "learn what life is about now." Here and elsewhere in Burnett's film, characters, especially men, assume that life is about violent attack and self-defense, predation and flight. Dismissing the wife's assertion that human life depends more on using one's brain than one's fists, the snazzily dressed men point at Stan's shabby clothes. Their contempt for the meager rewards of his labors parallels a gloomy line of reasoning from *Crowds and Power:* "Things which are particularly important for the practical existence of a group of men may be highly valued, but the greatest respect is always accorded to anything which has to do with killing. That which can kill is feared; that which does not directly serve killing is merely useful" (219). At the end of this sequence, the conflict modulates back to that between children and adults; Stan's son and daughter emerge only to be scolded by their mother and father—an anger referred, like the pain of a heart attack felt in one's arm, from the parents' dispute with their nasty, narcissistic visitors.

More than crowds, *Killer of Sheep* portrays packs, small groups that are confined rather than expansive. Human crowds, indeed, are present almost entirely by implication. "Hunting packs" and "war packs" appear most insistently in Burnett's film. Each is a "unit of action" that comes together for some form of predation. Canetti explains that "the choice of the term 'pack' for this older and more limited kind of crowd is intended to remind us that it owes its origin among men to the example of animals, the pack of animals hunting together. Wolves, which man knew well and from whom many of the dogs he uses derive, had impressed him very early. . . . A pack of hounds, trained to hunt together, is a living remnant of this old association. Men have learnt from wolves" (96).

These remarks highlight an intermittent motif that arises imagistically and aurally in *Killer of Sheep,* that of dogs. The first canine image is incongruous and a little mysterious: Stan Jr.'s young sister wearing a Halloween mask of a mournful hound. She appears to be more prey than predator, however, for her brother roughly grabs her face through the rubber muzzle. Still wearing the mask, she later stands sucking her fingers while on the sound track real dogs bark. When the image shifts to her father, the sound of dogs continues. We are made aware of the canine overtones of the relation of Stan to the docile animals that he dispatches when he complains, "I'm always awake." "Yeah," replies his friend, "countin' sheep." The barking had faded away, but at that moment an animal loudly barks and snarls.

Later in the film, three boys riding a bicycle are chased by a pair of dogs. When they abandon their bike and run, Burnett goes via a match cut from them to the slaughterhouse, where freshly killed sheep hang upside down, swaying before lines of glass brick in a motion that flows out of the panning shot of the boys racing past a picket fence. This visual analogy implies that children and sheep are both prey—whether of dogs or of industrial predators. Although Stan is always gentle and protective toward his daughter, she nonetheless intuitively understands the roles of predators and the chased, the strong and the weak, adults and children. She would rather be a dog than a sheep. But Stan Jr.'s rough handling of her and the casual shove that she receives from one of Stan's friends a few minutes later make clear that her hound-mask does not have the power to transform her from childish prey into hunter.

The attempt to escape becoming something's next meal is the most basic of the originary motives of crowd formation. A boy behind a scrapwood shield with his friends, sheep crowding together, children soaring one after another over rooftops, other sheep stampeding away—all manifest the instinct to find safety in numbers.

Escapes into crowds in *Killer of Sheep,* however, rarely achieve lasting success. In their outcomes, the very sequences in which crowd flights are portrayed demonstrate the futility of such attempts to get away. The boy cries when he is hit with a rock in both children's sequences; the sheep do not escape slaughter.

For the characters of *Killer of Sheep,* moreover, even ineffectual crowds are only temporary. Most of the time, Burnett's film suggests that

This is a mean old world,
Try livin' by yourself

—as Little Walter sings during infernal images of butchering. When Stan's wife returns from a thwarted excursion, the front door of their home is unlocked. "Stan Jr. left the house open," she says, with an anger once again simmering from previous frustration. "I'm going to kill that boy." Her threat echoes that which opens the film. In the next sequence, we see her come outside to summon her son, who escapes her on the roof with his friends, a refuge that recalls the "Shake a Hand" sequence. Yet though we do not see Stan Jr. come down from the roof, we will hardly assume that he and his companions have taken up residence there. Eventually, he will have to return to his home, with its threatening, reproachful adults.

The inescapability of poverty, predation, and conflict is emphasized by continual failures of the vehicles that might carry people away from such conditions; by the breaking down or loss of cars and bicycles—and even of skateboards. The plan to buy and install a used motor originates when a friend derides Stan and Bracy for having middle-class pretensions. "Man, I ain't po'," Stan protests, and he proposes to Bracy that they get the motor. After negotiating a price for it that literally includes the shirt off Bracy's back, they painfully haul it down a flight of stairs and onto Stan's pickup truck. The episode ends in inglorious self-cancellation when the motor falls to the pavement as they start to drive off. Its block cracks, rendering it useless. The labor and scarce money that Bracy puts into fixing his car, as the attempted outing to the country demonstrates, is also futile.

While Stan and Bracy wrestle the engine onto the truck bed, smashing Bracy's finger in the process, Burnett inserts a detail that links adult and juvenile futility, a series of boys tumbling off their skateboards on the street behind the men. Elsewhere, children seem equally immobilized. The sequence that begins with soaring children ends with a weeping, cowering, isolated boy. The gang of boys cannot push the boxcar. The three whom the dogs chase abandon their bike and run into a match cut that likens them to sheep being butchered. In an earlier sequence, a boy peddles up an alley and imperiously confronts a group of girls and younger children. A minute later he is running tearfully away, his bicycle left behind. "Come get your old raggedy bike," a girl shouts derisively after him—a childish taunt that anticipates, in the next sequence, the ill-fated adult project to buy the used motor, "What do you want with another raggedy-ass car for, huh?"

A comic episode precedes the picking up of the motor. Stan Jr. tells his sister that he needs some money—a desire symbolized by the ludicrous quantity of sugar he pours on his cereal. Burnett then cuts to a close up of the head of a woman who hears a shout from off-screen, "Get yourself together and get on out of here, 'cause you know you ain't no good woman!" She retorts, "You get yourself in line!" and the image shifts to her angrily pacing platform shoes as the sound track cuts to an exaggerated, comic blues. The woman strides haughtily past a man into a car, followed by her accuser, apparently humbled. She sits between two men in the front seat as we view them from the front across the hood, on which stands a can of beer. When the other passenger in the front seat leans forward to retrieve the beer, we realize that the car has no windshield. It is going nowhere, and is serving only as a dilapidated clubhouse. Its comic immobility foreshadows the probable end of the "raggedy-ass car" into which Stan and Bracy will not be installing a replacement motor, after all.

On the rare occasions when vehicles function, they eventually fail because of something like the absence of a spare tire. As it happens, however, characters' mobility does not ultimately much matter. One location appears very like another. When Stan stops at a liquor store to cash a check en route to getting the used engine, the sound track introduces another blues, "mean old 'Frisco, and that low-down Santa Fe"—equally uncongenial places that the train in the song separates as much as connects. Early in the film, we hear the dry grinding of a car's starter while Stan sits wearily at his kitchen table with his face in his hands. As he says something about getting ready to go to work, the engine finally catches; but far from escaping his plight, he is about to be thrust back into the job that devastates him. Neither he nor any of the other characters makes anything like an escape, not even an illusory one. Nothing that could take them someplace else works and no place in the film looks like someplace else anyway.

Indeed, the imagery and action of *Killer of Sheep* rarely refer to anything outside the neighborhood and its inhabitants. A train passes through and is stoned, but where it came from and where it may be going are of no concern. The one attempt that people make to leave the neighborhood is terminated by a flat tire and the lack of a spare.

The circumscription of the world in the film diminishes the issue of race; and to the extent that it is an issue, Burnett presents it with characteristic, reticulating irony. Excluding one of Stan's co-workers and a coarse, white boss-woman who appears sexually drawn to Stan in a rather idle way (as does another woman during the purchase of the motor), all the characters are African American. One might say that being black is prima facie a subject of *Killer of Sheep,* but such an assertion finds little support in a movie that neither avoids nor seeks racial questions. In practice, the film supports the obvious point—as Stanley Crouch once remarked—that African Americans have other things to worry about besides whites. Insofar as race is explicitly an issue, it is to a considerable degree linked with class: "You niggers are sick," says one of Stan's friends. "Now you think you're middle class." Just before the car sets off on its ill-fated excursion, an inebriated man rails, "Tell this nigger, y'all, that don't he know we can get fifteen years for him actin' [inaudible]" and continues, "We don't act like this no mo'." His diatribe appears to be occasioned by the prospect of leaving the black neighborhood for the world beyond.

Over images of children playing at a construction-demolition site, we hear a Paul Robeson recording of "The House I Live In." After celebrating democracy, various trades, "the children in the playground," and "all races, all religions," he concludes, "that's

America to me." Given the desolation of the site and the racial homogeneity of the children, the irony of Robeson's song appears obvious. But in Burnett's filmmaking an obvious irony is rarely the whole story. The children are playing together with rare harmony, and the next sequence of Stan at the slaughterhouse includes a fellow worker who is white.

Adjacency among the sequences of *Killer of Sheep* creates both linkages and contrasts—as likely to be ironic as straightforward, and likelier to be both at once. Additionally, the music track frequently complicates the ironies. Sometimes it partly transforms bleakness to beauty; at the least it usually comments upon the images it accompanies with an ameliorating expressiveness and dignity.

More uniformly ironic than the Robeson recording of "The House I Live In" is another in which he sings "Mother's been expecting me" and "all the friends I knew" while we watch a mass of sheep come into the slaughterhouse. On a repetition of "all the friends I knew," Burnett cuts to the front of Stan's home, where two dangerous-looking men arrive to try to convince Stan to join them in a job that requires someone who "won't blush to murder." A similar ironic relation exists between the plaintive music track and an image of banal violence when Stan Jr. encounters the young thieves: "I wonder / My little darling / Where are you tonight?"—a question that can refer equally to the robbers and to the boy. By contrast, the hymnlike version of "Shake a Hand" that accompanies shots of soaring children underlines at once the hope and the poignancy of the images. While Stan and his wife dance to Dinah Washington's "This Bitter Earth"—one of the few examples of diegetic music—the song articulates the sorrow of a life in which

Today you're young,
Too soon you're old

and the consolation that finding love with another person can offer. But the record ends and Stan detaches himself from his yearning wife, leaving her to memories of an emotionally richer time with her grandmother in the country. The reinforcement of the music track reverses and becomes dissonant with the image, thereby offering in succession a straightforward commentary and an ironic one.

Unable to break out of their isolated, decayed neighborhood with its scarcity and antagonism, the characters of *Killer of Sheep*

153

find themselves living as prey. The movie figuratively emphasizes their victimization, as we have seen, by identifying them with the title animal. The metaphor is traditional. As Northrop Frye observed, "Perhaps the use of this particular convention is due to the fact that, being stupid, affectionate, gregarious, and easily stampeded, the societies formed by sheep are most like human ones."[5] Georges Franju's short documentary *Le Sang des Bêtes* (The Blood of Beasts, 1949) juxtaposes abattoirs on the outskirts of Paris with impoverished suburban neighborhoods and shares with *Killer of Sheep* images of children, railroad trains, the slaughtering of animals, and an ironic use of music. It may be the most direct cinematic forebear of Burnett's film. But for all its ghastly insistence upon images of the dispatching and dismembering of horses, cattle, and lambs, it is a less rhetorically insistent work in terms of implied analogies between human and animal subjects. Nonetheless, the simile in Franju's film is explicit at least once: "*Les autres, comme des hommes, suivent. Ils bêlent, comme chantent des otages*" (The others [sheep], like men, follow. They bleat, as hostages sing). Such imagery is not uncommon in other films before or since *Killer of Sheep*. Metaphorical use of butcher-shop or abattoir imagery occurs, for example, famously in Eisenstein's *Strike* (1925), in Godard's *Weekend* (1967), Fassbinder's *In a Year of 13 Moons* (1978), as a variant via cross-cutting between Kurtz's death and the sacrifice of a bull in Coppola's *Apocalypse Now* (1979), and in Jonathan Nossiter's *Sunday* (1997).

Failed Transformations

Guilt in Burnett's picture attaches to the humans whom the film identifies with sheep or who identify themselves with their prey. This association may appear counterintuitive; we might suppose that guilt would result from regarding oneself as a predator or killer rather than as a victim. Canetti argues, however, that we do not feel guilt in cases where we do not feel any identification with our quarry. In practice, "feeling guilty and thinking of one's self as prey . . . are basically the same" (347). On the other hand, the disposal of insects or similar creatures considered vermin exemplifies killing without empathy and therefore has no potential for producing guilt. To avoid guilt, then, "Man easily persuaded himself to see as vermin everything which opposed him" (363).

Burnett's use of metaphor recalls what I take to be its narrative origins in the conception of metamorphosis, or what Canetti calls transformation, an act of understanding and identification in which "one body is equated with another" (340).[6] It is to that gift, "one of the great mysteries," that humans "owe what is best in themselves" (337). What is best in Stan is his unarticulated but powerful identification with the sheep that he slaughters, and the guilt that he consequently feels. What is best in us is reflected by the very existence of the film and by our responsiveness to it. We understand that we too are imaged by Burnett's movie.

But if Stan does not convince himself that sheep are vermin, neither has he access to exculpating transformations (which Canetti usually presents as being mythic or otherwise socially mediated). A predator who equates his body with those he slaughters, Stan feels like his own prey. Early in the film we hear him declare, "I'm working myself into my own hell." The inescapable grimness of life for him is contained in and symbolized by his daily killing of sheep. When he remarks to his wife that he needs to "find me a job"—as if he did not already have one—we infer that he regards what he does less as his employment than as his condition.

Stan does not flee into crowds but he shrinks from confrontation. His efforts to be free from giving or accepting commands lead him to isolation, depression, and rage. Despondent and apathetic, he can find "no peace of mind." Canetti's discussion of melancholia illuminates the sense of dead-end helplessness that threatens to consume Burnett's protagonist: "Melancholia begins when flight-transformations are abandoned because they are all felt to be useless. A person in a state of melancholia feels that pursuit is over and he has already been captured. He cannot escape; he cannot find fresh metamorphoses. Everything he attempted has been in vain; he is resigned to his fate and sees himself as prey; first as prey, then as food, and finally as carrion or excrement" (347). Most viewers will feel that Stan perceives the broad implications of what he participates in at the slaughterhouse. The melancholy last sequence shows him seizing sheep, then driving more inside to their deaths. It is backed up musically by Dinah Washington singing "Unforgettable." To Stan, the doomed animals are unforgettable indeed—as individual creatures and as emblems of himself and of his family and acquaintances.

This final sequence extends its implications retrospectively back to the next-to-last one. In the penultimate episode, a young woman with a crutch arrives at Stan's home to join a small gathering of neighborhood women. She whispers her pregnancy to Stan's wife, who relays the joyful news to the group. But the images of the succeeding sequence suggest to us the fate that the child will face in the world that Burnett's movie has portrayed.

The criticisms and self-justifications other characters direct at one another imply that they share Stan's desperation, though theirs might not be so quiet as his, nor as sharply felt. In Stan's kitchen, his friend Oscar declares, "I don't have any trouble sleepin'. I ain't ashamed of nothin' I can't help." A few minutes later, however, Bracy tells Stan that he has been "walkin' the streets all night. We passed here about three o'clock last night an' saw the lights on, but we decided t' keep on steppin'."

Stan's vision of a slaughter of innocents darkens every aspect of his life and becomes associated with what he calls his "own hell." The images and sounds of dogs, in addition to suggesting predation, recall classical dogs from Hades, or the "hell-hound on my trail" of the great bluesman Robert Johnson. Steam and low-key lighting in the slaughterhouse also invoke traditionally infernal images. Stan tells Oscar that he hasn't been in church since "back home. Since then I done a lot of things. Haven't done nothin' yet that'd make the Devil blush." His denial brings itself into doubt simply by being offered. Related to the demonic motif is a casual moment when Oscar greets Stan Jr. with "Hey, what's goin' on, Killer?" Since the boy is at that moment looking for his BB gun, the greeting is especially apropos. Stan Jr., like his father and the men surrounding him, seems destined to live as a predator among predators and, therefore, as prey. And living as prey is hell.

Double Crowds:
Men and Women, Adults and Children

Killer of Sheep embodies two of what Canetti identifies as "three basic antitheses. The first and most striking is that between men and women; the second that between the living and the dead; and the third that between friend and foe" (64). The contrast between living and dead is largely absent from Burnett's picture, although the wife's meditation on her country past and family may to a degree evoke it. The contest between friend and foe is recurrent. The most frequent division in *Killer of Sheep*, however, is that between women and men. Relations between the sexes are complex and various; they are in general mutually combative and competitive, but they can also be nourishing or consoling. In any case, the women and men of *Killer of Sheep*, and the gendered crowds they imply (and occasionally constitute), are almost always pointedly different from each other and frequently antagonistic.

Part of the male-female antithesis is the polarity between men as predators outside the home and women as caretakers within it. After we first see Stan at work among sheep carcasses and pans of organs, we are shown Stan's wife in the kitchen, cooking and attending to her appearance—activities evidently directed toward the anticipated return of her husband. At the same time, Stan's daughter in the laundry room is caring for her doll and singing. Stan's son, on the other hand, appears mostly outside the home, to which he returns briefly to get his BB gun. When the wife and Stan's violent friends dispute about living by the use of fists or brains, they typify the different dispositions of the sexes. The adjacent final sequences of the pregnant young woman and Stan in the slaughterhouse mark again the fundamental contrast in *Killer of Sheep* between the sexes.

The fact that the penultimate sequence shows only women and the last one only men reflects not just contrast but alienation. Women generally associate with women; boys run with boys, men with men. When Stan's daughter hangs about her father and his friends, her mother calls her inside. Although she says her daughter should not listen to "grown folks talk," the wife is not part of that male group either, and the film seems to suggest that "grown folks" at that moment means "men." Even in a brief party sequence that includes men and women together, the men roll dice while the women watch.

Within families, alienation between men and women is only slightly diminished. Despite some sexual tension between them, the men and women in the kitchen to which Stan goes for the used engine largely ignore each other. In his own home, Stan is mutely unresponsive to the affectionate or concerned gestures of his wife. A low camera and short focal-length lens underscore the separation of husband and wife at dinner. "I used to think you were just tired. . . . Don't nothin' ever make you smile?" When she continues, "Try to get some sleep. I can do dishes tomorrow," she intimates that she will go to bed with him. But her husband finishes his cup, rises from the table, and begins to work on the floor. A warm coffee cup reminded him earlier of "when you're makin' love, a woman's forehead." Evidently his wife no longer stirs him in the same way. In a later sequence, the wife is more direct: "Tomorrow's Saturday.

[Pause] Let's go to bed." Stan again fails to respond, though he does embrace his daughter when she comes to massage him—an action that seems pointed on both the father's and the girl's part, as if to suggest that she can console him, but his wife cannot. In each of these sequences, the context implies that the emotional toll of Stan's work is largely responsible for his impassivity or unexpressed hostility. This implication reminds us again that a fundamental contrast between men and women throughout the film puts men out in the world and women at home.

When Bracy finds Stan repairing the kitchen sink, he assumes that such labor must have been ordered by a commanding female: "See the wife got you towin' the cart." Later, when the wife looks into the room, she and Bracy nod coolly at each other, without speaking. Bracy's relations with his own spouse are not much warmer. When he finds her standing barefoot, he tells her to put shoes on. "Shit on you," she replies indifferently and walks away. As he works under the hood of a car, she stands complaining, "We need food in the house. You shouldn't have spent your last dime to get this car fixed. It ain't right."

Comic stereotypes of the war between the sexes in *Killer of Sheep* have the abrasiveness usual to such humor. In addition to the platform shoes sequence, there is an episode in which a uniformed man flees an angry woman with a gun, and another in which a voluptuous woman (who has just told Stan, "You'd be a good lookin' fella if you didn't frown so much") kicks a bandaged, hapless character who insults her after she rebuffs his advances. Sex in this episode provokes conflict, more violent than that between Stan and his wife, but not in quality wholly different. In another sequence, Stan's daughter asks, "Daddy, what makes the rain?" He replies, "Why, it's the Devil beatin' his wife." His rare spark of humor brings smiles from both wife and daughter, but the substance of his down-home proverb repeats the motif of routine conflict between men and women.

The boy who is driven from his bike by contemptuous girls begins the squabble by demanding, "Get out of my way, you skags!" Stan Jr. and Stan's friend, as we have seen, both treat the daughter with gratuitous roughness. Late in the film, a motley pack of boys emerges from a hole in the side of a house to throw dirt at a girl who is hanging laundry. The antagonism that largely defines adult relations between men and women persists among children.

"Hey man, why don't we go to the Bitsford Club, man, an' watch the 'ho's go in an' out," proposes a boy to his companions at the rail yards. Sex, that great reconciler of women and men, is portrayed as largely scopic or combative in *Killer of Sheep*. It is contemplated or indirectly proposed; but it does not occur, nor does sexual attraction bring men and women together. The sexual overtones of the liquor store boss's proposition that Stan come to work for her are more predatory than amorous; Stan and his wife seem to have reached a sexual impasse; and the woman who comments upon the pregnancy of the girl with a cane frames her acknowledgment in a martial metaphor: "I thought her old man was shootin' blanks. But I see he's droppin' bombs."

Conflict between the sexes, however, is not continuous or uniform; women and men sometimes offer each other mutual help and comfort. Stan—whom we first see on his knees under the kitchen sink—often adopts the concerned, helpful attitude that among other characters is largely within the domain of women. "Who did you?" he asks the man with head bandages, and he is outraged when the woman kicks that luckless figure. He "give[s] away things to the Salvation Army." Just after Bracy's wife has complained about a lack of money and food, Stan runs up to offer both: a little cash for Bracy and a can of peaches for Bracy's wife. Stan clearly wishes, despite his depression, to be a supportive husband and father. His fondness for his daughter, his dancing with his wife, and his responsiveness to both after the aborted outing all testify to his affection. At the same time, his wife cherishes and protects him, refusing to turn her feelings of disappointment into conflict and defending him from rascally acquaintances. Beleaguered as the central characters are, their home and family offer refuge from the world of anger and predation that seems almost uniform outside it. The degree to which such domestic consolations are seen as balancing the grimness of much of the rest of the film will depend upon the expectations of the viewer. One reader of this chapter found that it "shortchanges the sense of community and mutual reliance the film displays"; another felt that it understates the violence of Stan's world. The complex ironies of Burnett's film make such varying responses all but inevitable.

Children, despite their imitation of adult conflicts, often provide each other the aid and comfort that few seem to find at home. The mock battle of the second sequence is delayed while a boy who appears hurt is tended by his friend. When a child's voice is heard calling "Angie, Angie," Stan's daughter runs outside to join a very young boy; later she earnestly tells a friend who has missed school, "You gonna fall behind." Even the boys who dirty the girl's laundry look after one another; when the littlest one falls, the biggest comes to pick him up.

Throughout *Killer of Sheep*, however, children mostly repeat the actions of adults and the dynamics of adult relationships. Conversely, if children are in some respects little grown-ups or grown-ups in the making, adults often appear to be oversized children. "Hey Stan, can you come out an' play, man?" demands one of the thugs who comes to his house. Kids are not qualitatively different from adults, and they supply many of the clearest instances of the human tendencies that the picture dramatizes. The most emphatic equation of children and grown-ups is implied by their equivalent positions with respect to images of sheep. As the mathematical theorem of equivalence puts it, two quantities equal to a third are equal to each other. At the same time, as in all comparisons, similarity implies difference; and distinctions between adults and children—particularly distinctions regarding power—give rise to some of the most poignant moments of Burnett's deeply humane movie.

Point-of-view shots cast children as ingénue witnesses. The last image of the abandoned motor is a subjective shot through the eyes of Stan's daughter. As the truck drives away, the broken engine recedes on the street, its shrinking image accompanied by a wistful passage from a Scott Joplin rag. The daughter's cheerless gaze mirrors her father's stoic disappointment. Her presence modulates the sequence from something like Laurel and Hardy comedy into a more melancholy key, reminding us that the failures and disappointments she sees her parents suffer shape her expectations for her own life. Similarly, the sequence after the next one begins as what at first appears to be a broadly comic episode. A fleeing soldier apprehensively looks around the corner of a building at a pistol-wielding woman: *Amos 'n' Andy* stuff. But the episode is sharply altered in tone when Burnett unexpectedly introduces two children on a couch. A sleeping girl rests her head on her older brother, who sits with quiet, wide-eyed apprehension. The adults' conflict, promising rough comedy from the detached perspective of long shots, becomes painful with close-ups of the children's faces and an intercut extreme close-up of the strong, handsome face of their mother, watching them.

At play, children imitate their elders. We see Stan wrapping up a day's work at the slaughterhouse; next, over an exterior shot of the building, we hear girls singing,

This old man, he played one,
He played knick-knack on my thumb.
With a knick-knack, paddy-whack, give a dog a bone,
This old man came rollin' home.

Cut from the knacker's workplace to his house. There the wife works at being a mother and homemaker while the daughter plays at the same occupations. After Burnett shows Stan repairing the kitchen floor, he cuts to children hammering on scrap lumber and broken cinder blocks. Then back to Stan and his fellow workers at the slaughterhouse, cleaning meat hooks that tinkle like triangles.

Commands

Particularly relevant to Burnett's portrayal of children and their fate as adults are the psychic injuries inflicted by commands. These wounds become sites for stored emotional energy urgently awaiting discharge. The child who has obeyed a command becomes an adult who is compelled to reissue that same command, under the same circumstances. We see orders inflicted upon the children of *Killer of Sheep;* and we see the fated outcome of both children and commands in the adults who appear to be masters, but who in reality are replaying similar compulsions once inflicted upon them— whether long ago in childhood or in the daily indignities of their lives.

As Burnett's film does, so Canetti and the psychologist Alice Miller emphasize the scars that orders forced upon children leave in adult psyches. Canetti calls such scars "the stings of command" and Miller famously locates them in the injured, repressed inner child. Miller's description fits much of the action of *Killer of Sheep:* "Love and cruelty are mutually exclusive. No one ever slaps a child out of love but rather because in similar situations, when one was defenseless, one was slapped and then compelled to interpret it as a sign of love. This inner confusion prevailed for thirty or forty years and is passed on to one's own child."[7]

The boy's father in the opening sequence threatens to "beat [him] to death"; Stan Jr.'s mother is "going to kill that boy"; Stan advances threateningly toward his son in order to enforce his command. Among adults, threat also operates: the woman who drives the soldier from her home holds a pistol and the man in turn threatens to kill her; the usually mild-mannered Stan feels that he has the power to order a man who owes him money to "get on, nigger!"

Since "the source of a command . . . must also be recognized as something stronger than ourselves" (305), "those most beset by commands are children" (306). "From his earliest days stings of all kinds accumulate in him [a child] and it is round these that there form the compulsions and pressures of his later life. . . . They are what drive him towards this or that otherwise inexplicable deed or meaningless relationship" (318). The idea that childhood experiences shape adult compulsions is hardly original with Burnett, Miller, or Canetti. Distinctive, however, is the specificity with which they analyze the origins and operations of orders, their perception that the commands people suffer continuously impinge on their psychic lives, and the emphasis they give them in human emotional economies. Burnett's film opens with a boy suffering a primitive command from an overwhelming man and ends with Stan driving sheep into the slaughterhouse with commanding movements that are prelinguistic and designed to produce flight. In those final, archaic orders, we are vividly reminded that "beneath all commands glints the harshness of the death sentence" (304).

Bracketed and inflected by these images, the ordinary conflicts among the characters of *Killer of Sheep* should be at least partly interpreted as the consequences of commands. In some sequences, the application and results of visible commands are direct and encompassing; more often, sequences of events have multiple motivations. Only in a few episodes, however, is the concept of the command entirely absent. An "otherwise inexplicable deed or meaningless relationship"—say the railings of the man who talks about how people used to "get fifteen years" and how "niggers have changed" or the boy's aggression on the "skags"—may be seen as the reflection of some command that we can plausibly infer. In the cases just mentioned, the precedent commands would seem to be, respectively, the proscriptions that a black man, particularly in the rural South, would have obeyed in his youth and thereby carry within himself to adulthood, and the host of orders from adults that children are subjected to throughout the film. The residue that such commands leave are revealed, but they do not appear to be relieved either by the man's ravings or the boy's feckless attempt to boss the girls.

The sequence in which Stan Jr. is returning home for his BB gun reflects the workings of a series of commands. The form of the threat, "I cut your heart out, punk!" delivered to the man watering his lawn strongly suggests that the issuer is passing on an insult inflicted on him; "punk" hardly describes the tie-wearing, middle-class, middle-aged man, but it fits the frenzied young robber. To Stan Jr. one of the thieves insists, "You ain't seen nothin'!"—a command to keep quiet that the recipient immediately carries home and inflicts upon his younger sister, whom he literally muzzles.

Throughout *Killer of Sheep,* the overwhelming dynamic of transferred emotions accords with the analyses of thinkers like Miller and Canetti. The pervasiveness of commands, implied or explicit, combines with constant bullying downward—from men to weaker men or to women, to youths, to children, to smaller children, and so on. The pain and frustration of commands and threats cannot often be escaped or evaded. The job that gives Stan such anguish—his daily carrying out of painful, murderous orders—leaves him "feeling I might do somebody else some harm." At the bottom of this chain of orders and intimidation are the sheep—only slightly more helpless than most of the humans—penned up, uncomprehending, betrayed, and ultimately innocent. "Mother's been expecting me," sings Paul Robeson, as a herd of sheep ascends the ramp into the slaughterhouse,

> Father's waiting, too.
> Lots of folks gathered there,
> All the friends I knew.

The match cut from the fleeing boys to the swinging, freshly killed animals is then followed by a shot of boys on the porch of Stan's home standing on their heads, repeating the position of the sheep that we have just seen Stan hang upside down to kill. Together the sequences present human life as one arc in a circle of predation.

Transformation is functionally bivariate, leading either to guilt or to a unifying conception of the sympathetic wholeness of the world. Burnett's vision of human existence as contiguous with the abattoir—more subtly lethal than it, perhaps, but hardly gentler—does not exclude a simultaneous understanding of the aspects of life that are peaceful and loving. His vision is grave but not hopeless; he confronts the everyday evil of human beings without losing sight of what is appealing or compassionate in them, and without losing empathy with his subjects. The act of making *Killer of Sheep*, of comprehending in myriad "moving" photographs the world of its characters, is itself an act of courage that makes love possible. "To see is to retain—to behold," wrote Stan Brakhage. "Elimination of all fear is in sight. . . . There can be no ultimate love where there is fear."[8] The clear-sighted comprehension in *Killer of Sheep* of the world, its children, and its childlike adults embodies Brakhage's beholding. Two aphorisms from Canetti's notebooks, taken together, come close to summarizing the hard but affectionate understanding of life and people that informs Burnett's movie. "It turns out that we are really God's lowest creature, that is to say, God's executioner in his world."[9] *Killer of Sheep* testifies that if we are to find a less appalling role for ourselves, we must begin to come to terms with what we are, with the killers that we have become—for "hope can flow only from darkest knowledge."[10]

Changing Places:

Predation, Transformation, and Identity in Demme's *The Silence of the Lambs*

In light of the concept of transformation, we may reflect on the nature of the twenty-four frames per second that pass through motion picture projectors. The hundred-thousand-plus photographs making up a movie comprise more than so many pictures whose rapid succession dupes our overwhelmed optical pathways into seeing motion. If we recall the much-reproduced stop-action photographs that Eadweard Muybridge made in the last quarter of the nineteenth century, we may come to another, perhaps more fertile, understanding of what motion pictures do. They register metamorphosis. Each frame shows its instant moving toward the instant of the next. The blurring within frames that contain rapid motion makes their documentation of metamorphosis especially vivid. Like Canetti's "figures," the series of photos that constitute a movie signify "both the process of transformation *and* its result" (374). Siegfried Kracauer regarded the power of cinema to represent "the flow of life" as "a basic affinity of film. In a manner of speaking it is an emanation of the medium itself."[1]

Although different from most still photography in its capacity to record transformation, cinematography shares with its elder relative the power to fix an instant as an imperishable trace that is neither present nor past but outside of time (and therefore outside of place as well). To that capability, manifest but generally uncomprehended in its individual frames, cinematography adds the power of a multiplicity that returns its pictures to the universe of time and place, the universe of transformations. Its rapid succession of images turns a perishable moment into an imperishable past with respect to the frame that follows and a permanent future for the frame that precedes it. Amy Taubin writes of Jonas Mekas's filmmaking, "Like a still photographer, Mr. Mekas wants to capture the essence of the moment, but for him, that essence is the instantaneous transformation of present into past."[2] With cinematography, however, one can also look in the other direction, and see present and past as future.

Garrett Stewart has turned his attention to what he calls "the undervalued problem of the single frame" and to the relationship promised in the title of his book *Between Film and Screen*. It would be impossible to briefly summarize Professor Stewart's complex arguments or the points at which his interests intersect those of this study (some of which are noted elsewhere); but I should articulate a fundamental disagreement that is pertinent to the current discussion. Where I understand cinematography as recording and representing transformation, change in time, he sees it as embodying "a dying away in process."[3] His view of cinematography derives from a conception of still photography as intricately, perhaps "naturally," involved with death—a conception widely held among theorists and advanced with particular conviction by Roland Barthes and, following him, Susan Sontag.

This conception seems to me to be disputable; but, in any case, still photography and cinematography do not differ absolutely, and there are photographic and cinematographic practices that partake of both. In addition to series of stop-action photographs, we may count photos with long exposures that allow time to visibly paint its passing on light-sensitive materials, some sequences of still photographs, and double exposures (and uses of flash that amount to double exposures) as approaching cinema's tendency to render the world as a flow of transformations. Nonetheless, cinema's connection to metamorphosis is intrinsic to it and remains distinctive. In moving pictures, as Bazin remarked, "for the first time, the image of things is likewise the image of their duration, change mummified."[4] Bazin's countryman, Jean Epstein, also took note of the power of motion pictures to render change: "The cinema is a particular form of knowing, in that it represents the world in its continuous mobility."[5] Similarly, Stanley Cavell writes of "the *natural* evanescence of film, the fact that its events exist only in motion, in passing."[6]

The ability of the cinema to register both the process of change and its outcomes is evident in its concentration on the subtlest alterations of actors' expressions. "Man's perpetual readiness for transformation is clearly expressed in the mobility of his face." Canetti labels these fleeting changes of expression "seminal transformations" that occur in "unending succession" (374–75). A recent article provides clinical support for Canetti's assertions both as to the number, deep significance, and successive rapidity of facial expressions. Of particular interest is the writer's conclusion that facial muscles are connected to the autonomic nervous system and therefore that changes of expression work in both directions; that is, they can both express and cause emotional states. The involuntary expressiveness of our faces seems to have been evolutionarily programmed into our social constitution.[7]

The inherent tendency of motion pictures to render metamorphosis may be confirmed negatively, in their reversion to still photography through the freeze frame. The best known of freeze frames, that at the end of Truffaut's *The 400 Blows* (1959), simultaneously demonstrates the abrupt cessation of cinematic transformation and marks the end for Doinel (Jean-Pierre Léaud) of any significant change. The hopelessness of his situation is figured forth by the end of the possibility of transformations, the most radical hopelessness possible. Stewart, who gives this image extended attention in his book, characterizes it similarly as "sheared off both from the true past into which it cannot quite lapse and from the future it bars."[8] Truffaut's freeze frame strikes an especially ironic note because Doinel's story comes to its petrified conclusion by the sea, which, because of its constant motion, mystery, and traditionally protean symbolism, has through the ages been a preeminent image of mutability. Since *The 400 Blows,* the freeze frame has become a cliché at the end of movies, signaling the end of the story, the end of change, the end of images that have a future and a past.

Implicit in the materials and epistemology of cinema, metamorphosis also appears frequently as a central theme in filmic narratives. It is especially familiar from vampire and werewolf movies, from Cocteau's classic Orpheus pictures and *Beauty and the Beast* (1946), and from a multitude of science-fiction films of which various versions of *The Invisible Man* and *Dr. Jekyll and Mr. Hyde* are among the best known. *The Matrix* (A. and L. Wachowski, 1999) is a popular recent example.

An elegantly made and much commented upon crime-thriller, *The Silence of the Lambs* (1991) has particular thematic affinities with transformation and, as the genre of the film would lead one to expect, with predation and the terror of an unknown, malignant touch. In this respect and in several others, it resembles Burnett's *Killer of Sheep*, a film to which superficially it could hardly appear less similar. In Jonathan Demme's screen version of Thomas Harris's novel, all three principal figures are at once predator and prey; and all strive for some fashion of self-re-creation. As we shall see, their attempted metamorphoses often fail or have equivocal aims to begin with.

The camera that tracks the panting Clarice Starling (Jodie Foster) while she negotiates an obstacle course through misty woods invokes two familiar thriller expectations, each associated with predation. The audience is likely to suspect either that this as-yet-unidentified young woman will be attacked or that the shots following and running ahead of her will be revealed to originate from the point of view of some menacing stalker. As Carol Watts writes, "The assault course sequence . . . encodes a feeling of threat in classical fashion; the camera stalking the lone runner/victim through the woods."[9] When the man who appears simply issues her an order to report to a superior, the absence of any obvious threat feels like a reprieve. The assignment she receives, however, will ultimately fulfill the menace of the opening sequence, casting her as both quarry and hunter. Her second role is perhaps the less expected, but not uncommon for crime-thrillers; the heroines and heroes of Hitchcock's movies, for example, are often simultaneously pursued and pursuing. The title figure of *Killer of Sheep*, analogously, feels himself to be both predator and prey.

As the title of the movie suggests, lambs are the traditional victims with which Starling identifies and which she tries to save. In order to do the latter, she becomes a predator herself by joining the FBI, an agency of such defensive predators. A letter written at the start of the French Revolution and quoted by Canetti seems apposite: "Dear Friend, the wolves have always eaten the sheep; are the sheep going to eat the wolves this time?" (58). Attempting to save herself, Catherine Martin (Brooke Smith), the lamb that Clarice most urgently wishes to rescue, manages to achieve a similar transformation from prey into predator. She captures and threatens to injure "Precious," her abductor's toy poodle—a creature covered with fluffy white fur and as like a lamb as a dog can be.

Metamorphosing in the opposite direction from predator to prey, Jame Gumb, AKA "Buffalo Bill" (Ted Levine), screams along with his prisoner when she sees on the stones of her pen the bloodstains and broken fingernails of her predecessor. What he wants from Catherine, the lamb he has captured, is not her flesh but her pelt, her external identity. His victim, like Gretel in reverse, is being starved and dehydrated in order to loosen her hide for easier flaying; she is undergoing one forced transformation in preparation for a second, more horrible one.

An ambiguous imagery of birds extends the motif of prey capable of metamorphosing into predators. It is invoked most obviously in Clarice's last name, the significance of which is underlined when the renegade psychiatrist Hannibal Lecter (Anthony Hopkins) orders, "You fly back to school now, little starling. Fly, fly, fly. Fly, fly, fly." In its repetitions, "fly" suggests both motion through the air and the recourse of the threatened.[10] Confused, the lambs that Clarice as a child tried to save would not run; but, as Lecter tells his interviewer, "you could and you did." Catherine Martin's last name can also signify a bird, and the only name we hear for Starling's father, "Bill," carries faint overtones of a beak. The father of Buffalo Bill's first flayed victim raises pigeons. Attempting to secure Dr. Lecter's cooperation, Clarice tells him that his reward will include an annual vacation on an island where "terns nest." In all these instances, the avian images and allusions are one way or another associated with vulnerability or escape.

Birds can be predators as well as quarry, however, and some are both. One of several conspicuous Hitchcock allusions, the baleful stuffed owl in the "Your Self-storage" shed into which Starling ventures at Lecter's riddling instructions, has its wings spread, as if swooping toward prey. At the same time, it has been killed and stuffed. We will see similar spread-wing shapes created by the dead guard that an escaping Lecter hangs above his cell and when Gumb dances in front of his video camera, raising his arms and gown like wings.

Birds and related images of wings and flight consistently suggest the interchangeability of the identities of stalker and quarry, of the stronger and the weaker. Traditional symbols of the soul or psyche, the moths and butterflies that flutter through the movie also connect the imagery of wings and flight to the theme of fluid, changing identities. In Harris's novel, the transformation of Clarice from small bird to hawk, from game to hunter, evokes both the tradition of detective fiction and a fundamental understanding of human psychology: "Starling put her head back, closed her eyes for one second. Problem-solving is hunting; it is savage pleasure and we are born to it."[11] Like all people, Starling is congenitally both hunter and hunted.

Clarice pursues (and will eventually be stalked by) a quarry who, Dr. Lecter tells her, is motivated principally by the fact that "he covets." His eyes, like everyone's, "seek out the things [they] want." The desired outcome of covetousness is possession, and the radical form of possession is incorporation. Before he decides to shoot Starling, Gumb watches her, as he did Catherine Martin, through infrared goggles. Out of the darkness, his hand twice reaches for her. Whether his gesture expresses hostility or yearning hardly matters.[12] For the audience, his reaching embodies the most fundamental and powerful of human fears: "In the dark, the fear of an unexpected touch can mount to panic" (15).

The bizarre Gumb achieves incorporation externally rather than internally. In accord with the fluidity of predator-quarry identities throughout the film, he wishes to be wholly surrounded in his prey, to be swallowed by them. "Hannibal the Cannibal" more straightforwardly enacts the usual biological motive for predation. Unlike other serial killers, he observes, he did not keep trophies of his victims. "No," Clarice agrees, "you ate yours." He thirsts for blood. In Memphis he asks for a second dinner of lamb chops, "extra rare," which arrive virtually raw and which we later see sprayed with the blood of the guard he clubs to death. Taking a Gumbish turn himself, Lecter makes his escape by using the flayed face of the other guard as a mask. With grisly, unintentional humor, a young cop comforts the disguised killer, "You look real good." Lecter's intentional wit in the last line of the film is similar: "I'm having an old friend for dinner."

Threats of predation in *The Silence of the Lambs* are aimed at sexual possession as well as incorporation. When the petite Starling, dressed in blue sweat clothes, enters an elevator full of large red-shirted young males, we are conscious of a muted sexual threat. Later, another group of male trainees looks with interest when she and her friend Ardelia (Kasi Lemmons) jog past them. The circle of openly staring male sheriff's deputies who surround Starling look a little as if they might degenerate into what Canetti might have called a sexual "hunting pack." Dr. Chilton (Anthony Heald) tries to pick Starling up when she comes to his prison to interview Lecter, then turns hostile when she dodges his advances. During his second interview with Starling, Lecter suggests that the section head for whom she is working, Dr. Crawford (Scott Glenn), might want to "fuck you," and asks if the cousin to whose ranch she went as an orphan molested her. Miggs, Lecter's neighbor in prison, flings his semen at her as she walks by his cell. Most potentially alarming, though he says it sarcastically, is Lecter's murmured pleasantry when Clarice comes to his cage in Memphis, "People will say we're in love."

Catherine, the serial killer's "next special lady," first appears singing along with her car radio to Tom Petty. The words resonate ironically with the fate toward which she is driving:

> After all, it was a great big world
> With lots of places to run to.

Gumb's *nom de presse*, Buffalo Bill, "began as a bad joke in Kansas City Homicide. They said, 'This one likes to skin his humps.'" On this point, the screenplay alters the novel, which has Gumb's name originate as a reference to E. E. Cummings's poem "Buffalo Bill," a change that further emphasizes the threat of sexual predation in the film. After he has slugged Catherine into submission, Gumb cuts her blouse from her back to get a look at her hide. As he does so, a close-up reveals the tattoo between his thumb and index finger: "LOVE." The tattoo appears again when Gumb makes himself up to dance as a woman before his video camera. What he says tells us that he desires to be his own sexual prey, his own "special lady." "Will you fuck me?" he asks himself. A little later, "I fuck me. I fuck me so hard."

But, as in *Killer of Sheep*, predation is not the sole mode of sex and love in *The Silence of the Lambs*. The entomologist who shows interest in Clarice when she goes to have a pupa identified finds her receptive, as we infer from his presence at her graduation ceremony.[13] How does he differ from the sexual predators? He approaches without stealth, overtly. When Clarice asks him if he's "hitting on" her, he simply replies, "Yes."

Coveting begins, Dr. Lecter says, with the eyes. Lecter appeals to Clarice's experience both as sexual prey—"Don't you feel eyes moving over your body, Clarice?"—and as predator—"And don't your eyes seek out the things you want?" Eyes and looking receive emphasis in *The Silence of the Lambs* quite as insistently as in such models of scopophilia as *Peeping Tom* (Powell, 1954) or *Rear Window* (Hitchcock, 1954). Not only do people frequently stare at Starling, but the camera tends to stay on their faces for a few moments after she departs the frame, thereby emphasizing their watching. The abduction of Catherine begins with the camera scanning through Buffalo Bill's eyes, notably the green—perhaps envious—night eyes of his infrared viewers. The audience watches along with Gumb through the same green vision when he stalks Starling. In the storage garage the camera focuses repeatedly on eyes: Clarice Starling's, those of the stuffed owl, and the filmy, unnaturally wide-open eyes of a preserved head. The hometown of Gumb and his first victim harmonizes with the motif of eyes and seeing; it is Belvedere ("beautiful view"), Ohio.

The drawing that Clarice notices in Lecter's cell shows a scene in Florence, another beautiful view, "the Duomo seen from the Belvedere." Lecter in prison can prey only visually, and the camera, which repeatedly tracks into his eyes, makes one aware of his intense gaze. The camera comes especially close to his unblinking eyes when he insists that Starling tell him of the lambs and her attempt to save them. When he gives her in return the clue that will eventually lead her to Jame Gumb—"We covet what we see everyday"—the shots alternate between close-ups on the faces and eyes of the psychiatrist and his auditor. Her pupils are wide and receptive, his narrower, more focused; both watch intently, alert for the slightest sign that might lead to what they seek.

The urge to survive connects explicitly with looking and predation when Lecter asks his candid young visitor about the head in the bottle, "How did you feel when you first saw him, Clarice?" "Scared at first," she replies, "then exhilarated." Her exhilaration probably stems partly from her sense that she may have discovered something important. Canetti suggests that it also has a more fundamental origin: "The moment of *survival* is the moment of power. Horror at the sight of death turns into satisfaction that it is someone else who is dead. . . . Whether the survivor is confronted by one dead man or by many, the essence of the situation is that he feels *unique*. He sees himself standing there alone and exults in it" (227).

According to Dr. Lecter's impromptu profile of Clarice, if Gumb's "first principle" is that he covets, hers is the desire for "advancement, of course." She strives to escape the social fate to which she was born, "only a generation removed from poor white trash." As she struggles to rise above her origins, she also aspires to soar above her father professionally. He was a town marshal; she would be a special agent of the FBI. He was killed when two robbers emerging from a drugstore shot him. Will she be able to fly above that part of her heritage? Could anyone not want to try?

The camera serves as the agency of eyes and looking for any film. In *The Silence of the Lambs*, it focuses on the predatory potential of vision. It does so through point-of-view shots, emphasis on characters' watching, and, as we saw in the credit sequence, through its own actions. Its most direct association with death may be seen when it looks at Clarice from inside the car before she has entered and found the staring head. Logically, the shot makes little sense. Moreover, it defies one of the more frequently broken "rules" of cinematography, that the director should not put the camera in such impossible vantage points as behind the fireplace or looking out from within the refrigerator. Associatively, however, the shot anticipates the goggling eyes in the bottle and identifies the camera with them.

Shooting elsewhere from the points of view of Gumb and Lecter, the camera is further associated with the threat of death. Through shots that come from Starling's perspective, on the other hand, it is characteristically linked with the fear of attack. It twice assumes a subjective position within her memory: first, when she remembers herself on an ordinary day greeting her returning father, and later—more directly to the point of my present argument—when she recalls his funeral. The association with death of the second memory is obvious. Her first recollection has relevance to threat and fear also, for it takes place when Starling has just emerged from the basement cells of Lecter and his terrifying neighbors, nightmare creatures from whom a reassuring parent might protect a frightened child.

On its own, the camera pans across a river just after Clarice enters the house in which she will discover the Death's Head moth that tells her she has found Buffalo Bill. As the novel explains but the movie leaves us to notice ourselves, the moth's Latin name, *Acherontia styx,* invokes "two rivers in Hell. Your man, he drops the bodies in a river every time."[14] When the camera leaves Clarice Starling with Gumb, it shows the river, a swath of tripled railroad tracks, and a quiet, somewhat isolated house that offers nothing to raise suspicion. The camera appears for a moment to be abandoning her to a fate like that of Gumb's other victims. In doing so, it recalls a similar turning away of the camera in Hitchcock's next-to-last movie, *Frenzy.* In that instance, the camera tracks a serial rapist and killer up a flight of stairs with his next victim, then backs down the stairway, through the entrance hall, and out onto a busy street, unable to help or even to watch as the killer closes the door on the doomed woman. Demme's camera, by contrast, returns soon enough to the inside of Gumb's dwelling full of secret chambers, but a critical point has been made; no one outside the ordinary-looking house down by the tracks and the river will have any reason to go to Starling's rescue except, perhaps, for Dr. Crawford and his FBI team. But they are hundreds of miles away chasing a false lead.

Very much on its own, the camera stalks its proper quarry, its audience. It does so principally by deception, through editing that achieves the effect of dissimulation, the proverbial wolf in a sheep's fleece. Although purposefully misleading cutting occurs throughout *The Silence of the Lambs,* the most obvious and important instance takes place near the end of the film, when we are tricked into supposing that Crawford and a pair of SWAT teams in Calumet City near Chicago are entering the lair in which Gumb is about to slaughter Catherine. The slick playfulness of Demme's editing has a certain elegance, but it has the same primary purpose as any dissimulating, to make its witness—primarily the audience—feel safe. As Kurosawa dramatized in *Throne of Blood,* "Security is mortal's chiefest enemy." The editing could also be taken partly to represent Clarice's imagination of Crawford's operation, and therefore draws her into the same reassuring trap into which it is luring the audience. At the end of the sequence, a shot from behind Gumb as he opens the door to Starling reveals the hoax and the peril into which she, and we, have unwittingly fallen.

The cinematography, editing, and mise-en-scène of *The Silence of the Lambs* imitate and reinforce the fluidity of identities that characterizes its human figures. Color, of both light and objects, has particular importance. The contrasting, juxtaposing, and occasional apparent reversing of the symbolic associations of red and blue occur repeatedly throughout the film, from the blue-gray morning of its beginning to the blue-gray evening of its end.

Red in the cinema is frequently associated, as I observed in the discussion of *North by Northwest,* with the final horror of the inside of a predator's mouth. In consonance with fairly consistent practice in color cinematography worldwide and with the conventions of many cultures, *The Silence of the Lambs* connects red and orange with danger and predation while blue is given a variety of opposing associations: resistance, victimization, innocence, safety, counterattack. Pictures of Buffalo Bill's victims with red flayed flesh are pinned to an orange bulletin board; the whole contrasts with the cool, quiet, blue-lit halls of the FBI's "Behavioral Science Services." The early shot of Starling—small, female, clad in blue—standing demurely in an elevator filled with large red-shirted males establishes this contrast with respect to sex.

"Look deep within yourself, Agent Starling!" exclaims Hannibal Lecter, gnomically directing her to a self-storage facility. Within it—and perhaps within herself—she finds scarlet threats. The bodiless head under a red cloth is preceded by a sharp object that rips her pants and skin to draw red blood. "Even clothes give insufficient security," writes Canetti. "It is easy to tear them and pierce through to the naked, smooth, defenseless flesh of the victim" (15). Buffalo Bill does just that when he cuts through the orange print blouse of Catherine. The red-brown water of the Elk River disgorges the most recent of Gumb's victims, and a pink funeral home receives her body. Elsewhere red continues to signal danger: the red light as Gumb applies his makeup, another red light that illuminates Crawford within the airplane when he ignores Clarice's insight and goes to the wrong house in the wrong city, the red van that initiates the SWAT assault in Calumet City—doubly dangerous because it has gone astray.

The novel emphatically connects the crimson mouth of a carnivore with Lecter, who "touched the center of his red lip with his red tongue."[15] Unexpectedly, the movie more often associates him with cool colors and paints his tormentor, Dr. Chilton, in red and orange. Upon further reflection, we may find this reversal fitting; the egotistical Chilton preys on those in his power and seeks publicity for himself, while his most notorious prisoner has joined the side of those in pursuit of a serial killer. Out of the darkness of his cell, Dr. Lecter tells Clarice that her "bleeding has stopped," then emerges, illuminated by a blue light, in blue-green pants. Although he is on the hunt in the last sequence of the film, the light reverts to blue-gray as he follows Dr. Chilton. The audience is encouraged at this point to regard Lecter, like the police, as pursuing justice; hence the appropriateness of the blue cast and the crowd—executions derive from killing crowds—through which he follows his old tormentor.

The Death's Head moth, Buffalo Bill's *carte de visite*, also unexpectedly appears in a blue light. "So powerful, so beautiful," murmurs Gumb as he picks one up. The moths and their pupae are not predators but captives of the murderer. Another species that we might expect to be associated with hunting, cats, instead are cast as affectionate companions left desolate by Buffalo Bill's abductions.

When in his dangerous, predatory mode, Lecter appears in a literally different light. Under brilliant red and pink illumination at the Memphis airport, he arrives clothed in bright red pants, and he is transferred to a cage flooded with high-key, high color-temperature lighting. A little later, he will have murdered his two guards, killed two medical attendants, made his escape, and killed and robbed a passing tourist.

The huge red, white, and blue cloth that covers the old limousine in the storage garage joins opposing colors in the flag of the United States. So, less conspicuously, does the red tail of an American Airlines jet as it takes off among the blue lights of the Memphis airport. After Clarice has shot Gumb, the police arrive in a medley of red and blue. The cloth of the nation is woven of mixed fabric: assailants and victims, predators and protectors, outlaws and the enforcers of laws. In this respect, the complex chromatic symbolism of *The Silence of the Lambs* very much resembles that of *North by Northwest*. When the camera briefly tours Belvedere, Ohio, it shows an ordinary-looking town full of ordinary houses and ordinary people, colored in ordinary blues and oranges. The next-to-last sequence of the film, the graduation from the FBI's training center, mixes the same oranges and blues. The FBI, after all, serves as both hunter of the hunters and protector of the hunted. An agency of the U.S. government, it is composed, like its country, of human beings; and all people—potentially at least—are at once predator and prey.

Thematically at the center of *The Silence of the Lambs* we find what Canetti calls "transformation" (*die Verwandlung*, also translated as "metamorphosis," in the title, for example, of Kafka's most famous story). Closely related to the dynamics of crowds, in part because it "equates one body with another," transformation is also analyzed in *Crowds and Power* as a phenomenon of power. For Clarice Starling, Hannibal Lecter, and Jame Gumb, transformations, albeit in different forms, constitute fundamental motives and means. "If I help you, Clarice," says Lecter, bending to his own purposes her remark that "terns nest there," "it will be turns times two, quid pro quo."

"The lowly pun," writes Karen Mann, "may be the best emblem for the way meaning functions in the film."[16] Besides his occasional puns, Lecter conceals his meanings in another form of verbal metamorphosis, anagrams, which transform one word or phrase into another by rearranging letters. It is he who explicitly introduces the idea of metamorphosis, when he characterizes the evidence in the storage garage as "a fledgling killer's first effort at transformation." In his own practice of transformations, Hannibal Lecter divides into what we might think of as "blue" and "red" versions. As the former, he is an empathetic, preternaturally insightful psychoanalyst helping Clarice to understand and discover Buffalo Bill and to silence her torturing memory of screaming lambs. As a "red" transformer, he changes his identity to escape his captors and to stalk them (and others) in turn. A Jekyll and Hyde figure who metamorphoses spontaneously without the scientist's potion, he is both Dr. Lecter and "Hannibal the Cannibal."[17]

Crowds and Power begins its discussion of transformation by describing "the presentiments of the Bushmen," who "feel the distant approach of people whom they can neither hear nor see" (337). Their presentiments constitute "the initial stages of transformations" (340). Dr. Lecter, when he senses the approach of Clarice before he can see her, or when he remarks on a cut that he cannot know about, exhibits something similar to such presentiments. Similarly, he invokes the sort of feeling of another body that the Bushmen experience when he quizzes Senator Martin, Catherine's mother, as to whether she nursed her daughter and then asks her, rhetorically, "Tell me, Mom, when your little girl is on the slab, where will it tickle you?" The ring we later see in Gumb's nipple recalls Lecter's taunting of the senator.

Clarice's mentor and boss, Crawford, warns her against telling the renegade psychiatrist anything personal: "Believe me, you don't want Hannibal Lecter inside your head." But Lecter's cunning, his hyperacute perceptions, and his mastery of transformations and presentiments make Crawford's warning impossible to follow. With his capacity for empathy, Dr. Lecter achieves what Canetti calls "*clean* transformations; each creature whose coming the Bushman feels remains itself. . . . He can become this or that, but 'this' and 'that' remain separate from each other, for between transformations he always becomes himself again" (341). What the "blue" Dr. Lecter embodies could define the most understanding of therapists.

The Bushman's presentiments have another aspect, one in which "he also feels the dead animal, as an alien body pressed to

177

his own and in a state in which it can no longer escape him" (342). This phase aims at incorporation. It describes "Hannibal the Cannibal," the demonic "red" psychologist in whom "cannibalism and transformation have entered into a close alliance" (357). The talent that allows him to get into the heads of his prey at the same time bespeaks his kinship with them. In this movie of shifting, interpenetrating identities, Hannibal Lecter acts and suffers variously as predator, protector, and quarry.

The most gifted and sophisticated figure in *The Silence of the Lambs,* Lecter is also the most primitive and dangerous, a survivor of the sort Canetti describes whose passion for outliving through murder has become ungovernable. With each killing, such a survivor affirms his uniqueness and invulnerability. He evades "the terrible penalty for always having eaten" by transferring it to his victims. They, in turn, suffer "transformation into something which is eaten . . . the last, the transformation which ends all flight" (348).

Like the novice Buffalo Bill, Clarice is a "fledgling" at her profession. Whereas he raises lepidoptera, the idea of flying inheres in her last name. When Dr. Lecter raises the idea of transformation, she seizes upon it: "What did you mean by transformation, Doctor?" Her own "first principle," advancement, represents a difficult form of metamorphosis.

> Perhaps the most important of all prohibitions on transformation are the social. . . . It can be achieved only by undergoing a special initiation, and this is experienced as a transformation in the literal sense of the word. Often the candidate is thought of as dying in the lower class, to be brought back to life in the higher: death itself divides class from class. Transformation becomes a long and dangerous journey during which the novice has to undergo every kind of ordeal and terror. (380)

Like heroes of romantic myth, Clarice Starling descends into an underworld, Gumb's labyrinthine basement, in search of both a monster and her own self-realization. Plunged into absolute darkness and stalked to the point of death, she emerges from her ordeal to be certified, in the next sequence, a full-fledged agent of the FBI.

She is welcomed into its fellowship by her two mentors, the Doctors Crawford and Lecter, and by the memory of a dead parent; for to his own applause, Crawford adds, "Your father would be proud of you." Lecter, her antagonist as well as her instructor, telephones his congratulations by asking if she has achieved her other longed-for transformation, into one who hears not the screaming but the silence of the lambs. It was he, we remember, who mocked her "cheap shoes" and branded her—adopting an insulting drawl—as having sprung from "pore whaat trash." Now he renounces the power of the privileged, of the predator over former prey: "I have no plans to call on you, Clarice. The world's a more interesting place with you in it."

Buffalo Bill stuffs a pupa of the Death's Head moth into the throats of his victims. Since he first began to kill, according to Dr. Lecter, "the significance of the moth has changed: caterpillar into chrysalis or pupa, from thence into beauty. Our Billy wants to change, too."[18] But he is stuck in imitation: "Imitation relates to externals" (369). The female body-mask that Buffalo Bill is constructing from the epidermis of his victims will render him a woman in externals only. "Imitation . . . is nothing but a first step in the direction of transformation, a movement which immediately stops short" (370). Gumb wrongly believes that he is a transsexual. "His true pathology," Dr. Lecter declares, "is far more dangerous." Partly, at least, it is that of a survivor, a killer who has developed an insatiable passion for that intoxicating form of survival.

Whatever the complexities of Gumb's "true pathology," his imitation becomes "dissimulation . . . the hiding of a hostile figure within a friendly one" (371). When he abducts Catherine, he pretends to be an injured man grateful for help in loading his van. More profoundly, he aspires not just to capture and slay his victims—his killing is "only incidental," says Dr. Lecter—but to appropriate their sexual identities.

A skilled tailor, Gumb frequently appears in his basement sewing room surrounded by dressmakers' dummies, some of which wear scraps of human skin. His name invokes "gums," and his needles and scissors may be thought of as projections of his teeth. "The most striking natural instrument of power in man and in many animals is the teeth," writes Canetti. "It is probable that his teeth served him as a model for the improvement of his tools" (207). Gumb works in the nude, and makes horribly literal Canetti's observation that "clothes are men's second skin" (371).

By covering himself with a composite woman's skin, Gumb hopes to mimic the metamorphosis from pupa to the mature form of the captive moths he raises. He seeks beauty, certainly, but also adulthood; and his mannerisms often suggest an incongruous juvenility. (We may remember here the juvenility of many of the trapped adults in *Killer of Sheep,* and also, in a comic setting, the similar characterization of Sturges's boyish heroes.) Gumb's transformation, however, goes backward. Like Gregor Samsa, he devolves from a person to a grotesque insect, bug-eyed in his infrared viewing apparatus, a creature of the dark.

Contiguous sewing and moth rooms serve as both workshops and emblems for Gumb's urgently desired transformation. A Death's Head moth lighting on a spool of thread tells Clarice that she is in the presence of the serial killer. Gumb is identified with his victims through the same vectors. He engorges them with pupae and he seems to have shared with some of them his passion for sewing. The head of his first victim is found in a car full of partly dismembered mannequins, and a friend of the first young woman to have been flayed declares, "Sewing was her life." When Clarice is searching that girl's sewing room, she discovers why Buffalo Bill "skins his humps." The wallpaper there, significantly, is covered with pictures of butterflies. The dead girl also wanted to change. In her desire for self-transformation, she is like Jame Gumb, like Clarice Starling and Hannibal Lecter, like humankind itself.

Painted butterflies, reflections in mirrors, and images in general (what I have called "internal artifice") are associated throughout *The Silence of the Lambs* with the desire for transformation and its incidental terrors. We first meet Buffalo Bill's victims on an FBI bulletin board in horrific photographs. The bedroom of the young seamstress is filled with snapshots of herself with friends and family. Clarice also finds there a set of photos, secreted in a music box lid, of the young woman posing semi-nude. In those pictures, we see that she is somewhat overweight, which the frequently shown school yearbook shot of her appealing face conceals. The yearbook photo, that is to say, transforms her into a more conventionally attractive girl than she really was. Conversely, the other photos, perhaps taken by Gumb (like those he did of himself, they are Polaroids) make her appear less attractive.

The association of images with predatory dissimulation and with the transformation of living beings into provender connects with the hunter's attempt to avoid the guilt of murder. As *Crowds and Power* and *The Silence of the Lambs* both assert, the predator attempts to conceive of his prey as inconsequential, an insect or even something inanimate. The phrasing of Gumb's commands to Cath-

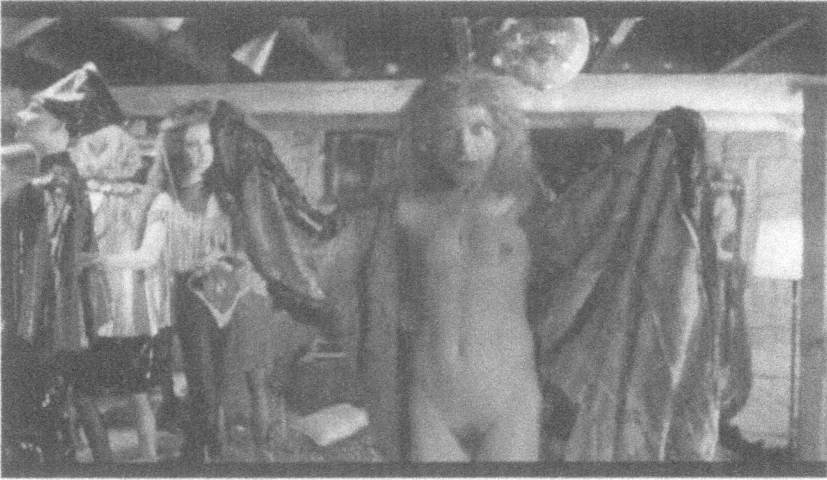

Attempted transformation

erine exemplifies that desire to dehumanize: "It rubs the lotion on its body."

In his cell, Dr. Lecter makes drawings, substituting memory for the view of the world that he lacks and thereby transforming himself from a prisoner into a free man. Dr. Chilton shows Starling a photo of the nurse Lecter savaged, but the camera does not reveal it to us. Rather, it transposes the expected role of predator onto Dr. Chilton, as we have seen, by showing him in orange-framed surveillance monitors.

Dancing before his video camera, Gumb does his female imitation to a song that wails, "I'm cryin', cryin', cryin'. . . ." His genitals concealed behind his closed thighs, he strikes poses that recall Diane Arbus's photograph of "A naked man being a woman." His Polaroids of himself, which we briefly see on the walls of his sewing room, document the same attempts at transformation, attempts that stop at the stage of imitation. During the sequence in which these shots appear, and at other times in the basement chamber of horrors, the editing cuts rapidly among Gumb, his captive, and his dog. The acoustic cutting is equally rapid among Gumb's ceremonial music and murmuring, the cries of Catherine, and the whimpers of Precious. Such editing effectively equates one body with another.

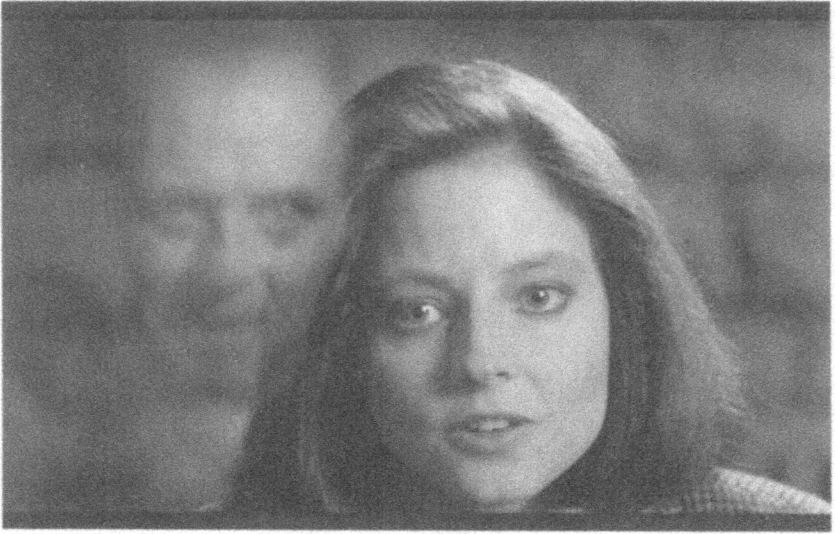

Identity and separation

Images of drawings, photographs, and video displays; abrupt acoustic transitions; assertive, sometimes deceptive, cross-cutting; all implicate the process of moviemaking itself in the processes of transformation. Most obvious, film translates a three-dimensional spatial world into a two-dimensional image. The powers of editing and of such transitional devices as fades and dissolves allow for the juxtaposition, mixing, and equation of places and characters.

The Silence of the Lambs is edited largely by straight cuts, but one striking shot approximates a double exposure. The camera is aimed at Clarice from Dr. Lecter's cell. As he offers her the key to unlocking the mystery of Buffalo Bill, his reflection on the Lucite barrier appears next to and slightly overlaps the image of her face. The interpenetration of identities in *The Silence of the Lambs* is made visible by the doubled image. At the same time, it suggests that the two identities have "equal importance; neither is ranked higher than the other and neither is hidden behind the other" (374). The image of the two faces figures the overlap of identities and the sympathetic capacity of human beings to get into each other's heads. It also makes visible the transformative energies of the world and serves as an emblem for the capacity of motion pictures to record and imitate those sympathetic transformations.

Power, the opponent of empathy and an inveterate constructor of barriers, "wages continuous warfare against spontaneous and uncontrolled transformation" (378). Because the arts, including movies, have their basis in transformation and must therefore be fundamentally egalitarian, power will find in them especially dangerous enemies. It feeds on death, the stopping of all metamorphoses. Dr. Chilton, with his passion for prison cells, for restraining masks, straps, and binding garments, and with his punitive removal from Lecter's cell of any aids to imaginative transformation, is placed squarely on the side of power and against metamorphosis. That placement largely accounts for his being so unsympathetic a figure—innocuous as he may seem in comparison to his prisoner or to Jame Gumb.

The survivor, the power-monger par excellence, experiences the death of others as "the moment of power" (227). For such survivors as Gumb and the "red" Lecter, killing has become an insatiable passion. Buffalo Bill will never stop his murdering, as Clarice suggests to Crawford, because he has developed "a taste for it." Even in the isolation of his jail cell, Lecter manages to kill Miggs by "whispering to him all afternoon," finally convincing him to commit suicide by swallowing his tongue, a kind of self-cannibalization.

Crowds and Power does describe a sort of survival that is regenerative rather than predatory, one in which the living regard the dead as individuals rather than as masses of vermin or malignant crowds. Writing of the ancestor cult of the Chinese, Canetti observes, "There is thus a close and mutually rewarding link between the modified form of survival enjoyed by ancestors and the pride of the descendants" (272). Similar in western culture is "immortality," which the living confer upon "the dead who offer themselves as food to the living . . . a reversal of sacrifice to the dead, which profits both dead and living" (278). Clarice's relation to her father has the form of such a mutually fortifying connection between an ancestor and his surviving progeny. Buffalo Bill's pickling of heads and donning the skin of his victims enacts a horrific, coercive parody of such immortality.

In her orientation toward death and the dead, Clarice emerges as the sole hero of *The Silence of the Lambs*. Although she admits to having felt fright and then exhilaration at the sight of the bottled head, her relation to the dead is everywhere else sympathetic, nourishing and nourished. She does not, as she tells Crawford—using a perfectly apt verb—"spook easily." On the contrary, she moves empathetically among the perished, whom she even joins by simulation when, during a drill, she is ambushed: "You're dead, Starling!" She never forgets the individuality of those whom Buffalo Bill has murdered. Her concern for them resembles concern for the living. Taking custody of the corpse of one of Buffalo Bill's victims, she tells the local officers, "There's things we need to do for her. I know that y'all brought her this far and that her folks would thank you if they could for your kindness and sensitivity. And now, please, go on now 'n' let us take care of her." A little later, we see her in a natural history museum comfortably traversing a hall of enormous skeletons. Her reciprocal relationship with the dead attaches to her father via the recollections that come to her at moments of stress or sorrow.

Of the predatory claws that dart out from darkness to ambush us, few are more dreaded than those of the dead, the monstrous quasi-dead, or their more realistic representatives, murderous psychopaths. At a particularly frightening moment in *The Silence of the Lambs*, Hannibal Lecter's hand seizes that of his guard, whom he handcuffs to the bars of his cage and whom he will later kill and partly flay. In contrast to that terrifying grasp, Demme sets a close-up of the graduation handshake between Crawford and Clarice—calm, cordial, and, perhaps most important, initiated by her. That clasping of hands certifies Clarice's transformation into an FBI agent and reverses the terror of the grip of the unknown. The only amorous males in attendance are the entomologists from the museum, clearly invited guests. The food being consumed is a cake decorated with the great seal of the organization whose full membership she has attained. The courting is mutual and the eating is communion, not predation.

The day may come when Clarice will have to track Hannibal Lecter. (Indeed, it has come—in a manner of speaking—via a sequel, Ridley Scott's 2001 *Hannibal*.) At the end of Demme's film, however, the time of reckoning for Hannibal the Cannibal seems far away—as does Lecter after he breaks off his telephone call to amble in leisurely pursuit of the succulently nasty Dr. Chilton, a bully who richly deserves to be consumed.

The Silence of the Lambs remains a film of motion and of the transformations of time, persons, and places until it fades to black and disappears. Just before the closing credits, the camera completes its last movement, a crane shot that tracks back and up from the scene on the street below and that reverses the downward tilt with which the picture begins. Despite the camera's immobility during the credits, however, the screen remains full of activity. No freeze-frame could conclude this motion picture of constant metamorphoses, both in the world it portrays and in its fluid portrayal of that world. The wind tosses palm fronds continuously while the closing credits roll up the screen, appearing at the bottom and disappearing at the top. Their movement parallels that of most of the pedestrians on the street, the majority of whom enter the street from below and disappear up-screen, in the direction taken by Dr. Chilton and his pursuer. Lecter transforms himself into an anonymous tourist, and this protective coloration allows him to blend into the crowd to escape those who might want to seize him as he stalks his old nemesis. The location has changed from the United States to the Bahamas, Dr. Chilton from warden to prey, and Dr. Lecter from Chilton's prisoner to his hunter. The transformations that have composed the main themes of the action continue, still ruled by the fluid dynamics of the eaters and the eaten—the predator always aware that his role might be reversed and the latter always obeying the command to flee and hoping to metamorphose from potential food into the one who eats. In *The Silence of the Lambs,* separating those roles remains a difficult task.

Concluding Thoughts

This book argues that attending to representations of crowds, power, and transformation can lead us to new or clarified perspectives on the cinema. Although *Crowds and Power* does not serve as the only guide for the analyses in this study, it is by far the most important one. With its examination of the drive to form crowds, its articulation of the kinds of crowds and their dynamics, and its inspection of their origins in packs, *Crowds and Power* offers film studies a multitude of productive insights. Perhaps the most precious metal cinema scholars can mine from Canetti comes from his understanding of the radically opposed relation between crowds and power. The human talent for transformation allows crowds to form; but dealers in power must try to suppress it, for crowds realize the profoundest possible equality. Movies depend upon and celebrate transformation and, therefore, crowds; both comprise central, recurrent themes in the history of cinema—as does their antagonist, power.

The identification of movie audiences with actors and actions on screen may be experienced as a crowd phenomenon, an individual one, or both. Comic films usually encourage mass identification—that is, a sense that one is participating both with the crowd depicted or implied in the film and with the audience in the theater. Tragic or ironic pictures, given their emphasis on alienation or ambiguity, elicit a more individualistic response. All movies, of whatever genre, facilitate the imaginative experiencing of others as ourselves. They encourage, in short, transformation.

Crowd themes appear with special clarity in film comedy. Most comedies, as Northrop Frye showed, end with the reintegration of the protagonists into a new or revived society.[1] Moreover, comic protagonists usually exhibit an extraordinary capacity for transformation, a talent often crucial to resolving the conflicts that drive the plot. The gift of film comedians for metamorphosis signals their readiness for change and their ability to experience other personae. This readiness has an important social component: "It is the influence of one man upon another which stimulates the unending succession of transformations" (375). Comic metamorphosis usually erupts in response to another person; the aptly named "double-take" serves as a good example.

Most film comedians rely on an aptitude for rapid transformation. Typically, they have startlingly mobile faces and body language that is expressive and eccentrically graceful. Recall performances of Charlie Chaplin, Imogene Coca, Lucille Ball, Red Skelton, Joe E. Brown, Richard Pryor, Peter Sellers, or Jim Carrey (add your own examples). On their extraordinarily mobile faces, transformations occur as quickly as they are often extreme. The silent film demanded especially communicative body language, which it got from such stars as Harold Lloyd and Buster Keaton. The athletic, inventive Keaton was sometimes called The Great Stone Face, but his subtle modulations of expression suited the capability of motion pictures to magnify small gestures and achieved a paradoxically great effect. Mae West mastered a similarly expressive facial economy in the early sound era. Because of the frequent transformations of comic heroes and heroines, one could say that the welcoming or newly created crowd surrounding them at the end of their films represents an outward manifestation of crowds already existing within them. The externalization of "the spots" in *The Miracle of Morgan's Creek* makes literal that merging of an internal with an external crowd.

Henri Bergson famously emphasized the importance of adaptability to human identity, and inflexibility as the cause of certain sorts of ludicrousness. For Bergson, flexibility comes from the élan vital; for Canetti, as we have seen, the power to experience multiple identities underlies what makes humans human (and humane). Comedians often behave with mechanical inflexibility, as Bergson notes, but their power to ultimately prevail in comic narratives results from overcoming their rigidity and achieving its opposite. The fulfilled romantic love that usually accompanies their triumphs at once rewards broadened identity and embodies a sexually achieved transformation. It is the essence of fusion with another.

Comedies imitate the creation of a crowd, typically achieving at their conclusions maximum human density and equality. At the beginning of most comedies, an old crowd has stopped growing, has become exclusionary, and is wont to issue commands—often in the form of manifestly ridiculous laws or rules. It has become one side of a pair of antagonists: the old versus the young, men versus women, the corrupted and disillusioned versus the innocent, the givers of orders versus the receivers, and so on. The formation of a new crowd or the unifying of antagonistic groups reasserts the inherent equality of human beings. The meek and weak who win out tend to be those who have previously evaded the most commands. They can triumph because they do not suffer the stings of command, nor pass them on, nor create spaces around themselves that cannot be crossed. (Roger Thornhill, as we saw in analyzing *North by Northwest,* ultimately comes to exemplify such a comic hero.) Tragedy reverses this action. Typically, givers of commands withdraw or otherwise become separated from the groups around them and are themselves finally overwhelmed by the retributive stings of the universe, its justice, *logos,* or natural law. Comic heroines and heroes, by contrast, are frequently saved at crucial moments by outlandish coincidences—the more implausible, up to an extreme point, the better. The salvation of the hero of *The Life of Brian* (Terry Jones, 1979) by a group of joy-riding aliens from outer space who happen to pass at a crucial moment takes this tendency about as far as it can go.

Transformation usually includes rejecting or escaping power. The authoritarian inflexibility of antagonists in movies of diverse genres embodies the hostility that power feels toward metamorphosis. Since metamorphosis is at the center of crowd formation, crowds resist power. Power, which desires isolation and uniqueness, in return opposes transformation and its attendant crowds, albeit that it may sometimes find using them expedient.

In motion pictures, transformation can be effectively caught, held, and examined. As I observed at the start of the previous chapter, all but the first and last frames of any shot are at once Present in themselves, Past to succeeding frames, and Future for preceding ones. As a result of their imaginative mastery of time, movies have had from the beginning an affinity for historical epics, elaborately authentic-looking period pieces, and stories of time travel. The dissolve, one of cinema's showier transitions, has come to signify a change in time and, usually, an associated change in place. For science-fiction films and others in which metamorphosis is directly represented, the dissolve has historically been the technique of choice—though modern digital resources have displaced it in contemporary practice.

Let us briefly review where we have been. The structure of *Potemkin* becomes clearer when we understand it as an anatomy of crowd formation, crowd characteristics, and the revolutionary transformation of the masses. Its portrayal of mass dynamics accords, quite precisely, with Canetti's systematic understanding of how crowds achieve their goals and transform themselves or are thwarted and disintegrate. Another silent film of enduring appeal, *Intolerance*, has been somewhat resistant to formal explication. Its unity-in-multiplicity comes into sharper focus as we trace its portrayals of the complex relations among crowds, power, and individuals.

The films of Preston Sturges, from the perspective of crowd theory, are quintessential romantic comedies. They typically trace the protagonist's opening loss of social position, his descent into danger and extreme ostracizing (or its threat), and the concluding triumphant—often improbable—social transformation that allows him to claim a lover and preeminent status in a crowd that adoringly surrounds him and that he has to a considerable degree brought into creation. Sturges's comedies elevate the loss and regaining of the protagonists' stature within crowds to an importance equal to the traditional achieving of individual identity and winning of a fortune and a lover or bride. Like comedies throughout cultural history, their happy endings are authorized and intensified both by crowds within the narrative and by appeals to the audience witnessing it. Power is not much of an issue in Sturges's madcap world, but to the extent that it does appear, it is ridiculous and minimally threatening. As Aristotle observed, comedy imitates "a kind of error or ugliness that is neither distressing nor destructive."[2]

The tragedy of *Throne of Blood*, on the other hand, shares with *Intolerance* a nearly linear alignment between increasing power and increasing isolation and paranoia. Unlike Griffith's epic, however, Kurosawa's redaction of *Macbeth* has at its center the machinations of the dead—a crowd that few critics have identified as such, though in folklore, religion, and literature such a conception is common. Similarly, the correspondence between power and isolation in *Citizen Kane* is stark, but *Crowds and Power* allows us to see it more exactly and in the broader cultural contexts invoked by Canetti's work. Most remarkably, Welles embodied within the central figure of Kane the conflict between crowds and power that is usually divided between protagonists and antagonists, or between groups and individuals. Accompanied by Canetti, we can also better comprehend Kane's ambivalent relation to crowds and his inability to achieve the transformations that are forbidden to the possessors of great power.

At the thematic center of *North by Northwest,* we find crowds and their relation to individuals and the hunting packs that threaten them. Its comic plot is resolved, as one would expect, when the now-married couple finally escapes the antidemocratic, antilove packs of the Professor's predators on one side and Vandamm's murderous organization on the other. At the same time, the protagonist undergoes a loss of identity that precedes and ultimately leads to his transformation from the rather frivolous, belatedly immature playboy at the beginning of the film into the clearsighted believer in marriage of the conclusion.

Killer of Sheep is easy to admire but difficult to analyze. Its series of thematically linked episodes invokes the fear of predation that Canetti identifies as forming the deepest stratum of the human psyche. It images at once the fear of being captured and the guilt of preying on other beings. Afflicted by that fear and guilt, Stan's depression answers to Canetti's factoring of melancholia as the feeling that all flight is cut off and all transformations out of reach. Predation is also at the center of *The Silence of the Lambs,* but the centrality of transformation to it has mostly gone unnoticed, despite the frequency with which that film has been analyzed. Metamorphosis in Demme's film has an intimate connection to stalking and incorporation. Prominent details of imagery—birds, moths, and butterflies, for example—can be more fully understood when perceived in such a context, as can subtler aspects, such as the color symbolism that organizes much of the cinematography. The central figures of the film, Lecter, Gumb, and Starling, all seek metamorphosis. The transformations they aspire to and their successes or failures may be very different, but they share the same basic desire.

Could one arrive at these understandings without *Crowds and Power*? Presumably so, since all are supported by textual details that "are there." But the realities depicted in pictures, as Canetti said, can sleep until someone views them with "the experience that awakes them."[3] On this point, I can speak only for myself. For me, "the experience that awakes them" has been reading *Crowds and Power.* Whether or not I could have reached such understandings without its stimulus is arguable; the main point is I didn't. I did not see—or anyway, make sense of—most of what I discuss in my explications until I put the films in the vicinity of Canetti's thinking. (Nor have other critics observed these themes and structures of imagery, so far as I can tell by my surveys of existing criticism.) Where I did see, my perception was sharpened and extended.

By way of offering a final example of such an extension, let me return for a few paragraphs to *Citizen Kane*. All viewers will realize that the banquet sequence in that film celebrates the protagonist's power, his belief that he has conquered the world of New York newspaper publishing. Reference to Canetti places this action in larger contexts, both in Welles's film and in human culture.

Recall Charles Foster Kane's isolation in the midst of crowds that he himself convenes and leads, and the increase of his isolation as his power grows. That Kane's best friend, Jed Leland, pulls away from him during this episode dramatizes the exultant publisher's alienation even as his power to assemble and direct crowds reaches a climax. A similar loss of personal connection coupled with increased public power is shown when his first wife reads a rival newspaper at breakfast. The readership of newspapers is a particularly potent modern crowd, and that of Kane's paper has been rapidly increasing about the time his wife deserts it.

Especially germane to the banquet scene are Canetti's observations that "everything which is eaten is the food of power," and that consumption is one of the ways that power displays its authority (219). Kane himself consumes little during this scene, but it nonetheless underscores "the connection between power and digestion" (219). "It is no longer necessary that his [a ruler's] girth should be greater than that of everyone else. . . . He transfers the satisfaction of repletion to his court, to those who eat with him, only reserving the right to be offered everything first" (220). At this stage of his career, Kane has minions to eat and drink for him—minions, moreover, whom he likens to more food. "I felt like a kid in front of a candy store," he declares, recalling how he looked at a photo of the staff of New York's most prestigious newspaper six years earlier. "Well, I got my candy, all of it." The owner of these journalistic comestibles reserves the right of first choice to another variety of bonbons, the harem of dancing girls whom he embraces while his companions feast. Additionally, much of the table conversation is devoted to Kane's upcoming trip to Europe and his plans for prodigious appropriation of its antiquities and works of art. From a Canettian viewpoint, Kane is more than an especially interesting, dictatorial parvenu; he enacts rituals of power that he shares with rulers throughout human history and across many cultures.

How Canetti's thought illuminates various strands of imagery, character, and theme will vary from strand to strand and from movie to movie. In some cases, it provides a shortcut to interpretations more difficult to reach without it; in others, the insights it suggests seem unimaginable without Canetti's guidance. In any case, I hope this study has shown that the central concepts of Canetti's "first masterpiece of crowd theory"[4] can broadly expand our understanding of the representation of crowds, power, and transformation in the cinema—and of the cinema itself.

Afterword: On *Crowds and Power*

Born in Bulgaria into a community of Sephardic Jews in 1905, Elias Canetti moved with his family to England when he was about six. His father suddenly died a year later and the family moved to Vienna; Canetti attended schools there and in Zurich for the next fifteen years or so. To satisfy his mother's insistence that he learn something of practical value in the world, he earned a Ph.D. in chemistry at age twenty-four. He never practiced a scientific profession, however, and upon finishing his doctorate, he became what he would remain the rest of his life, a writer. Within a few years he completed his one novel, *Auto-da-Fé* (*Die Blendung*), a comic, dreadful, intensely imagined work that is perhaps the least known of the great monuments of modern European literature.

He fled the Nazis in 1938, returning to England where he lived for most of the rest of his life. Canetti authored a number of rarely produced plays, several books of aphorisms and meditations, three volumes of his memoirs through about age thirty-one, a short travel book titled *The Voices of Marrakech,* and a number of essays. He wrote in German, his fourth or fifth language, but the one in which he lived from age eight until he moved permanently to England. All his published writings have been translated, some with his advice, into English. At the center of his oeuvre stands *Crowds and Power.* To it he devoted thirty-five years, much of that time to the exclusion of other work. In 1981, Canetti was awarded the Nobel Prize for Literature. He died in August 1994.

Since its publication in 1960 (English translation, 1962), *Crowds and Power* has attracted admirers around the world, especially in Europe. In North America, it has been less noticed or discussed. Given the originality and trenchant independence of Canetti's work, along with the difficulty of classifying it and finding a place for it among dominant structuralist and postmodern social theories, its neglect is not wholly mystifying. On the other hand, the twentieth century is widely acknowledged as a century of crowds and concurrently of appalling abuses of power. Within that context, one might have expected more impact from what J. S. McClelland called the "first masterpiece" of crowd theory.[1] Richie Robertson, writing on "Canetti as Anthropologist," observed, "Much of the book anticipates trends in the human sciences that have developed only since its publication."[2] He concluded by hoping that if Canetti missed his moment, his time may nonetheless be yet to come. The publication during the 1990s in Germany of a dozen books on Canetti indicates that his importance has been growing there; and the number of non-German contributors to a 1995 volume of essays on *Crowds and Power* suggests that the wave of his influence is propagating elsewhere as well.[3] A multitude of articles and Web sites in a remarkable number of languages confirm the widening interest in Canetti's thought. In 2000, David Darby, a Canadian scholar, edited a collection of *Critical Essays on Elias Canetti*.[4] The Italian journal *Running New* devoted an issue in 2002 to the subject "Elias Canetti, The Anthropology of Evil and Metamorphosis."[5] As of 2005, the centenary of Canetti's birth, essays, new books, and conferences devoted to his work continue to multiply.

The rhetorical form of *Crowds and Power*, many of its central subjects, and its methods are disorientingly original. Whether Canetti's great work should be considered anthropology, literature, sociology, philosophy, psychology, a mix of those, or something else altogether has been less a matter of dispute than puzzlement. "*Crowds and Power* is a work without a clear position between literature and science."[6] Its argument follows lines neither straight nor circular; it neither progresses by logical steps nor returns regularly to one governing idea. My preference in spatial analogies, for what it may be worth, is for an ellipsoid with foci of crowds, power, and transformation, such that wherever on the curve of Canetti's exposition one may be, the influence of those three centers of gravity will be felt in various proportions.

As to the question of what *Crowds and Power* may be, the answer seems to me straightforward if somewhat arcane. Formally, *Crowds and Power* fits comfortably into the casual, encyclopedic literary habit that Northrop Frye identified as the "anatomy." More commonly encountered in fictional or religious incarnations like Spenser's *Faerie Queene*, Rabelais's *Gargantua and Pantagruel*, James Joyce's *Ulysses* and *Finnegan's Wake*, or the Bible, the anatomy also occurs in the form of compendious meditations on a central subject or a set of related themes. Nonfictional instances in English include

Robert Burton's *Anatomy of Melancholy*, Carlyle's *Sartor Resartus*, and Frye's own *Anatomy of Criticism*. Like other encyclopedic, culture-defining literary forms, the anatomy as Frye analyzes it (and as his work exemplifies) aspires to contain a significant part of the world in terms of a category of human understanding and imagination. That is not to say that an anatomy like *Crowds and Power* presumes to set forth every possible human world, but that the world it defines is large, of broad and deep significance, and illuminated by the wide-ranging study of its subject. In Burton's case, that means "human society is studied in terms of the intellectual pattern provided by the conception of melancholy," an understanding that produces a "comprehensive survey of human life."[7] Carlyle's work takes clothes and their construction to organize the world, and Frye's anatomy is informed by an understanding of human culture studied through literature broadly conceived as "an order of words," the "total coherence" of which the critic attempts to articulate.[8] For Canetti's anatomy, the lenses that bring into focus and make coherent vast bodies of disparate human experience are crowds and power and their intertwined origins in the deepest levels of human nature, especially in that imaginative human capability Canetti called transformation. Within the anatomy of *Crowds and Power* lies the potential for a Canettian aesthetics, biology, history, political science, psychology, and so forth. By all indications, Canetti was dauntingly erudite in a number of languages, and he was more than capable of bringing to the genre of the anatomy the encyclopedic knowledge that it requires.

In passing, one might note that the anatomy is practically congruent with a parodic encyclopedic tradition, generally called "Menippean satire" after the lost works of its putative first practitioner. Among the best known of such works are *Don Quixote, Candide,* and *Finnegan's Wake.* If *Crowds and Power* rarely shows its kinship with the zany humors of Menippean satire openly, that branch of its family nonetheless contributes something to Canetti's mode of thinking in his own nonfiction anatomy. Menippean satire characteristically delights in confronting logic and ideology with inconvenient, recalcitrant facts—as does Canetti. That tendency has a playfulness to it, a benignant mischievousness, which is very much a part of Canetti's thought and informs all his writing with wry skepticism toward attempts to make the world conform to any system of verbal order, including his own.[9] We mistake Canetti's spirit if we assert, as David Denby did in an otherwise appreciative and illuminating essay, that "Canetti is hardly given to self-mockery" or that his work is "humorless, almost haughty."[10] Frequent self-directed ironies in his *Memoirs* contradict such a judgment, as do the appalling comedy of *Auto-da-Fé* and the eccentric, exuberant playfulness of the dramas and aphorisms. Even in *Crowds and Power,* which contains Canetti's most uniformly direct writing, his ludic, often ironic cast of mind contributes a detectable undertone. The aside on comedy that appears in the second volume of his *Memoirs* applies to *Crowds and Power* as well as to his other works: "Comedy lives for me, as when it began with Aristophanes, from its *universal* interest, its view of the world in larger contexts. However, it should deal boldly with these contexts, indulge in brainstorms that verge on madness, connect, separate, vary, confront, find new structures for new brainstorms, never repeat itself and never get shoddy, demand the utmost from the spectator, shake him, take him, and drain him."[11]

As Frye notes, "the word 'anatomy' . . . means a dissection or analysis, and expresses very accurately the intellectualized approach of this form."[12] At the same time, however, the anatomy gives paramount importance to the data of experience and resists reducing particularities to homogeneity. When forced to choose between intellectual system and fact, the anatomist invariably chooses fact, however ill it may fit prevailing systems of causality or classification, including his own. Canetti shares the anatomist's predisposition. Of Stendhal, a writer whom Canetti particularly admired, he wrote, "He experienced it [life] with exactness and depth . . . [and] he allowed everything that was separate to remain separate, instead of trying to construct spurious unities" (277).

For Canetti's thinking, two qualities of the anatomy are especially congenial. First, the encyclopedic form encompasses a diversity of data and points of view. Anatomies aim neither for theoretical or methodological uniformity nor for rhetorical closure. Second, their contents are always to some degree arbitrary. (Recall the joke about the man who was introduced to encyclopedias when, lonely in a strange city, he picked up a volume entitled "Girls to Grab.")

Closed intellectual systems, as far as Canetti is concerned, serve themselves rather than multifaceted reality. "The balance between knowledge and ignorance determines how wise we get," he wrote in 1942. "Ignorance must not be impoverished by knowledge."[13] Again, "Thoughts fitting together into a system are irreverent. They gradually exclude the unsaid and then leave it behind, until it dies of thirst."[14] Twenty-two years later, five years after the appearance of *Crowds and Power,* Canetti, probably speaking of himself, noted that "his insights always struck him as suspicious whenever he managed to defend them convincingly."[15] Within *Crowds and Power* itself, Canetti repeatedly calls his thoughts tentative. One should not mistake the vigor with which Canetti expresses his ideas for arrogance or dogmatism. He gives his speculations the advantage of their most precise, powerful articulation; but he repeatedly labels them tentative and refuses them systemic closure.

Crowds and Power splits roughly in half, with the dynamics of crowds and packs serving as the dominant subject of the first half and those of power and transformation occupying the remainder. A short epilogue concludes the main text, which is followed by a bibliography—chiefly citations of original sources. Canetti introduces the bibliography of ten pages: "It contains, first, all the books from which I have quoted; second, all the books which have played a decisive part in shaping my thought, original documents of a widely diverse nature, relating to myth, religion, history, anthropology, biography and psychiatry. . . . Finally . . . a few recent works which contain reliable surveys of unfamiliar civilizations" (485). Notably absent are the names of crowd theorists, historians, psychoanalysts, and others whose interests intersect Canetti's and with whose writings he was surely familiar: Marx, Le Bon, Reich, Hitler, Freud. As Roberto Calasso notes, "These screaming omissions contributed to no small degree to the suspicion and alarmed headscratching with which the book was received by academics."[16] Equally out of consonance with modern academic practice is Canetti's sparing use of endnotes.

Not counting the epilogue, *Crowds and Power* is divided into eleven titled sections, the first four of which are concerned with crowds and packs while the remaining seven chiefly address power. All eleven sections are further divided into what are, in effect, essays with titles that announce their topics. Most are short, from two or three to as many as ten or fifteen pages. The largest section and the one with the most essays, twenty-four, is the first, "The Crowd." Including the epilogue, the 107 essays that compose the 546 pages of *Crowds and Power* are rarely sutured together. As Youssef Ishaghpour writes, "Each section, each paragraph remains tied to others, but is in itself an independent whole, a figure in a constellation of differences: there is no thesis or conclusion into which particular parts disappear."[17] Because Canetti subscribes to no totalizing concept or system, his meditations may be addressed in parts without violation of their spirit of inquiry. Like Stendhal, he allows what is separate to remain separate.

Even when Canetti appears to be abstracting and systematizing his understanding of crowds, he simultaneously complicates and particularizes it. In his long analysis of crowds, the permutations of their fundamental forms are numerous and are geometrically multiplied by further, secondary distinctions. What's more, after describing the four main attributes of crowds, Canetti restores their mystery with a pair of sentences that explicitly prevent closure. "There is, however, another tendency hidden in the crowd, which appears to lead to new and superior kinds of formation. The nature of these is often not predictable" (29). Canetti never explains this enigmatic remark. The wide window overlooking uncertainty remains uncurtained.

In practice, self-commentary of any kind is largely absent from *Crowds and Power*. Recounting his youthful attraction to the "strength and recklessness" of Georg Grosz's drawings, Canetti identifies a habit of mind that persists to a considerable degree in his later writings: "A truth that mediated, that weakened, that explained, that excused was no Truth for me."[18] The actions and circumstances *Crowds and Power* describes are spared any systemic spider web that might ensnare and embalm them. Descriptions of events or cultures—Mary Douglas's of the Lele, for example—are frequently quoted or paraphrased with only slight commentary. Readers are trusted to draw their own conclusions. As a result, *Crowds and Power* has a literary density, the quality of a primary text rather than a commentary.

Nor does Canetti assert that the truth of any topic may be encompassed from a single perspective. The human talent for transformation, an idea of central importance for Canetti, must be by its nature protean, polymorphous, difficult to fasten down and comprehend. "The most hopeful course" toward understanding any complex phenomenon, as Canetti writes about transformation, "is to approach it from several different angles" (337). If some of those angles tack away from previous observations, so be it. The conscience of words derives from their responsibility to reality, not to themselves.

Since they represent open, expansive worlds rather than closed ones, encyclopedic literary forms must be incomplete and, indeed, uncompleteable. As narratives, they tend to break off more or less arbitrarily or to end tentatively, often with a promise of later continuation. *Crowds and Power* makes several references to another volume, which never appeared, and ends with an epilogue that offers no very specific prescriptions.

Canetti remains true to his modesty. Despite the penchant of readers for demanding, and authors for offering, the final truth of things, he refuses to claim closure. From his perspective, the human urge to embrace systems of thought that promise to explain everything leads to the chasing of chimeras. Nonetheless, *Crowds and Power* often asserts and always assumes the existence of a human nature found in all cultures. This assumption puts Canetti at odds with thinkers who give more emphasis to cultural determinants of human subjectivity and behavior. The view of humans as critically formed by highly specific cultural practices flourished throughout Canetti's life. Canetti's understanding of people reverses these assumptions; he analyzes diverse cultures and practices as specific manifestations of the shared dynamics of crowd and pack formations, and of the impulse toward the maladaptation of power.

Although many twentieth-century thinkers have embraced assumptions about humanity that favor cultural determinism and deny "essential" human attributes, Canetti clearly believes that all people share at least some fundamental qualities. The opening sentence of the second essay asserts the existence of one aspect of a general human nature: "The crowd, suddenly there where there was nothing before, is a mysterious and universal phenomenon" (16).

The biological basis of crowds, Canetti repeatedly asserts, may be observed in other animals as well as humans. Indeed, some aspects of crowds include inanimate as well as living nature. Crowd symbols are "collective units which do not consist of men, but which are still felt to be crowds" (75). Because they "shed a natural light" on crowds, they offer profitable insights into actual human crowds. Such symbols provide objective correlatives for aspects of crowds and thereby allow us to visualize their dynamics. As Canetti writes, "The specific nature of this coherence [of people in a crowd] is unknown. The sea, while not explaining, expresses it" (80). Crowd symbols are more than cultural or artistic conventions. They reflect, as well, something of a shared nature not only among human beings but also among nonhuman organisms and things.

Human packs, which derive in part from the examples of other animals, are the oldest, most limited form of crowds. They therefore illuminate with particular clarity the origins and inner workings of larger, more complex crowds. Packs exemplify "one of the main theses of this enquiry. All four main types of pack exist everywhere there are human beings" (120). Warning against dismissing African kings as irrelevant to modern experience, Canetti observes, "It is not for a European of the 20th century to regard himself as above savagery. His despots may use more effective means, but their ends often differ in nothing" (411). As is usually the case when Canetti turns to examples distant in time or place, the discussion of African tribal rulers both underlines the universality of the illustrated phenomena of crowds and divests them of their concealment in familiar trappings.

The approach Canetti takes to understanding packs, crowds, and even crowd symbols exemplifies his approach in general. He attempts to observe his objects of study from positions both outside and within. "One must stand apart, a devotee of none" (169). But at the same time one "should allow each to unfold in one's mind as though one were condemned to actually belong to it" (169). As he writes in *Notes from Hampstead*, "The passion with which one possesses every object and the passion with which one distances oneself in contemplation of it—that is everything."[19]

Like all original thinkers, Canetti sometimes ignores or flouts "common sense"—as we call widely accepted dogma and shared prejudice. Taken seriously, *Crowds and Power* has plenty to raise doubts in anyone. But Canetti addresses scant attention to opposing views and engages in almost no polemics. Such rhetoric would constitute a version of the inward-turning system that he finds inimical to a true comprehension of reality. Eschewing self-conscious dialectics, Canetti adopts a persona that speaks with the blunt concreteness of someone who knows the extent of both his understanding and his ignorance, someone who invites his readers, without elaborate apology or coaching, to make their own judgments. His investment in such a persona has behind it the capital of more than thirty-five years of experiencing, observing, reading, thinking, and writing. One might argue that Canetti's omission of theorists like Freud and Marx from his exposition and his bibliography must be, by implication, polemical; but I believe that it rather has to do with fundamental rhetorical decisions and with a disinclination to become involved in defensive quibbling or self-justification.

For all that, we have no reason to regard Canetti as writing *ex Olympia* or from some dim, distant intellectual Zembla. Early in *Crowds and Power* he addresses what has been the central focus of most previous crowd theorists, the problem of mob violence. Canetti's idea of the crowd's discharge (*"Entladung"* also means "eruption" or "release") raises the issue of the mass's famous attraction to destruction. This quality of crowds, Canetti notes, is often mentioned and deplored "but never really explained" (19). Unlike earlier crowd theorists, Canetti views this phenomenon not only from the outside, but also from within. From the point of view of the crowd itself, the noises of its rampage "are the robust sounds of new life. . . . Everything shouts together; the din is the applause of objects" (19). The crowd's instinctive goal is to efface "established and universal visible and valid distances"; its breaking and burning amount to constructive actions in which "the discharge accomplishes itself" (19). Canetti neither deplores nor excuses this behavior. Rather he reports and analyzes it according to the motives and qualities of crowds that he has already set forth. "To the crowd in its nakedness everything seems a Bastille" (20). Of his own attitude, he writes, "Concerning crowds, I have lost my earlier prejudices; for me, the crowd is neither good nor bad but simply *is*, and our current blindness about crowds I find unbearable."[20]

Freud, of the preceding Viennese generation, had considerable influence on Canetti's conception of his enterprise, however little the younger man may have turned to him for a theoretical framework or for specific interpretations of human behavior. In the second volume of his memoirs, Canetti reflects, "Since Freud's ideas [of crowds] did not suffice for me, failing to explain the phenomenon that was most important to me, I was sincerely, if naively, convinced that I was undertaking something different, something totally independent of him. It was clear to me that I needed him as an adversary. But the fact that he served as a kind of model for me—this was something that no one could have made me see at that time."[21]

How was Freud a model for Canetti? Both were trained as scientists and tended to favor thermodynamic modeling of human emotional energy. More profoundly, Canetti would have admired Freud's courage and independence. Although Canetti must have been repelled by Freud's passion for encompassing theories, the psychologist's willingness to question, modify, and even wholly scrap his theories in the face of circumstances that they could not accommodate would have been congenial to Canetti's respect for concrete reality and his conviction that language and intellectual systems must follow the facts of the world, not precede or pretend to convey existence upon them.

As a writer on crowds, Freud served almost wholly as adversary. In *Group Psychology and the Analysis of the Ego,* Freud had asserted, "Such a limitation of narcissism [in a crowd] can, according to our theoretical views, only be produced by one factor, a libidinal tie with other people."[22] Canetti cannot have admired the precedence Freud gave to "our theoretical views," which he felt that Freud used to explain crowds away. "What I missed most in Freud's discussion was *recognition* of the phenomenon. This phenomenon struck me as no less elementary than the libido or hunger. I didn't set out to get rid of this phenomenon by tracing it back to special constellations of the libido. On the contrary, the point was to focus on it squarely, as something that had always existed, and that existed now more than ever."[23] On the other hand, Freud had commented on the profound equality among members of crowds, the absence of sexual love between members of certain groups, and the disintegration of a group when it succumbs to panic—all observations that accord with Canetti's in *Crowds and Power.*

A careful reading of *Group Psychology and the Analysis of the Ego* reveals why it was finally of so little importance to Canetti's thinking. In the first twenty-five pages, Freud asks provocative questions about what a group is, how it influences the mental state of the individuals who comprise it, how one might distinguish between "very fleeting groups and extremely lasting ones," "homogeneous and inhomogeneous ones," "natural groups and artificial ones," and so on. He also promises "to lay particular stress upon a distinction to which writers on the subject have been inclined to give too little attention; I refer to that between leaderless groups and those with leaders."[24] But he does not deliver on this promise, and he fails to return to many of the distinctions and questions that he raises early in the work. Rather, he finally more or less "get[s] rid" of groups as a fundamental human quality by concluding that they are defined and motivated by the common libidinal orientation of their members. Freud, in short, returns to individuals.

Canetti, on the contrary, finds crowds to be as elemental to human identity as individuality. When he personifies crowds throughout *Crowds and Power,* he does not do so simply as a figure of speech, expressing something like "the crowd acts as if it were a single entity." While Canetti always remains aware of the individuality of particular persons, he simultaneously understands crowds to be a fundamental human configuration. It is as answerable to human nature to declare "a crowd wants" as it is to say "a person wants."

Crowds and Power has strong affinities with some central ideas of a Marxist descendent of Freud, Norman O. Brown, although neither Brown nor Canetti give any indication of familiarity with each other. Brown asserts in Life against Death that "man entered social organization in order to share guilt. Social organization . . . is a structure of shared guilt."[25] Since Canetti believes that guilt originates in "feeling like prey" and that people form crowds in order to escape that feeling, Brown's insight fits with Canetti's. Canetti finds in transformation the very basis of what makes humans human. (He calls it "Verwandlung," the word that Kafka used as the title of his most famous story, "The Metamorphosis.") Similarly, Brown speaks of "metamorphosis, or symbol formation; the origin of human culture."[26] Both Canetti and Brown, finally, may be considered to be what Ernest Becker calls "literary men." They share with other "literary men" the view of human civilization that Northrop Frye articulated in Fables of Identity: "The imaginative or creative force in the mind is what has produced everything that we call culture and civilization. It is the power of transforming a subhuman physical world into a world with a human shape and meaning, a world not of rocks and trees but of cities and gardens, not an environment but a home."[27] (Canetti would probably not include the adjectival formation "subhuman"; there is little in his writing to suggest that he regards humankind as especially elevated among animals or within the matter and energy of which the comprehendible universe is composed.)

Brown quotes approvingly from a letter Blake wrote to Butts in 1800, one that expresses an idea closely related to Canetti's crowd symbols:

Each herb and each tree,
Mountain, hill, earth and sea,
Cloud, Meteor and Star,
Are men Seen Afar.[28]

Considering leaders to be secondary in the creations of crowds, Brown presents a view that is very much in tune with Canetti's:

"This original approach to mass psychology developed in Spinoza's *Ethics* does not, as even Freud's does, envisage dependence on a leader, or head, as the origin or essence of mass formation."[29]

Ernest Becker, disciple of Otto Rank, is one of the few social philosophers who cites Canetti. He argues in *Escape from Evil* that human behavior—especially the violence that people do to each other, their fellow creatures, and their environment—is fundamentally motivated by the fear of death and "the inevitable urge to deny mortality."[30] Such a view accords with Canetti's central hypothesis that crowd behavior derives largely from the fear of being seized by unknown predators—a motive that also lies behind the pathologies of power.

At his most specifically Canettian, Becker writes, "Seen in these stark terms, life on this planet is a gory spectacle, a science-fiction nightmare in which digestive tracts fitted with teeth at one end are tearing away at whatever flesh they can reach, and at the other end are piling up the fuming waste excrement as they move along in search of more flesh."[31] Quoting Rank, Becker sets forth an understanding of sacrifice that practically duplicates that of *Crowds and Power* (though it lacks Canetti's further understanding of sacrifice as a crowd phenomenon): "'The death fear of the ego is lessened by the killing, the sacrifice, of the other; through the death of the other, one buys oneself free from the penalty of dying, of being killed.'"[32]

Canetti's thoughts on the causes of war are also largely congruent with Becker's analysis of human evil. Writing about double crowds and their relation to war, Canetti observes that people wish to kill, and therefore become aware that they can be killed, which motivates most of their excuses for going to war. The intensity of war, Canetti continues, derives from two causes: the desire of two opposed crowds to persist as crowds (an attribute of all crowds) and the desire of the people who compose them to forestall death (67–73).

Among Canetti's contemporaries, Siegfried Kracauer was especially attracted to some of the phenomena to which Canetti devoted decades. Kracauer, however, addressed such subjects mostly in occasional essays, a very different genre from Canetti's long meditations, and he wrote for different times and readers. He does not often follow his insights about mass media into their complicated implications and he sometimes indulges a moralistic attitude foreign to the author of *Crowds and Power*. Canetti, who regarded the impulse to make judgments as "a disease," would never title an essay "The Little Shopgirls Go to the Movies" nor condescend as Kracauer did to "their silly little hearts."[33]

Jessica Benjamin, D. W. Winnicott, and Alice Miller, among relatively current psychologists, have clear affinities to Canetti's understanding of human personality and the dynamics of human interactions. When Benjamin analyzes the dysfunctional psychological development that leads to the sort of person who desires to control other people without really acknowledging them, one is reminded of Canetti's assertion that power involves the dehumanization of other people, their reduction to "vermin" or "trash." "Domination," Benjamin writes, has to do with "the fantasy of omnipotence. For the person who takes this route to establishing his own power, there is an absence where the other should be."[34] Like Canetti's conception of transformation, what Benjamin calls "the transitional object" serves healthy human development as "a means of passage toward the awareness of otherness, toward establishing a boundary between inside and outside. But it is precisely an intermediate experience in which that boundary has not yet hardened."[35]

Benjamin's view of such a "transitional object" is influenced (as she acknowledges in general) by the psychology of D. W. Winnicott, who wrote, "Only gradually do we demand of the developing individual that there shall be a fully acknowledged distinction between external reality and inner psychic reality; indeed there is a relic of the intermediate substance in the cultural life of grown men and women . . . which most clearly distinguishes human beings from the animals (religion, art, philosophy)."[36] Though this looks to some extent like Canetti's idea of transformation, it would probably be unpalatable to Canetti, because it subsumes transformation into a general view of psychic development, rather than granting it the status of a basic means for connecting self and other. More fundamentally consonant with Canetti's thinking is Winnicott's observation that "integration brings with it an expectation of attack."[37]

Neither Canetti nor Alice Miller are unusual in their emphasis on childhood experience as a critical determinant of later behavior, but both give extreme emphasis to such influences and to the scars that commands forced upon children leave in adult psyches. Canetti calls such scars "the stings of command" and Miller famously locates them in the injured, hiding inner child. Miller comes close to Canetti when she declares, "Love and cruelty are mutually exclusive. No one ever slaps a child out of love but rather because in similar situations, when one was defenseless, one was slapped and then compelled to interpret it as a sign of love. This inner confusion prevailed for thirty or forty years and is passed on to one's own child."[38] Of special importance, from a Canettian point of view, is Miller's phrase "and then compelled to interpret it as a sign of love." For Canetti, commands set virtually permanent barbs into their victims—but only if they are obeyed. The bearers of such stings will compulsively attempt to remove them by reenacting the same commands in similar circumstances on a new victim. Miller is more optimistic than Canetti about the chances for stopping the cascading proliferation of evil commands across generations, but her sense of their etiology and effects is close to his.

The force of commands that do not intend to kill or lead to killing "is almost invariably in excess of what need be used to bring about the desired action and this is the real reason why a command leads to the formation of a sting" (331). Logically, a command that is not followed cannot cause a sting because, far from having extra force, it lacks the energy to penetrate its target at all. When Canetti urges that in order to master power we must confront command—as he does in the last sentence of *Crowds and Power*—we should remember this analysis. The excess force would seem to be the death threat that, according to Canetti, underlies all commands. Its removal, like the removal of the possibility of killing from the sublimated war crowds of political parties, would be essential to the establishment of a truly humane society.

The relatively abstract and philosophical discourse of Michel Foucault, the most influential theorist of power of the recent past, contrasts sharply with the concrete, literary mode of Canetti's writing. Comparisons between them are not easy to make. Nonetheless, they converge at some points, for example as regards the use of inquiry as an instrument of power, a theme that Foucault explores in the *History of Sexuality* and in *Discipline and Punish*. Foucault's concept of the will to knowledge and his understanding of disciplines that exercise their power by probing and examining have strong affinities to Canetti's understanding of questioning, especially when it is used in the service of a paranoid compulsion to discover and eliminate those whom the questioner assumes to be enemies. Discussing the power profile of "Hobbes's asocial man," Robertson asserts that "Canetti's conception of power is similarly asocial." "For an account of the distribution of power within institutions, where it eludes the complete control of any individual," he writes, "we have to go to Nietzsche's modern disciple Michel Foucault."[39]

My suggestions about Canetti's relation to other thinkers can only be fragmentary, partial, and preliminary. The place of *Crowds and Power* in the long history of crowd theory is illuminated by J. S. McClelland's *The Crowd and the Mob from Plato to Canetti*. Petra Kuhnau's *Masse und Macht in der Geschichte* (insofar as my limited German allows me to comprehend it accurately) relates Canetti's thought in detail to the scientific, psychological, anthropological, and sociological climate of the time during the long incubation of his great work. Michael Mack "provides an account of the intellectual and historical context of *Masse and Macht*" that is especially valuable in its discussion of Canetti's relationship with Franz Baermann Steiner.[40] Johann P. Arnason and David Roberts, the aim of whose book is "to open up Canetti's work to the wider context of social theory," invoke a different set of thinkers: Hannah Arendt, Emile Durkheim, Thomas Hobbes, Horkheimer and Adorno, Serge Moscovici, and others.[41] In noting some affinities between Canetti and others who have thought about crowds and power, I intend to indicate a few points at which his concerns intersect theirs. I am convinced that Canetti's place in the history of ideas will eventually be an important one. That degree of knowledge about his work, however, awaits a broader audience; a wider and more thorough understanding of *Crowds and Power* and Canetti's other writing; and further demonstrations of the capacity of his thought to shed light on individuals and society, history, politics, and the arts.

Canetti's writing is distinguished by a particularity to which he was firmly committed. "Among the most sinister phenomena in intellectual history," he writes in *The Conscience of Words*, "is the avoidance of the concrete."[42] Canetti insists that words arise from real actions and things and that they must revisit those springs of meaning if they are to retain their vitality. Ishaghpour, an articulate reader of Canetti, emphasizes the poetic concreteness of the writing in *Crowds and Power*. He notes that Canetti is not a theoretician in the ordinary sense of that word; on the contrary, "in *Crowds and Power* one encounters forms and images, not concepts, which according to Canetti himself, are inherent in power and incapable of comprehending the objects with which they are concerned."[43] Canetti's "'*pensée poetique*' privileges images over concepts, objects over deductions."[44] His thought is attached to things and actions, not to methods, to critiques of understanding, or to deconstruction. In *Crowds and Power*, "The reflected image replaces the concept; constellations of form replace systematic discourse. This produces a unique richness, diversity, and intensity. It is the difference between *Crowds and Power* and what we are used to in philosophic or anthropological writing; but it also accounts for the strangeness of *Crowds and Power*."[45]

Canetti's commitment to the concrete in *Crowds and Power* underlies the frequency of lightly explicated recounting of source materials. Introducing the story of a punitive expedition by one South American tribe against another, Canetti states that "the account was taken down word for word from a Taulipang man and it contains all that one need know about the war pack" (99). Following the Taulipang warrior's narrative, Canetti simply retells it, adding emphasis to some incidents. No more commentary is required, for this report of a war pack "is the most truthful, because most naked" (103). Canetti's attitude toward the teller of that story implies his intentions in his own writing: "It contains nothing extraneous; nothing has been improved or glossed over by the narrator" (103).

Beyond his passion for the concrete, Canetti's commitment to myth reflects a genuine epistemology. After recounting a story of the South American Uitoto, Canetti remarks, "The concentration of this myth, where everything really important is enacted within the body of the snake, is completely authoritative; it is truth itself" (257). In the second volume of his memoirs he writes, "The true reason for my fascination with this original trend in Chinese philosophy was (without my realizing it) the importance of *metamorphoses* here. It was, as I see today, a good instinct that drew me to metamorphoses; my probing kept me from giving in to the world of concepts."[46]

This formulation—"kept me from giving in to the world of concepts"—reflects one of *Crowds and Power*'s central purposes, resistance to power. Edgar Piel declares that "*Crowds and Power* was . . . written (as he [Canetti] tells us in the essay on Hrdlicka) 'in the undisguised hope of putting an end to power.'"[47] The principal instrument of power, command, has become "the most dangerous single element in the social life of mankind" (333). Yet Canetti does not wholly disavow command, but argues for its radical amelioration by reducing the fierceness and persistence of the "sting" through which command endures and propagates. "We must have the courage to stand against it and break its tyranny" (333). The last sentence of *Crowds and Power* iterates one of its central purposes: "If we would master power we must face command openly and boldly, and search for means to deprive it of its sting."

Canetti rarely indulges in exhortations like these. He avoids them because they have an affinity with the closure and conceptual systematizing that he finds inimical to understanding. He also avoids such prescriptions, I think, because they come close to making judgments, which he finds incompatible with the pursuit of truth. Rather than turning to conventional commentary and meta-commentary upon his sources and his own arguments, Canetti emphasizes specific actions, objects, and occasions of transformation. In the fluid dynamics among and within packs and crowds, and between people and the creatures and inanimate objects with which they interact, he finds crucial truths about the human condition. Knowledge of reality may be mediated by words, but it can also be obscured or usurped by them. Humankind's best hope for progress toward a peaceful, creative world comes not from the pre- and pro-scriptions of systems, but from apprehending its own nature. "There is no other hope for the survival of mankind," Canetti wrote, "than knowing enough about the people it is made up of."[48] One of his aphorisms, dated the year that *Crowds and Power* was published, speaks eloquently to the purpose of that work and its mode: "Hope can flow only from darkest knowledge, otherwise it will become a derisive superstition and speed up the destruction that looms more and more ominously."[49]

Conventional history, which Canetti sees as the tendentious simplification of the past, aims to show through the discovery of "laws" and causal systems the inevitability of what has happened. The determinism that historians favor, however, reduces complex reality in the service of concepts. The opening lines of Robert Frost's "Directive" expresses an attitude Canetti would have found congenial:

> Back out of all this now too much for us,
> Back in a time made simple by the loss
> Of detail . . .

In their desire to conceive the past as inevitable, most historians impoverish reality and discount freedom. "History," Canetti mused in 1950, "portrays everything as if it could never have become otherwise. Yet it could have happened in a hundred different ways."[50]

Worse, like an obsequious courtier, history prostitutes itself shamelessly to power. At the end of his discussion of a notoriously murderous, self-aggrandizing Sultan of Delhi, Canetti remarks, "Muhammad Tughlak has been defended and justified by modern historians, those eulogists of power, on grounds of his *time* and/or *necessity,* which, in their hands, can assume any and every shape" (434).

Within the broad unity of its concerns, *Crowds and Power* employs multiple perspectives. Any commentary must be equally flexible both when adopting the perspectives that Canetti provides and when importing others that seem relevant. Canetti's thought, like the crowds, power, and transformational dynamics it illuminates, is complex and multifaceted. The depth and resonance of *Crowds and Power* and the astonishing stamina, patience, and open-mindedness that Canetti brought to it guarantee that any interpretation or redaction must be partial and limited. Yet its compression, density, and resonance have to some extent worked against it in North America, where the academic near-monopoly on intellectual life has meant that works of a kind unfamiliar or unfashionable in university circles tend to be dismissed. It is not surprising that most of the limited attention that Canetti and *Crowds and Power* have had in the United States and Canada has come from independent intellectuals and writers relatively unsubmerged in the conventions and fashions of academic institutions. It is time for North American academics to catch up with the thinkers and writers elsewhere who have recognized the depth and relevance of Canetti's thought. We deprive ourselves of a great, original mind if we ignore Canetti because he does not fit current notions of what theory or cultural criticism should look like. Like all true thought, that of *Crowds and Power* and Canetti's other writings grows in relevance and power as the years pass. As he wrote in his notebook for 1969, "If there is one thing I never want to be, it is 'timely.' For any time should suit me."[51]

Appendix: Summary of *Crowds and Power*

A few miscellaneous preliminaries:

1. The summary is for the convenience of the reader who has never read *Crowds and Power;* it may also serve as a quick review for those familiar with Canetti's work. Obviously a précis that reduces its subject by more than an order of magnitude cannot fully represent, let alone substitute for, Canetti's dense and eloquent original.

2. The absence of most of the myths, historical incidents, or anthropological summaries that Canetti uses to expound his understanding of such things as transformation is necessary for brevity, but reduces the vitality of Canetti's thought. A few of those myths are summarized in the sections of this book that analyze particular films.

3. I generally quote *Crowds and Power* from Carol Stewart's translation. On occasion, however, when Canetti's German seems especially vivid or crucial, I provide it, using the 1960 edition (Hamburg: Claasen Verlag).

4. I have placed my comments in parentheses where it may not be clear if remarks are my own rather than Canetti's.

The Crowd: "The Fear of Being Touched"

From the first sentence of the first essay of *Crowds and Power,* Canetti's attack is direct, concrete, compact: *"Nichts fürchtet der Mensch mehr als die Berührung durch Unbekanntes"* ("There is nothing that man fears more than the touch of the unknown"). He offers no prefatory survey of previous crowd theorists, no general remarks about humans as social animals, or their xenophobia, or what it really means to know something or someone. Canetti goes straight to the basis in human nature for the forming of crowds and seeking of power, the description and analysis of which will occupy the next 500 or so pages of his magnum opus. The instinctive terror of being seized by an unknown agent underlies both the communal response of crowd formation and the aggressively individualistic drive to accumulate power. Coalescing into a crowd counteracts people's terror of being touched; the lust for power pathologically exaggerates that fear into what Canetti identifies as an obsession with survival—preferably survival *alone.*

In support of his opening assertion Canetti appeals to shared experience:

> There is nothing that man fears more than the touch of the unknown. He wants to *see* what is reaching toward him, and to be able to recognize or at least classify it. Man always tends to avoid physical contact with anything strange. In the dark, the fear of an unexpected touch can mount to panic. Even clothes give insufficient security: it is easy to tear them and pierce through to the naked, smooth, defenseless flesh of the victim. (15)

Because of this fear, humans create spaces around themselves, shut themselves in closed houses, take offense if brushed in public by a stranger, and hasten to offer apologies when they accidentally cause the contact. "The whole knot of shifting and sensitive reactions to an alien touch . . . proves that we are dealing here with a human propensity as deep-seated as it is alert and insidious" (15).

Although Stewart renders the title of the opening essay of *Crowds and Power* simply as "The Fear of Being Touched," Canetti's original German describes its full subject: "*Umschlagen der Berührungsfurcht*"—which may be rendered literally as "Reversals or Sudden Changes of Touch-Fear," a title that stylistic grace can hardly tolerate, but that represents Canetti's words and the contents of the following discussion more accurately than the economical and idiomatic but misleading title in English. Given that we are talking about the opening premises of Canetti's argument and that his book will focus on the many transformations undergone by crowds, packs, and the morphologies of power, the disappearance of the *Umschlagen* from the English title represents a significant omission. (Later in *Crowds and Power,* Stewart translates "*Umschlag der Meuten*" as "The Transmutation of Packs.")

Canetti's title also anticipates his fundamentally dynamic understanding of crowds and power and their various species, permutations, and transmutations. The abrupt reversal of the fear of being touched into its opposite takes place only in a physically and psychically dense crowd. "As soon as a man has surrendered himself to the crowd, he ceases to fear its touch" (15). Indeed, as Canetti later asserts, people crave the crowd more as they experience it more.

The Crowd: "The Open and the Closed Crowd"

Although many twentieth-century thinkers have embraced assumptions about humanity that favor cultural determinism and deny "essential" human attributes, Canetti clearly believes that all people share some fundamental qualities (the biological basis of which, he occasionally argues, may be observed in other animals as well). The opening sentence of the second essay asserts the existence of one aspect of a general human nature: "The crowd, suddenly there where there was nothing before, is a mysterious and universal phenomenon" (16).

Having presented the underlying basis of crowd formation in the fear of being seized by something unknown, Canetti turns to the first of many distinctions he will make among crowds and their workings. As soon as a crowd comes into existence, "it wants to consist of *more* people: the urge to grow is the first and supreme attribute of the crowd" (16). Indeed, the open crowd exists only as long as it is swelling: "It disintegrates as soon as it stops growing" (16). As a result, any open crowd must not only be fated to a relatively brief existence, but it will be more or less aware of the threat of its dissolution.

The closed crowd renounces growth and accepts boundaries in order to prolong its existence in time. "The natural crowd [that is, the crowd before accruing traditions or other constraints] is the open crowd" (16). The closed crowd, by contrast, is the institutionalized crowd. It focuses on the repeated coming together of a limited number of reliable members, a repetition that makes its periodic dissolution temporary and preserves the crowd potentially in its absence as well as kinetically in its presence.

This distinction is of great importance for the scope of Canetti's argument, because it brings into the purview of crowd-analysis groups and institutions what few before *Crowds and Power* would have considered to be crowds at all: the Catholic Church, for example, along with nations, tribes, ethnic groups, and so on. All these Canetti will examine as closed crowds, groups that have suppressed the desire to grow in favor of the desire to persist, but that in other respects share the dynamics and attributes of the natural open crowd.

The Crowd: "The Discharge"

A crowd truly comes into being at the moment when all feel themselves to be one and the same, when differences and inequalities among its members disappear. These distances are chiefly "imposed from outside; they are distinctions of rank, status, and property" (17). (All crowds, then, are in a sense what Canetti will later analyze as "reversal crowds"—as the *"Umschlagen"* in the title of the first essay prefigures.) But "this blessed moment" of absolute equality, self-transcendence, and freedom "is based on an illusion; the people who suddenly feel equal have not really become equal; nor will they *feel* equal forever" (18). The crowd anticipates and dreads its disintegration, which it can forestall only by continuing the process of discharge through gaining new members—a source that must eventually run dry.

The Crowd: "Destructiveness"

The idea of the discharge (*"Entladung"* also means "eruption" or "release") raises the issue of crowds' notorious penchant for destruction. This quality of crowds, Canetti notes, is often mentioned and deplored "but never really explained" (19). From the point of view of the crowd itself, however, the noises of its rampage "are the robust sounds of new life. . . . Everything shouts together; the din is the applause of objects" (19). The crowd's instinctive goal is to efface "established and universal visible and valid distances"; its breaking and burning amount to constructive actions in which "the discharge accomplishes itself" (19). Canetti neither deplores nor excuses this behavior. Rather he reports and analyzes it according to the motives and qualities of crowds that he has already set forth. "To the crowd in its nakedness everything seems a Bastille."

The Crowd: "The Eruption"

Population growth in modern times and the concentration of people in urban areas have made experiences of open crowds more frequent and familiar. Effective as closed crowds may be in perpetuating themselves, they cannot entirely stifle the desire for "the crowd abandoning itself freely to its natural urge for growth" (20). "All the rebellions against traditional ceremonial [sic] recounted in the history of religions have been directed against the confinement of the crowd" (21). Since the French Revolution, we have come to recognize as a facet of modernity the recurrent formation of open crowds that desire to experience their "animal force and passion" (22). As we have seen, however, the discharge of the open crowd threatens to result in its dissolution. Its best hope for persistence "lies in the formation of double crowds, the one measuring itself against the other" (22). (Nations at war, groups in commercial competition, or rival religions are examples of double crowds.) The possibility for dynamic stasis between two open crowds leads to the subject of the next essay.

The Crowd: "Persecution"

Related to the double crowd's self-definition by its opposition to another group, a sense of persecution characterizes what Canetti calls "the inner life of a crowd" (22). Besides threats to it from outside (or from achieving its goal, then dispersing), the crowd's continuation is further jeopardized by the fact that within every member lurks an individual, "a small traitor who wants to eat, drink, make love, and be left alone" (23). From this circumstance develops a paranoia that sees everywhere the simultaneous threat of enemies without and subversives within. When Canetti comes to discuss power, we shall see striking similarities between this aspect of the crowd and the paranoia of power-seekers.

The Crowd: "Domestication of Crowds in the World Religions"

"A sense of the treacherousness of the crowd" (24), and its disintegration when growth slows or stops, lead world religions to substitute the repetition of regular, predictable assemblies for the exhilaration of unrestrained growth. A sudden attempt from outside to prohibit or suppress such self-restrained religions, however, will cause them to erupt again into a secularized open crowd, with its "unique and violent feeling" (25).

The Crowd: "Panic"

The most abrupt, explosive disintegration of crowds occurs from within when they become dangerous to their members individually—as might happen in a burning nightclub with few exits. The personal boundaries of individuals become painfully clear as the crowd itself comes to resemble a terrifying wildfire. "That emphatic trampling on people, so often observed in panics and apparently so senseless, is nothing but the stamping out of fire" (27).

The Crowd: "The Crowd as a Ring"

A crowd in an arena is doubly closed: first, because it occupies a limited number of places and, second, because its attention is fixed exclusively on the center of the arena and itself. It turns its back on the rest of the world. Only within the stadium can it experience discharge. This short essay on the crowd as a ring, with its description of an intensely focused, doubly closed crowd, effectively ends the characterization of open and closed crowds with which *Crowds and Power* begins. The remaining fourteen essays of the first section outline other characteristics that distinguish crowds; if they are not precisely secondary, they are perhaps not quite so fundamental as the division between open and closed crowds.

The Crowd: "The Attributes of the Crowd"

Uncharacteristically schematic, this essay summarizes the qualities of crowds as they have been thus far described and outlines distinctions based on those qualities. All crowds have in various degrees and proportions 1) the desire to grow; 2) equality—"one might even define a crowd as a state of absolute equality" (29); 3) density; and 4) direction, so essential for the existence of a crowd that its "fear of disintegration means that it will accept *any* goal" (29). The division between open and closed crowds has to do with growth. The attributes of density and equality are referred to by the descriptors "rhythmic" and "stagnating." A rhythmic crowd—of people dancing, for example—enacts density and equality to engender a crowd feeling. A stagnating crowd puts off its discharge, the moment of absolute equality, in favor of a long period of density. The distinction between "slow" and "quick" crowds refers to the quality of direction, to the nature of the goal. Quick crowds are familiar in modern society: they include political, sporting, and bellicose crowds. The slow crowd is oriented to a distant goal; examples include "religious crowds whose goal is heaven, or crowds formed of pilgrims" (30). The slow crowd gathers gradually, like tributaries flowing into a river moving toward a distant sea.

While Canetti appears to be abstracting and systematizing his understanding of crowds, he simultaneously complicates and particularizes it; the permutations of crowd qualities have already become numerous and will be geometrically multiplied by further distinctions. What's more, Canetti restores mystery to crowds with a pair of sentences that explicitly prevent the closure of his perceptions into a hermetic system. "There is, however, another tendency hidden in the crowd, which appears to lead to new and superior kinds of formation. The nature of these is often not predictable" (29).

The Crowd: "Rhythm"

Rhythm begins with feet, those of humans and of the animals they have lived among. Rhythmic crowds enact density and equality and, through repetition, imitate growth. This essay contains the first of *Crowds and Power*'s many anthropological examples, a description of the *haka*, a war dance of the New Zealand Maoris. Of particular importance in this case is "the extreme *ramification* of equality" by the synchronization of arms, legs, fingers, toes, tongues, and eyes (33). Through this rhythmic expression, the members of the tribe feel themselves to be a crowd and appear invincibly unified to outsiders.

The Crowd: "Stagnation"

The stagnating crowd is focused on density and puts off discharge. Audiences at concerts, crowds of witnesses at public executions, and religious gatherings at which people "stand together before God" all exemplify this peculiarly passive, compressed crowd. The discharge, when it finally comes, is likely to be concentrated and brief. "The crowd pays for the lengthened period of stagnant expectation, which it will have enjoyed intensely, with its own immediate death" (35). Worldwide, the most widely shared conception of the stagnating crowd may be found in the idea of the crowd of all the dead, who lie together in the earth awaiting Resurrection and the Last Judgment.

The Crowd: "Slowness, or the Remoteness of the Goal"

Similar to the stagnating crowd in its postponement of discharge, the slow crowd moves across vast distances for an extended time toward a goal so remote that discharge is sublimated in extreme cases into an ideal, unlikely to be found in this life. The slow crowd may be closed like the Exodus of the Children of Israel from Egypt; or it may be open, like a network of streams gathering together to form a mighty river. But in any case, the invisible goal is far away in time and, often, in place.

Like a goal, a crowd may be invisible, and the preeminent invisible crowd, the idea of which is found wherever humans exist, is the crowd of the dead. Many peoples imagine their dead as warriors, repeatedly fighting opposing hosts of the dead. Other invisible crowds are composed of spirits, both demonic and beneficent. Today, "for most of us, the hosts of the dead are an empty superstition" (46); the most important modern invisible crowd has become posterity. Demon hosts of yore have been replaced in modern times by bacteria and viruses, as invisible, multitudinous, and diverse in malignancy as their predecessors. A particularly pure and dense human crowd, known since the invention of the microscope, may be found in the ejaculated crowd of spermatozoa, 200 million of which go together toward a single goal and each of which carries within it its own crowd, the genetic record of its ancestral heritage.

(With the fall of the "evil empire" of the Soviet Union, the United States lost its primary opposing crowd; as a result, one could observe in political rhetoric more frequent invocations of the invisible crowd of posterity, with virtually all proposed social action appealing for justification to a rather abstract "our children." As of September 11, 2001, however, a new oppositional crowd appeared, Al-Qaeda in particular and terrorists in general. The eagerness and even joy with which many Americans and their leaders embraced the new war against this enemy, and the reemergence of an ostentatious patriotism that had flag makers running triple shifts, stands witness to the crowd passion that lies just under the surface of nations. The simultaneously aggressive, demonstrative piety that emerged also exemplifies the readiness of religions to enlarge and solidify their groups by defining them in opposition to a hostile counterpart, in this case "fundamentalist" Islam.)

The Crowd: "Classification of Crowds according to Their Prevailing Emotion"

Canetti turns from the forms of a crowd to what it "feels, what its content is" (48). Although the feelings of crowds are often mixed, five main types can be distinguished according to their dominant emotional content. The most ancient, preceding the emergence of humanity itself, are the baiting and flight crowds. The other three, more recent and uniquely human, are the prohibition, reversal, and feast crowds.

The Crowd: "Baiting Crowds"

"Hetzmassen" is difficult to translate; besides "to hunt," *hetzen* means "to hurry" and "to stir up hatred." All these senses operate in Canetti's conception of the baiting crowd, which forms "with reference to a quickly attainable goal" and "which is out for killing" (49). This powerful ancient crowd goes back to the hunting pack among men and takes many cues from similar packs among animals. Its dynamics illuminate some of the most notorious crowd behaviors: war, religious persecution, lynching, riots against minorities. The actions and emotions of *Hetzmassen* have a great deal in common with the dynamics of power.

Within the goal-oriented baiting crowd, direction, density, and equality coincide; it also grows rapidly, "because there is no risk" (49). The idea of sacrifice is closely allied to Canetti's conception of the baiting crowd, which chooses the victim to stand in for others it does not dare to kill or to deflect the threat of its members' deaths onto another person. But the success of a baiting crowd, the killing or ostracism of its victim, finally leaves its members feeling more vulnerable. The insistence on public justice derives from the equality of the baiting crowd and the public execution of criminals from its direction. In modern life, the baiting crowd "is preserved in the newspaper reading public [we can add the consumers of television and other media]. . . . One is tempted to say that it is the most despicable and, at the same time, the most stable form of such a crowd. Since it does not even have to assemble, it escapes disintegration; variety is catered for by the daily re-appearance of the papers" (52).

(This essay suggests that any assessment of Canetti as an apologist for crowds would be inaccurate. The baiting crowd loves power and is dominated by the terror of death and by survival-lust. Therefore, it is primarily destructive, neurotic, and in bad faith. Canetti regards it as dangerous and contemptible, but not as a perversion of crowd feeling. The baiting crowd is, in its emotional content, originary and fundamental.)

The Crowd: "Flight Crowds"

Flight crowds make up the other original, even prehuman, class of crowds. They remain familiar in contemporary life. Created by a threat, the flight crowd is overwhelmingly dominated by direction away from danger. It is among the most dense and diverse of crowds. Should a flight crowd be repeatedly blocked, it will become confused about its direction and disintegrate into a panic. A flight crowd disperses when its goal of safety is achieved, when the threat disappears, or when its members are physically unable to go on.

The Crowd: "Prohibition Crowds"

The prohibition crowd arises when "a large number of people refuse to continue to do what, till then, they had done singly" (55). Strikes are the most familiar modern prohibition crowds. A "negative crowd," the prohibition crowd is notable for its focus on equality—as always, closely tied to the idea of justice—and for its aversion to destruction. When thwarted, assailed, or besieged, however, it is likely to revert to destruction, especially within its own sphere. (Recent urban riots in the United States and elsewhere often seem to begin with prohibition crowds that disintegrate into violent open crowds when the authorities attempt to disperse them. In any case, their destruction of their immediate environs has been an almost uniform feature of such riots.)

The Crowd: "Reversal Crowds"

Recalling the prohibition crowd, the more active and aggressive reversal crowd generally arises in a stratified society when many "sheep" turn against a few "wolves." Such crowds frequently arise as a "collective deliverance from the stings of command." In revolutions, baiting crowds are most visible, but reversal crowds provide their underlying motive and staying power. Another kind of reversal crowd arises during religious revivals. It reverses previous defiance of divine commands, frequently after mimicking a blocked flight from God's fearful wrath. The loss of consciousness sometimes caused by such extreme fear simulates mass "deaths" that precede being "born again" into obedient piety.

The Crowd: "Feast Crowds"

The celebratory feast crowd displays great density, equality, and growth but has little need for direction. Its members bridge usually inviolable social strata and sometimes also erase the antagonism between the crowds of the living and the dead. During traditional festivals, past and present "feasts call to one another; the density of things and of people promises increase of life itself" (63).

The Crowd: "The Double Crowd: Men and Women, The Living and the Dead"

As Canetti has already noted, the best chance for the persistence of open crowds lies in the formation of double, opposing crowds of roughly equal strength. The structure of the double crowd begins with three archetypal antitheses: women/men, the living and the dead, friend/foe. (The rise of militant feminism since about 1960 provides examples of the first that are closer to us than Canetti's anthropological ones.) "The age-old antagonism between the living and the dead" forms an intermittently active double crowd. The pair is unbalanced, however, because the army of the dead is always larger and more powerful than that of the living, who are consequently "always on the retreat." War, "the most violent expression of what seems the inescapably dangerous essence of double crowds" (66), provides the subject of the following essay.

The Crowd: "The Double Crowd: War"

"One would give much to understand and to be able to dissolve it" (67). War aims to transform an enemy crowd into a heap of dead. Each side wishes to be a larger living crowd than the other. The remarkable duration of wars derives from their origin in crowds, for all crowds wish to persist and to grow. (History bears witness that wars have a way of spreading as their double crowds grow.) War crowds ultimately form because of "the individual's cowardice before death" and his secret understanding that his own desire to kill means that he himself can be killed. But the sequence of thoughts is always publicly reversed: it is the enemy who kills or desires to kill and who must therefore be attacked. The enormous passion for war comes from two sources, the desire of people to forestall death through the deaths of others and their desire to act as a crowd. "As long as the war lasts they must remain a crowd, and the war really ends as soon as they cease to be one" (73). (The disintegration of the American war crowd that defined itself in opposition to the communists of North Vietnam, and its decreasing ability to portray that enemy as a threat, led to the end of the Vietnam conflict. That war remains an apt illustration of Canetti's central tenets.)

The Crowd: "Crowd Crystals"

A reduction of closed crowds to small, rigidly limited groups, crowd crystals serve in times of need to precipitate crowds. The crowd crystal is all limits, adopted from inside rather than imposed from outside. Exemplars of crowd crystals include soldiers and religious devotees like monks. Of astonishing historical durability, crowd crystals may exist for long periods in obscurity until conditions are right for them to stimulate the growth of a new crowd.

The Crowd: "Crowd Symbols"

Of particular usefulness to any Canettian analysis of art or literature, crowd symbols are "collective units which do not consist of men, but which are still felt to be crowds" (75). Because they "shed a natural light" on crowds, they offer profitable insights into actual human crowds. Such symbols provide objective correlatives for aspects of crowds and thereby allow us to visualize their dynamics. As Canetti writes, "The specific nature of this coherence [of people in a crowd] is unknown. The sea, while not explaining, expresses it" (80). This essay describes eleven examples of crowd symbols, both natural and created by humans: fire, the sea, rain, rivers, forest, grain, wind, sand, the heap, stone heaps, and treasure. Behind each of these symbolic crowds one can recognize the "concrete crowd" it figures forth.

Detailed affinities with human crowds make fire an especially important and malleable crowd symbol. Like crowds, "fire is the same wherever it breaks out: it spreads rapidly; it is contagious and insatiable; it can break out anywhere, and with great suddenness; it is multiple; it is destructive; it has an enemy; it dies; it acts as though it were alive, and is so treated. All this is true of the crowd" (77). Furthermore, crowds, like fire, can be damped down and tamed, seek enemies, and have their "own restless and violent life" (77). Their similarities have led to a close alliance between human crowds and fire; indeed, "the human urge to *become* fire, to reactivate this ancient symbol, is still alive" (79). Hopeless, besieged cities incinerate themselves, as do desperate kings and their courts. (One recalls here the 1993 example near Waco, Texas.)

In its waves, the sea is multiple and moving; it is also dense and cohesive. In Shakespeare's *The Comedy of Errors,* it serves as a crowd symbol threatening the individuality of one of the protagonists:

> I to the world am like a drop of water
> That in the ocean seeks another drop,
> Who falling there to find his fellow forth,

Unseen, inquisitive, confounds himself.
(I.ii.35–38)

The sea provides the crowd an image of its own insatiability.

Rain stands for a crowd at its moment of discharge and also suggests its disintegration—just as those two events are closely connected in actual crowds. Rivers emblematize the crowd's direction and its formation. Procession-like, they suggest "the crowd in its vanity, the crowd exhibiting itself" (83). It is a slow crowd (except when flooding, when it would suggest the voracity and discharge of a quick open crowd).

Upright like humans but taller, the forest inspires awe. In its resolute and multiple immobility, it has come to symbolize the protective power of the army. (Hence the power of the inspired idea that Birnam Wood should uproot itself to attack Macbeth.)

Grain fields are pliant and submissive. In them people "readily see their own equality before death . . . [especially] a common death in battle" (85). (So our cliché for the bringer of mass death, the Grim Reaper with his scythe.) On the other hand, heaps of grain may stand for increase, both in their abundance and in their multiplication when the seeds are planted.

Wind emphasizes the direction of crowds and stands for the invisibility of masses of spirits or the dead. Flags make wind visible and mark the air of nations as theirs. Wind is animated by its multitudinous voices: sighs, howls, murmurs, roars.

In the tiny sameness of its grains, sand is an image of crowd equality. As a desert, it can grow dangerously, like humanity's teeming minuscule enemies: locusts and other insects, bacteria, and viruses. Alternatively, the immense numbers of its grains make it a symbol of growth and of progeny.

Heaps of substances significant to humans are emblems of density and growth and, in their uniformity, of equality. They suggest the rhythmic crowd in its creation and, as the heap is used up, in its periodic decrease. The stone heap, by contrast, is meant to endure. It is an indestructible tribute to "the rhythmic exertion of many men" (88). (Architecture, especially the monumental variety, appears to be the ultimate expression of a crowd represented by a stone heap.)

Treasure, too, is a kind of heap; but while it may represent crowd growth, it also partakes of power in its secrecy and distrust. In times of severe inflation and the consequent deflation of monetary value, treasure turns into a flight crowd of frightened, depreciated, humiliated persons.

For Canetti, the membranes separating human experiences and attributes from those of other animals, of plants, and of the nonliving universe are permeable. Thus "crowd symbols" are more than cultural or artistic conventions—though they are certainly that. They reflect, as well, something of the universally shared identity not only among human beings but also among non-human organisms and things.

The Pack: "The Pack: Kinds of Pack"

Both crowd crystals and crowds derive from packs. Like crowds, packs wish to be larger, but they lack the additional people required. Growth and density, though desired, can only be simulated; equality and direction dominate. Unlike such group concepts as tribe, kin, or clan, the pack is a unit of action rather than of static relations. Found wherever humans live in groups and deriving in part from the examples of other animals, packs are the oldest, most limited form of crowds. They therefore illuminate with particular clarity the origins and inner workings of larger, more complex crowds.

Canetti identifies "*four* different forms, or functions" of packs. "They all have something fleeting about them, and each changes easily into another" (94). They are 1) the hunting pack, whose object is the capture and distribution of prey; 2) the war pack, a sort of double pack that, like the hunting pack, intently pursues an object or goal, in this case the destruction of an enemy; 3) the lamenting pack, which responds to the dying or death of a member; and 4) the increase pack, which, in dances and other rituals, manifests the intent to grow. The fluid transmutation of these packs into each other prefigures "the instability of the far larger crowd" (96). Furthermore, "their mutations often give rise to peculiar religious phenomena," particularly when hunting packs turn into lamenting ones. (The imagery of The Book of Psalms repeatedly illustrates fluid changes among pack-functions, especially among war, lament, and increase packs or crowds.)

The Pack: "The Hunting Pack"

When prey is sighted, the hunting pack (like a baiting crowd) comes together with the goal of killing. After the prey is dispatched, distribution occurs according to laws that are complex and variable among different packs, but that are always a part of the hunting pack. "The two decisive factors," invariable among all hunting packs, "are the *sighting* and the *killing* of the prey" (98).

The Pack: "The War Pack"

War packs consist of opposing hunting packs, "both of them out to do exactly the same thing to each other" (99). A South American Taulipang man's account of a night attack on the rival tribe of the Pishauks makes up most of this essay. The account "contains all that one need know about the war pack" (99). The goal of "the sixteen men . . . was the annihilation of the hostile pack so that nothing, literally nothing, of it should remain. They describe their own actions with relish; it was the others who were, and remained, murderers" (103). In this story, one can recognize the features of war and the war crowd as Canetti described them earlier.

The Pack: "The Lamenting Pack"

Continuing the anthropological mode of the previous essay, Canetti begins with the description of a death in the Warramunga tribe of Australia. Like all packs, that of lamentation and complaint generates intense group excitement. Even before the dying Warramunga man expires, the tribe forms a lamenting pack that through its density tries to absorb him. Not only do they surround him, wailing and lacerating themselves, but a number of them literally throw themselves onto the dying man. After his death, the lamenting pack turns abruptly to "frightened rejection and isolation of the *dead*" (106). (It thus contains some of the aggressive elements of growth, density, and incorporation of a hunting pack, along with the defensive reactions of a flight crowd or of the living half of a double crowd of the quick and the dead.)

The Pack: "The Increase Pack"

A formation of greater complexity than the other three packs, the increase pack has propelled the spread of humanity and the enrichment of civilizations. Few in number compared to the creatures around them and desiring to be more, early humans incorporated their fellow creatures imaginatively into themselves by transformation. Indeed, it was through the development of transformation, the unique "gift and pleasure" of humankind, that full human identity came into being. All myths, rites, beliefs, and ceremonies express the desire for increase. Totems that identify human beings with particular abundant animals or with other numerous phenomena include many creatures and objects that persist as crowd symbols.

The Pack: "The Communion"

The common meal presents a special increase ceremony. A hunting pack changes to an increase pack, and the animal that it consumes is made to feel honored so that it will revive and allow itself to be hunted again. Such feasts evolve into religious communions that aim at the increase of the faithful and consume the symbolic flesh of a god whose resurrection the faithful relate to their own.

The Pack: "Inward and Tranquil Packs"

As the four main qualities of crowds (growth, density, equality, direction) give rise to distinctions among types, so packs can be classified according to the contrasting qualities of outward/inward and tranquil/noisy. Outward packs (often hunting or war) move toward a goal; inward ones (predominantly lament, increase) are concentric and introspective rather than acquisitive. The communion is a transition between outward and inward packs, generally from a hunting to an increase pack.

The distinction between noisy and tranquil (or expectant) packs is exemplified, for the former, by the strident pack of lament or the intrinsically noisy ones of hunting and war; and for the latter, in the patience required when the goal of the pack is "not attainable by rapid and intense activity" (115). This distinction roughly parallels that between quick and slow crowds; Canetti notes that such "expectation and stillness . . . has entered into those religions which profess belief in another world" (116).

The Pack: "The Pack's Determination: The Historical Permanence of Packs"

Determination with respect to their objects characterizes all packs, which repeat themselves in human life as constantly as other basic vital processes. Packs often function as crowd crystals and they preserve "many of the genuinely archaic elements still persisting in modern cultures" (117). Common nostalgia for a simpler, more natural life has underlying it the desire to live again in isolated packs. (Utopian communes, survivalist camps, and small groups of militiamen all exemplify returns to pack living.) The lynch mob is a particularly shameful, if unashamed, primitive pack that continues to erupt in modern life.

The Pack: "Packs in the Ancestor Legends of the Aranda"

Two legends of Australian aborigines, retold by Canetti in this essay, exemplify a mythic understanding of the origins of hunting and increase packs, and of transitions to lamenting packs. They also contain hints of war packs. In these legends, Canetti finds evidence for "one of the main theses of this enquiry. All four main types of pack exist everywhere there are human beings" (120). The development of different religions varies according to the predominant packs and modes of transmutations from which they arise. The most important are religions of lament and increase, but religions of hunting and war also exist.

The Pack: "Temporary Formations among the Aranda"

The configuration of certain of the Aranda's "multiform" feasts and ceremonies express meanings in the grouping of their participants as well as in their actions. Ceremonies that involve single-file processions evoke migration. Those featuring running and dancing in circles stabilize and protect performances enacted in the center, where "they are applauded, reverenced, and taken possession of" (123). (These ceremonies recall the "doubly closed crowd" that gathers at an arena.) Lying down in a row for many hours "could be an enactment of death," followed by resurrection when the novices jump up at last (123). A dense square suggests a protective formation for movement in hostile territory. The densest formations, the swaying cylinder and the "chaotic heap on the ground," remind Canetti respectively of "an extreme example of a rhythmic crowd" and of the lamenting pack that encloses and lies on a dying man. "With him in its midst, it resembles and recalls the heap of the dead" (124).

The Pack and Religion: "The Transmutation of Packs"

Canetti's commitment to his formalism and his conviction about the existence of universal aspects of human behavior are explicit in this brief introductory essay. Transformation of packs "occurs every-

where. . . . Without precise knowledge of it, no social event whatever, of any kind, can be understood at all" (127). When a group's
transmutations become fixed, they turn into rituals and become the
core of its faith. This section sketches "a few social and religious
structures with reference to the nature of the packs prevailing in
them" (128). Enticingly, Canetti promises an exhaustive interpretation of religion "in a separate work." But that work has never appeared.

The Pack and Religion: "Hunting and the Forest among the Lele of Kasai"

Chiefly description that is quoted or paraphrased from Mary Douglas's study, this essay leaves the reader to work out most of the implications of the data. Because its social identity is reaffirmed by
each hunt they undertake, the Lele have developed a true hunting
religion. Their social structure illuminates the development of the
forest as a crowd symbol. The forest contains for the Lele everything they most value and also the fearful spirits by whose suffer-
ance they are allowed to hunt.

The Pack and Religion: "The War Booty of the Jivaros"

Among the tribes of the Jivaros of South America, the practice of
blood revenge is the cement of society; the war pack makes up their
principal unit of action. When successful, it returns with the sev-
ered heads of enemy warriors, which are shrunken and finally become the central attraction of a ceremonial feast. The war pack thus
transmutes into an increase pack in a ritual that expresses the dynamic of the Jivaro religion.

The Pack and Religion: "The Rain Dances of the Pueblo Indians"

Because of the gentle nature of rain and the imaginative transformation into rain of Pueblo Indians in their dances, the outward
and noisy packs of hunting, war, and lament have mostly atro-
phied. The social and religious practices of Pueblo Indians derive almost entirely from increase packs. Rain comes from the blessings of
ancestors, so the people of the Pueblo have a nourishing relationship with their dead. Their important crowds, each of which leads
to the next, occur in the following sequence: ancestors → rain →
maize → children. "Rain and maize have made them gentle; their

life depends entirely on their own ancestors and their own children" (137).

The Pack and Religion: "On the Dynamics of War: The First Death—The Triumph."

The pack dynamics of war begin with a first death that precipitates a lamenting pack; that pack transforms into a war pack whose goal is revenge. From the war pack, if it is victorious, comes an increase pack that ceremonially confronts the enemy with its decrease and with the triumphant crowd's enlargement through the capture of prisoners and goods. Among peoples who depend upon conquest for much of their growth, "a kind of state religion of war develops, with the speediest possible increase as its aim" (140).

The Pack and Religion: "Islam as a Religion of War"

For all religions, invisible crowds have central importance; but for Islam especially they are opposing double crowds, "fated to be separate forever and to fight each other. . . . The double crowd of the Last Judgment is prefigured in every earthly battle" (142). During the pilgrimage to Mecca, Islam temporarily becomes a slow crowd and days of peace reign. Most of the time however, as the Koran makes clear, Islam conceives itself as a war crowd devoted to the defeat and subjugation of infidels.

The Pack and Religion: "Religions of Lament"

How does the notably transient lamenting pack give rise to religions of lament, which have a "peculiar persistence during millennia" (143)? All form around a legend of a man or god whose death is absolutely "the one death which should not have taken place" (143). The dynamics are related to those of war, which begins, we recall, when people desire to kill and therefore become conscious that they can be killed. In religious formations, a hunting pack seeks to expiate its guilt by forming a lamenting pack around a figure who takes responsibility for them on himself. They thereby hope to redeem themselves from guilt which, as Canetti observes elsewhere, arises when people feel like prey (I hunt; therefore I can be hunted). Religions of lament must consequently remain "indispensable to the psychic economy of men for as long as they remain unable to renounce pack killing" (145).

The Pack and Religion:
"The Muharram Festival of the Shiites"

Although most Islamic sects display the traits of a religion of war, the large Shiite branch has become "a religion of lament more concentrated and more extreme than any to be found elsewhere" (146). "The 'afflictions of the family of the Prophet'" form the central theme of the Shiites, whose members embrace a corresponding sense of persecution. The bulk of this essay consists of a description of the festival that commemorates the martyrdom of Husain. In these mass rites, the lamenting pack is enlarged into the crowds of a religion of lament.

The Pack and Religion:
"Catholicism and the Crowd"

The deliberation, calm, and spaciousness (there is room for everyone) of the Catholic Church derive from its unequaled defenses against the violent volatility of the open crowd. Its rituals are "temporal lament mummified." Communication among the congregation is hindered and while "communion links the recipient with the vast, invisible church, . . . it detaches him from those actually present" (156). Usually precise and slow in its workings, the Catholic Church keeps in reserve the crowd crystals of its monasteries and religious orders. In times of danger from outside or accelerated defection from inside, the members of these orders are enlisted to reactivate the Church's latent open crowd. "The most spectacular example of such conscious crowd formation on the part of the Church is the Crusades" (158).

The Pack and Religion:
"The Holy Fire in Jerusalem"

The catastrophe of 1834 in the Chapel of the Sepulcher illustrates the fluid rapidity with which crowds can transmute among forms. During the descent of the Holy Fire, the lamenting crowd becomes one of triumph. Because of "elements of contention inherent in the ceremony"—the presence of antagonistic Turkish soldiers policing the ceremony—the 1834 event saw the crowd of triumph change into a flight crowd and then, its escape blocked, disintegrate into a panic that left a heap of hundreds of dead worshippers.

The Crowd in History: "National Crowd Symbols"

Attempting to understand important differences among nations, one must consider their crowds and crowd symbols. Only when the symbol of a nation changes does its consciousness of itself also change. Like religions and other crowds, all nations wish to increase, but what they wish to increase *as* has been little noted. The approach Canetti takes to understanding crowd symbols exemplifies his approach in general. He attempts to observe his objects of study from positions both outside and within. "One must stand apart, a devotee of none." But at the same time one "should allow each to unfold in one's mind as though one were condemned to actually belong to it" (169).

Among examples of national crowd symbols, the sea serves the English, who feel themselves ships' captains devoted to its conquest. The crowd of the Dutch "equates itself with the dyke and together they withstand the sea" (172). Germans conceive themselves as an army, more specifically as a marching forest in which each feels safe and at one with his compatriots and forebears. The crowd symbol of the French, revolution, is of recent vintage—specifically, movement toward the Bastille. The national cohesion of the Swiss is felt in their impregnable mountains, "linked like the limbs of a single gigantic body" (175). Spaniards feel themselves to be both the matador and the admiring crowd at a bullfight. Torn between the symbols of ancient Imperial Rome and the Catholic Rome of St. Peter, and pulled also between national unity and cities "haunted by greater memories," modern "Italy may serve as an example of the difficulty a nation has in visualizing itself" (177). (The history of governmental instability in Italy since the publication of *Crowds and Power* would appear to support Canetti's observation.) "Jews are different from other people, but, in reality, they are most different from each other" (178). Nonetheless, the image of the Exodus, a slow crowd moving for generations toward a promised land, has become at once the crowd symbol and the torment of the Jewish people.

The Crowd in History: "Germany and Versailles"

Following the Franco-Prussian War (1870–71), the national symbol of Germany was the army as a closed crowd, one that became open with the outbreak of World War I (and that presumably returned to being a closed crowd at its end). The disbanding of the German army by the "*Versailler Diktat,*" however, produced the birth of National Socialism, for "every closed crowd which is dissolved by force transforms itself into an open crowd to which it imparts its own characteristics" (181). The Nazi Swastika combines the threat of punishment with "a hidden reminder of military discipline."

The Crowd in History: "Inflation and the Crowd"

"A crowd phenomenon in the strictest and most concrete sense," inflation depreciates the crowd symbol of treasure and creates a newly equal crowd, because everyone is impoverished. Each member "cannot help feeling its degradation as his own" (186). This crowd will not forget its depreciation and will seek "to find something which is worth even less," reduce it to absolute worthlessness, and throw it away. The "something" that Hitler and the Nazis found was the Jews.

The Crowd in History: "The Nature of the Parliamentary System"

Political opponents parallel war crowds, but they all belong simultaneously to a single crowd in their immunity from death inflicted by the government or each other. A democratic decision is embraced not because it is necessarily the wisest, but because it "derives from the renunciation of death as an instrument of decision" (190). Anyone who corrupts the democratic process "lets death in again without knowing it" (190).

The Crowd in History: "Distribution and Increase: Socialism and Production"

Justice, which Canetti explicitly contrasts with "that terrifying growth called power," originates when people recognize the necessity of sharing. It ultimately derives from the distribution phase of the hunting pack. Its modern sibling, the obsession with production, derives from the increase pack. The proletariat is particularly associated with increase, and thus socialist regimes share with capitalist ones "the *hubris* of production" (191).

The Crowd in History: "The Self-Destruction of the Xosas"

Although its placement after an essay on production might imply that the Xosa's self-destruction can stand as a parable for frenetically producing and consuming societies, Canetti emphasizes "with what consistence and precision events follow upon each other in a crowd" (197). The dead ancestors of the Xosas promised in visions to join their posterity in evicting the colonial Whites, but they deceived the living in order to swell their own crowd. The Xosas starved in immense numbers after destroying their own cattle and grain. Anticipating later analyses of power, Canetti notes that Commander Kreli, who led his people into disaster and death, "survived by many years" his tribe's catastrophe.

The Entrails of Power: "Seizing and Incorporation"

The story of the Xosas includes a meditation on the "death sentence" under which all domestic animals live and how "the *force* of the hunter has become the *power* of the herdsman" (199). It therefore serves as an apt transition from the first of Canetti's great subjects, crowds, to the second, power.

Canetti returns to the first idea of his first essay, touch and seizure by the unknown, but his perspective is now partly shifted from that of fearful prey to predator. Yet even as a predator a person remains frightened; for the persecutions "he actively undertakes, he also experiences passively in himself" (203).

All active power occurs in six overlapping phases. "First there is the lying in wait for prey. . . . The next thing is the first *touching* of the prey" (203). The act of seizing follows, then the beginning of incorporation in the mouth with its dreadful teeth. "*Smoothness* and *order*, the manifest attributes of the teeth, have entered into the very nature of power" (208). These qualities inform power in various ways, from such tangible manifestations as prisons and military formations to abstract ones like ideas of smooth and efficient functioning. (In Psalm 57 we read of "the sons of men, whose teeth are spears and arrows, and their tongue is a sharp sword.") The fifth stage of power occurs on the long "road that the prey travels through the body" (209). The end of power is excrement, "the compressed sum of all the evidence against us . . . our daily and continuing sin and, as such, it stinks and cries to heaven" (211).

The idea of power includes as well a less "glorious but no less essential form" that consists of the power to avoid falling victim to an aggressor.

Unlike most crowds and packs, power turns away from transformation or increase. It desires only itself and, far from becoming one with its prey, it wishes to reduce other living creatures (includ-

ing people) to vermin that it can crush and discard as so much excrement. Only in such isolation of self and reduction of others can
power escape guilt, which arises when one feels like prey.

Concluding, Canetti asserts "that *all* the phases of this process
. . . must have their correspondence in the psyche" (210). The etiology and symptomatology of power set forth in the rest of *Crowds
and Power* ferrets out and explores these correspondences. Nothing
more clearly signals Canetti's general attitude toward power as a
mental illness inherited from our history of physical predation
than his assertion that "the symptoms of *melancholia* are especially
illuminating in this context" (211). More insistently, however, he
equates power with acute paranoia.

The Entrails of Power: "The Hand"

"In more than one respect man's hands have been his destiny"
(219). This essay is divided, unusually, into a general introduction
and five subtopics. With its opposable thumb, the hand originated
in trees, grasping and releasing branches. This rhythm is recalled
today in trading (or shopping). The hand's first weapon was a stick
detached from a tree and later refined into spears, bows and arrows,
and so on (American Indians are said to have called rifles "fire
sticks"). Through all these transformations, the weapon "remained
what it had been originally: an instrument to create distance, something which kept away from men the touch and the grasp that they
feared" (212). (The imagery of the hominoid's bone-stick weapon
and its technological descendents in Kubrick's *2001: A Space Odyssey*
is congenial to a Canettian analysis.)

"The Patience of the Hand." Besides its early violent activities,
"the hand has found other ways to perfect itself and these, in all
cases, are ways which renounce predatory violence" (213). From
these patient works arises "the only world in which we care to live,"
a world of creation. The Bible suggestively attributes the making of
humankind to a divine "potter whose hands are skilled in shaping
clay" (213).

In "The Finger Exercises of Monkeys," which begins with the
grooming that is the principal social activity of these primates,
Canetti locates the origin of the hands' training in skillful patience.
As humans observed the various forms taken by their own manipulating hands, they were inspired to create objects and symbols.

"The Hands and the Birth of Objects." Shaping hands give rise
to both the things that humans create and the language into which

they transform them. "*Words* and *objects* are accordingly the emanations and products of a single unified experience: *representation by means of the hands*" (217).

"Destructiveness in Monkeys and Men." In contrast to the delicate grooming activities of the hand, the "hardening exercises" that have to do with sticks and with testing and breaking objects has led to "a separate destructiveness of the hand, not immediately connected with prey and killing" (218). The mechanical inventions and other technology that derive from these exercises, however, can develop in particularly dangerous ways because their absence of any intent to kill leads to a mindless and automatic quality when they are used for killing. "No one actually intends anything; it all happens, as it were, of itself" (218). (Again Kubrick comes to mind, for both *2001* and *Dr. Strangelove*.)

"The Killers are always the Powerful." What is patient and peaceful is merely useful, but what kills is feared. Dismaying as his interpretation of human history may be, however, Canetti's desire to live in a world shaped by the hand's patience encourages us to imagine a world ordered otherwise. While "those who devote themselves to killing . . . have power" (219), they represent only part of the complex destiny we hold in our hands.

The Entrails of Power: "On the Psychology of Eating"

Because "everything which is eaten is the food of power" (219), the connection between food and power is strong and close. Some tribes choose champion eaters to be kings, and a trace of this tendency remains in the association of gluttons (or their refined counterparts, gourmets) with ruling classes. The caricature of the big-stomached, cigar-puffing plutocrat illustrates Canetti's point; the possessor of power has eaten much and well. The hostility conveyed reflects the assumption—often made explicit by an accompanying sketch of a pair of ragged children or an impoverished adult—that "those who have eaten do not mind stumbling over the hungry" (222).

Sharing food leads to intimacy and is of special importance for the cohesion of the family. Because the mother literally gives of herself to be eaten, she exercises the most intense power in the family, even if the more obvious power of the father appears greater.

Laughter, which originally "contained a feeling of pleasure in prey or food which seemed certain" (223), has come to substitute symbolically for predation. The sudden feeling of superiority in which Hobbes located the origin of laughter remains benign only because we do not treat the literally or figuratively fallen object as prey. "We laugh *instead* of eating it" (223).

The Survivor: "The Survivor"

Canetti's word, "Überlebende," recalls the "Übermensch," with its horrifying twentieth-century associations. Canetti's survivor is no less horrifying. "The moment of *survival* is the moment of power" (227). Whatever distress the survivor may feel at the surrounding dead is quickly replaced by the consciousness that *someone else* is dead and by a feeling of his own uniqueness. The lowest form of survival is killing, which fills the survivor with an incomparable, addictive feeling of strength. (The insatiable appetite of movie audiences for violence perhaps has to do with survival.) After a battle, a survivor stands exultant while the dead lie helpless, without consciousness. His death has been deferred; he is the chosen of the Gods. (Canetti's analysis brings to mind religious conceptions of the superior Chosen to whom is granted eternal life while infidels and the faithless suffer endless death.)

The Survivor: "Survival and Invulnerability"

There are two ways, generally speaking, to fend off danger: first, to flee or otherwise keep it at a distance; second, to seek and confront it. The second is the way of the hero, whose victories as they succeed one another increasingly fill him with the survivor's wondrous feeling of invulnerability.

The Survivor: "Survival as Passion"

Passion for survival can become "dangerous and insatiable" in those who, like famous commanders and conquerors, frequently survey heaps of dead. It is also a dangerous cultural passion, especially evident in the adulation accorded by history to such men whose "fame depends in the end less on victory or defeat than on the monstrous number of their victims" (231).

The Survivor: "The Ruler as Survivor"

The autocrat, a "paranoiac type of ruler," uses every means, including his power of life and death over his subjects, to keep danger at a distance. He needs a certain number of executions, for his sense of survival must be fed. Those he has killed become his truest, most dependable subjects. The terror the Emperor Domitian inflicted on his noble subjects at his famous "Funeral Banquet" exemplifies the absolute power in which the paranoiac ruler glories. At night in a pitch-black room, Domitian's noble guests found place markers shaped like gravestones, naked servants painted black, and funereal accoutrements. After hours of expecting execution, the guests were returned to their homes and sent valuable gifts. Mercy, the fact that the autocrat may allow his subjects to live, only multiplies his sense of power. "He is able, as it were, to dispatch them from life to death and then to bring them back to life again" (234).

The Survivor: "The Escape of Josephus"

Trapped by enemy Romans, Josephus wishes to surrender; but his men, who are determined instead to commit suicide, refuse and threaten to kill him. Since there is no hope of escape, he proposes that the cornered Jews draw lots; as each draws the fatal lot, a companion will kill him until there remains only one, who will kill himself. This arrangement means that only the last to die must transgress the divine proscription against self-murder. When the lots "fall out" so that Josephus and just one other remain alive, Josephus persuades his last compatriot to surrender with him. As a prisoner, he ingratiates himself with the Roman commander and thus escapes death again. His deception perfectly illustrates the nature of the survivor. Like all such leaders, he pretends that he will be the first to die, but he actually sends his people to die ahead of him, thus prolonging his own life. He survives the deaths of both his enemies and his own people, thereby growing stronger himself. "Enemies he can use openly. . . . His own people must be used secretly" (241).

The Survivor: "The Despot's Hostility to Survivors: Rulers and Their Successors"

Muhammad Tughlak, Sultan of Delhi, and other ancient rulers illustrate Canetti's proposition that despots have a profound hostility to survivors, for such rulers "regard survival as their prerogative" (242). Conflicts must inevitably arise between rulers and their heirs, both of whom have the despot's passion for survival, "the specific passion of power."

The Survivor: "Forms of Survival"

Of the 200 million spermatozoa that set out together, only one reaches the egg (among a woman's ova, too, only a small proportion will ever be fertilized). To survivors, then, all owe their lives.

As to both killing and witnessing, more or less blamelessly, the deaths of others, Canetti observes that "the most elementary and obvious form of success is to remain alive" (249). From "plague-heroes" who survive massive natural catastrophes through people who witness the deaths of friends, relatives, and parents, no one is entirely free of the desire to survive, to outlive others, however concealed that desire may be. What has been called "the instinct of self-preservation" does not accurately reflect our competitive, often aggressive wish "to stay alive so as not to have others surviving [us]." Only surviving those who lived and died before our time can be wholly innocent—that is, without the survivor's wish to extend his life beyond the lives of others.

The Survivor: "The Survivor in Primitive Belief"

The ubiquity of various forms of survival is illustrated by myths and beliefs from the Marquesas of the Pacific; the Murngin of Australia; Fiji Islanders; the Uitoto, Taulipang, and Caraibs of South America; the Bantu of Africa; and the "many tribes all over the world [that] attribute their origin to one couple which alone remains alive after some great catastrophe" (258). The essay ends with the story of a Caraib man left alive by the triumphant enemy Cabres to witness the slaughter and cannibalization of all other members of his immediate tribe. This "enforced survivor" is sent back by the victors to recount to other Caraibs what he has seen. Far from being intimidated, however, they return with him to exterminate the man-eaters. Canetti's conclusion is enigmatic, but seems to offer hope that humanity might be able to turn its passion for survival to creative account. "The Caraib who was forced to climb the tree served both sides, friend and enemy alike. If we have the courage, there is an immense amount we can learn from his dual role" (262).

The Survivor: "The Resentment of the Dead"

(The German title here is more striking: "Die Toten als die Überlebten," literally "The Dead as Survivors.")

Because they have been survived, the dead are assumed to be envious and vindictive. The living everywhere fear the dead and create rites and cults to propitiate them. Studies of peoples in India, China, and Africa provide examples of how uneasy survivors deal with their dead. Among the Chinese, who have particularly well developed ancestor cults, the living and the dead have a "close and mutually rewarding link. . . . Survival loses its crowd characteristics . . . and thus it ceases to be murderous" (272). Like several other essays in which Canetti confronts predominantly distressing human characteristics, this one ends by noting that alternative, happier configurations are possible.

The Survivor: "Epidemics"

Thucydides recounts the intoxicating sense of power that results from surviving a plague: "They themselves were so elated at the time of their recovery that they fondly imagined that they could never die of any other disease in the future" (273). The survivors of epidemics, mass suicide, and battles experience a similar euphoria.

The Survivor: "Cemeteries"

People's feelings of reverent awe in cemeteries cover a "secret satisfaction" both that they have already lived longer than did many buried there and also that they stand alive among the crowds of mostly long-dead people lying in the ground.

The Survivor: "Immortality"

In contrast to survival, those who seek immortality neither contemplate killing nor desire to live on alone. As exemplified by the writer Stendhal, such a person takes with him into the future his contemporaries and offers himself to posterity "as food to the living . . . a reversal of sacrifice to the dead" (278). In doing so, he strives not so much for present fame, but rather "chooses the company of those to whom he himself will one day belong, men of earlier times whose work still lives, who speak to him and *feed* him" (278). As in Chinese ancestor cults, immortality aligns the living and the dead in trust and mutuality. In this essay many readers see Canetti's own ambitions. More directly, it offers a prescription for confronting the prospect of death without turning to survival, the passionate pathogen underlying the disease of power.

Elements of Power: "Force and Power"

Like several similar passages, Canetti's etymological discussion—here of *Macht,* the word for power, which derives from a root meaning "to be able"—is dropped from the English translation. Physical force applies to what is immediate in time and space; power is more extended in both directions. A cat, for example, uses force to seize a mouse; but its playing with the captured prey, watching and controlling it at a distance for an extended time, may be understood as power. Should the mouse come close to escaping, the cat again pounces; power tends to revert to force during crises.

In religions, most believers experience God as power—continually and distantly watchful—"but there are those for whom this is not enough" (282). Calvinists and Moslems most clearly exhibit the desire to feel God's force actively and continuously. Such people experience everything that happens as a direct expression of God's will. "It is as though they were already in God's mouth, to be crushed in the next instant" (282).

Elements of Power: "Power and Speed"

Speed in pursuit and in grasping is relevant to power: the speed of lions, wolves, leopards, tigers, birds of prey, arrows, horses, and now machines. Especially fast and powerful is lightning, often thought of "as a supernatural command" (as in Hawthorne's *The Scarlet Letter*). A despot, always conscious of his own dissimulation and expecting the same of others, cherishes speed for the sudden unmasking of opponents.

Elements of Power: "Question and Answer"

"All questioning is a forcible intrusion. When used as an instrument of power it is like a knife" (284). (Orwell's *1984* terrifyingly dramatizes Canetti's insights into questioning as a weapon of attack and oppression.) Answers are acts of submission that restrict the mobility of the responder. Like prey, he is inspected and named prior to being tasted or dissected. Questions, like the abrupt touches of strangers, "are to some extent restricted by the forms of civilization" (288). (In the United States one is constitutionally protected from the obligation to respond to questions with potentially self-incriminating answers.) No truly religious person can ever presume to question God. Among the defenses against questioning, upon which personal freedom depends, are silence and secrets; but both are dangerous to their possessor. Behind all the questions that power asks are purposes; none are idly curious. (What of disinterested questions that seek only knowledge? Like the patient skills of hands, they serve neither force nor power; hence, though they may be useful, they seem childish and arouse no fear. Such questions remain, as we say, merely academic.)

Elements of Power: "Secrecy"

Secrecy crouches in ambush at the center of power, safe from discovery. The magic of the medicine man or the distant foreigner are secret and hard or impossible to discover. "It is only a step from the primitive medicine-man to the paranoiac and from both of them to the despot of history" (292). Silence, the instrument of power's secrecy, isolates its possessors and inhibits their self-transformations, for silence is literally and imaginatively motionless. Like a crowd whose growth is forcibly inhibited, secrecy is inherently explosive. All concentrated secrets must ultimately bring disaster to everyone whom they concern. (Sam Spade, in Huston's *The Maltese Falcon*, understands the explosiveness of secrets; they are almost the only things that he truly fears.)

Let us define the *concentration* of a secret as the ratio between the number of those it concerns and the number of those who possess it. From this definition it can easily be seen that modern technical secrets are the most concentrated and dangerous that have ever existed. They concern *everyone*, but only a tiny number of people have real knowledge of them and their actual use depends on a handful of men (296).

Elements of Power: "Judgment and Condemnation"

The "cruel pleasure" of judgment stems from a disease to which hardly anyone is immune. It originates in the desire to form hostile packs with the judge implicitly belonging to the superior group. In extreme circumstances, the "good" pack may feel that it must attack—that is, pass a death sentence on—their "bad" opponents.

Elements of Power: "The Power of Pardon: Mercy"

Mercy is a concentrated expression of power, for it presupposes knowledge and condemnation. "Many prohibitions exist only to enhance the power of those who can punish or pardon their transgression" (298). Supreme power manifests itself in commuting a death sentence at the last instant, thereby approximating resurrection. Although "persons of paranoid structure," like despots, might sometimes grant mercy, they never truly forgive or forget.

The Command: "The Command: Flight and Sting"

Commands predate speech. All derive from a disparity of strength between two participants, one of whom must flee its predator. Thus Canetti calls the original command a "flight-command," and concludes that "beneath *all* commands glints the harshness of the death sentence" (304). Commands are directed from the stronger to the weaker, who experience the actions they undertake because of them as "something alien." Commands initiate action and brook no contradiction. Those who issue commands (like survivors) grow stronger with each order that is obeyed. Every command consists of momentum (*Antrieb,* perhaps better translated as "drive" or "impetus" here) that "forces the recipient to act" and a sting that "sinks deep into the person who has carried out the command and remains in him unchanged. In the whole psychological structure of man there is nothing less subject to change" (305). Stings may be excised only by passing them on to someone else exactly as they were received. All people have a deep urge to be free of their stings. The most free, however, are not those who rid themselves of their stings, but those who manage to evade them in the first place.

The Command: "The Domestication of the Command"

To remove the open threat of death from command, the stronger links it with a promise of food; "instead of serving its master as food, it [the commanded] is itself given food to eat" (307). But even the substitution of rewards for threats does not change entirely the nature of a command, which still contains an element of threat. (Recall that all domestic animals—and perhaps most humans—live under threat of a death sentence, however distant and implicit it might be.)

The Command: "The Recoil: The Anxiety of Command"

"A command marks not only its victim, but also its giver" (308). The anxiety of command arises from the issuer's assumption that "all those he has threatened with death, are still alive and still remember" (308–9). The anxiety of command is stronger in those who originate commands, rulers, than in those who only pass them on. It can increase in concentration until it causes madness. (Canetti cites "certain of the Roman Emperors"; we might add such people as Stalin, FBI director J. Edgar Hoover, or Pol Pot, for whom the accumulated anxieties of command seem to have led to increasingly erratic, paranoid, and often murderous behavior.)

The Command: "Commands Addressed to More than One Individual"

As individual flight and mass flight are fundamentally different, so are commands made to an individual and to a crowd. Unlike an army, in which commands are passed down vertically through individuals, a command spreads horizontally through a crowd. Because it "is immediately diffused, no sting is formed" (310). Commands addressed to large numbers of people are intended to bring crowds into existence. When the commander is successful, those who follow his orders do so happily, for he creates and sustains them as a crowd.

The Command: "The Expectation of Commands"

A soldier, conditioned to act only on commands, constantly expects and even longs for them. Having incorporated a vast number of prohibitions, negative commands, he receives positive commands to action as a relief from compelled stasis. Soldiers of equal rank have equality and armed forces have direction, but armies rarely seek to act as crowds. The command in an army must be transmitted and followed exactly, regardless of the number of soldiers to whom it is issued. (In order to maintain discipline, an army must avoid the pervasive equality, diffusion of command, and disappearance of stings that occur in crowds.)

The Command: "Expectation of Command among the Pilgrims at Arafat"

After standing most of the day upon Mount Arafat, the pilgrims' "collective expectation increases the effect of the divine command to such an extent that it reverts to what all command originally was: a command to flee" and "everyone flees as though possessed" (314). At a succeeding stop in Mina, the pilgrims sacrifice many animals and share the flesh. This progression is predictable, for as Canetti observed earlier, "religious sacrifice springs from a state of crowd fear. It serves to halt the pursuit and, for a while, still the hunger of the hostile power" (309).

The Command: "Discipline and the Sting of Command"

An army employs the manifest discipline of commands and a secret discipline that functions through promotion, which allows a soldier to pass on to others below him his stings of command. In every soldier the desire to transfer stings to subordinates inevitably becomes intense, for his own stings "must accumulate to a monstrous degree" (315).

The Command: "The Mongols: The Horse and the Arrow"

The astonishing discipline of Mongol soldiers derived from the fact that they were immediately able to pass on the commands they received to the horses on which they sat. They also passed on commands against their enemies through the arrow, "the exact image of the original, non-domesticated command" (318). Like the original flight-command, an arrow either kills or leaves a scar (a sting). Mongol ferocity came from their facility in passing on their stings.

Most people, especially as children, are "crammed full of the stings of command" (318). Life can become a long struggle to rid ourselves of these stings, driving us "towards this or that otherwise inexplicable deed or meaningless relationship" (318).

The Command: "Religious Emasculation: The Skoptsy"

Like soldiers, the Skopets are commanded to offer themselves as victims, but they had to enact the command—castration for men, cutting off breasts for women—directly upon themselves, thereby leaving a scar, the visible (if usually hidden) sign of the command's sting. They could pass it on only by converting others to the sect, so that they would accept the same command. A member of the sect of assassins, whose command to kill usually guaranteed his own death as well, passed on the sting of his own death sentence by murdering another before he died.

The Command: "Negativism in Schizophrenia"

Since stings result only from carrying out commands, they may be evaded by either refusing to hear or declining to obey them. In their extreme negativism, schizophrenics isolate themselves from commands and achieve an immobility much like that of a soldier

awaiting orders. At the opposite pole, a condition of extreme sug-
gestibility, the schizophrenic escapes into imaginary crowds to
evade his stings and thus becomes responsive to the "voices" that
such persons often report. (Schizophrenics' paintings frequently
suggest crowds by multiplying lines to turn one object or creature
into many repeating or nesting ones.)

The Command: "The Reversal"

Indian treatises on sacrifice make clear the permanence of stings
and the fierce determination of their sufferers to rid themselves of
them by reversal. "'Whatever food a man eats in this world, by that
food is he eaten in the next world'" (324). The Sanskrit word for
flesh, *mansa,* splits its syllables to mean "me-he." In the afterlife,
the sting of the death sentence will be reversed: "he-me." As I ate
him, so now he eats me.

The Command: "The Dissolution of the Sting"

A sting can recognize and seize upon only the specific situation in
which it was inflicted, like an antibody that can recognize and attach itself only to a specific pathogen. Its possessor will express the
original command onto someone else and thereby rid himself of it.
Frequently repeated commands, however, may obscure the original
situation(s) and make reversal impossible. Liberation from all stings
can be achieved in crowds—especially in a reversal crowd that
"comes in existence for the joint liberation of a large number of
people from the stings of command they cannot hope to get rid of
alone" (328). Such a crowd may attack persons of the ruling class
or, "in the most concentrated case," a king, "the ultimate source of
all commands" (329). In the killing of a king, "the most inclusive
sting . . . is removed from those who have jointly had to bear it"
(329).

The Command: "The Command and the Execution: The Contented Executioner"

Because the executioner quickly inflicts the death threat implicit in
every command on his victim, no sting forms. He becomes, as well,
a sort of survivor.

The force of commands that do not intend to kill or lead to
killing "is almost invariably in excess of what need be used to bring
about the desired action and this is the real reason why a command
leads to the formation of a sting" (331). (A command that is not

followed cannot cause a sting because, far from having extra force, it lacks the energy to penetrate its target at all. When Canetti urges that to master power we must confront command—as he does in the last sentence of *Crowds and Power*—we should remember this analysis. The excess force would seem to be the underlying death threat. Its removal, like the removal of killing from the sublimated war crowds of political parties, would be essential to the establishment of a truly humane society.)

The Command: "Commands and Irresponsibility"

Even ordinarily good "men who are acting under orders are capable of the most appalling deeds" (331), because commands and stings are experienced as alien by those who receive them. Because of the stings they have accumulated, moreover, they not only lack sympathy for their victims but regard themselves as the true sufferers. The command, "in the compact and perfected form it has acquired in the course of its long history, . . . is the most dangerous single element in the social life of mankind" (333). Canetti does not prescribe abolishing it but rather ameliorating it, preventing commands and their stings from penetrating "more than skin deep," so that they "can be removed with a touch" (333).

Transformation: "Presentiment and Transformation among the Bushmen"

All humans possess the talent for transformation but "few are aware that to it they owe what is best in themselves" (337). It has given us enormous power over other creatures, but it remains "a great mystery and . . . [is] extremely difficult to understand. . . . The most hopeful course is to approach it from several different angles" (337).

The first angle comes from the folklore of Bushmen. The presentiments by which they recognize the approach of an animal or another human are felt in their own bodies, *as* the body of the other. "*One body is equated with another*" (340). Yet each body also remains itself. As hunters, the Bushmen also feel presentiments of dead prey, the weight of the dead animal and its warm, fresh blood. These "two different phases . . . together contain the Bushman's whole relation to the animal and the entire process of the hunt" (342).

Transformation: "Flight Transformations: Hysteria, Mania, and Melancholia"

Like the oldest crowd, the flight crowd, transformations in order to escape danger are ancient and universal. Such transformations take two forms: the linear, which involves changes of place as well as of form and which is often part of hunt narratives; and the circular, which happens on one spot and consists of "frustrated attempts to escape on the part of the prisoner" (345) who is eventually compelled to submit to the demands of the captor. Attacks of hysteria may be equated with desperate circular flight-transformations. Mania partakes more of the transformations of the pursuing hunter; it "is a paroxysm of desire for prey" (347). When flight-transformations are felt to be useless and are abandoned, melancholia ensues. Guilt—like debt, to which it is conceptually and semantically related—is equivalent to "thinking of oneself as prey" (347). "This transformation into something which is eaten is the last, the transformation which ends all flight. It is to avoid it that, in whatever shape offers, everything living flees" (348).

Transformation: "Self-Increase and Self-Consumption: The Double Figure of the Totem"

The Aranda bandicoot myth and the Lukara witchetty grub myth of Australia illustrate from another angle the origin and meaning of transformation. In both, the first awareness of other creatures by the ur-ancestor (and therefore the first true self-consciousness) arrives through a feeling of a crowd on the skin. The two kinds of creatures that subsequently form the basis of the animate universe, people and the prey on which they live, spring from the same ancestor whose every cell is potentially one or the other. The restriction to a single transformation, as in these myths, constitutes a totem, a crystallized metamorphosis that can be passed on to posterity. A third myth varies the story when "the thing which is eaten eats back" (357). All three stories powerfully link humans with what they eat via imaginative transformations. In a later development, the clan avoids consumption of their totem animal except in occasional ceremonies through which "the kinship remains real and the animal which is oneself can be made to increase" (358).

Transformation: "Crowds and Transformation in Delirium Tremens"

The hallucinations of all alcoholics have shared features that allow one to study crowd processes and transformations as they appear in the minds of individuals. The dynamics of crowds and of transformation, in practice, are so nearly allied "that it is best not to separate the two" (359). From the general descriptions of delirium tremens, we observe frequent diminution of crowds into masses of insects, small animals, and vermin. The transformation of one's enemies into such alien, hostile, useless creatures "is one of the central myths in the history of human thought" (363). It is, simultaneously, "the exact model of the dynamics of power," for the alcoholic, like a despot, is isolated from the metamorphoses that he intimately witnesses and even causes; "they do not transform *him*" (363).

Transformation: "Imitation and Simulation"

The isolation of the alcoholic from his own imaginative metamorphoses and the pathological distortion of crowd processes prompts Canetti to consider what we might call transformation infected by the disease of power. Imitation, which relates only to externals and does not experience the object from the inside, remains no more than a truncated step toward transformation. Simulation goes a bit further, but those who practice it stop midway between imitation and transformation and are concerned less to become something else than to conceal their own identity. A special form of imitation, dissimulation, hides a hostile reality within an apparently friendly figure. It has become integral to power. A despot is limited to simulation and especially dissimulation. He cannot achieve transformation, for he always "remains conscious of his inner hostility to others . . . which is his true nature" (373).

Transformation: "The Figure and the Mask"

The figure and the mask are to representation what transformation and imitation/simulation are to action. As exemplified in the divine animal-human images of ancient religions, the two aspects of the figure (lioness and woman, for example) are of equal importance. Crystallized like a totem, the figure expresses both the process and the result of transformation.

Although it creates a kind of figure, "the *mask* is distinguished from all the other end-states of transformation by its rigidity" (374). Directed outward, it fixes a distance—one frequently charged with menace—between itself and the spectator. It separates. Wearers of a mask must fear unmasking and thus retain two separate identities, an outward and an inward one. They cannot achieve the free, open equality of identities represented by other kinds of figures. When the mask is not taken up to intimidate or isolate, however, it has constructive uses: in ceremonies it can reassure spectators by interposing itself between them and an awesome or dangerous power. Drama began with and continues to depend upon the mask.

Transformation: "The Power of Unmasking"

Like the paranoid, the despot sees disguised enemies everywhere. Along with his own dissimulation, he fights his enemies by unmasking them and by waging "continuous warfare against spontaneous and uncontrolled transformation" (378). Behind every disguise, paranoid unmaskers know that they will find "always essentially the same enemy" (378).

Transformation: "Prohibitions on Transformation"

A social and religious phenomenon of great importance, prohibitions on transformations have an ancient origin in the idea of metamorphosis through sexual intercourse and in the fear of irregular or forbidden kinds of copulation—the supposed sexual union, for example, of witches with the Devil. In societies, prohibitions on transformation serve existing hierarchies and thereby resist equality (like that found in crowds). The strength of the urge toward a particular transformation is closely related to the strength of its prohibition. (In some modern societies, this postulate would seem to be confirmed by the simultaneous obsession with preventing the use of certain drugs and the equally intense obsession with using them.)

"The two best articulated forms of power known to the older civilizations are primarily differentiated by their contrasting relationships with transformation" (381). The *"master transformers"* appear in the form of such escape artists as the Trickster of the North American Indians; they achieve great power as Shamans, who can summon spirits to serve their transformations. At the opposite pole are rulers to whom all self-transformations are forbidden, even as they command it in others.

Why, Canetti asks, might humans desire to prohibit transformation? Early man was perhaps "made uneasy by the increasing fluidity of his nature . . . and this inevitably aroused in him a desire for solidity and permanence" (382). (The last transformation, we recall, is death, a transformation into something that is eaten. We note again the intricate connections among survival, the prohibition of transformation, and power.)

Transformation: "Slavery"

For slaves, as for children and domestic animals, commands and food come from the same source; unlike children, however, slaves are prohibited from transformation. They may not grow up or develop the differentiation of personality that Canetti identifies as characteristically human. (Canetti's discussion here makes the sensitivity to the diminishing epithet "boy" of African American men, the descendants of former slaves, even more understandable.) In the institution of slavery one can find the foundations of state tyranny.

Aspects of Power: "Human Postures and Their Relation to Power"

Among the "many silent configurations of power" are various human postures. Standing, especially when somewhat isolated but within the sight of others, suggests independence, potential energy, and the capacity to represent (to "stand for") someone or something. Sitting on the ground "denotes an absence of needs, a turning in on one's self" (393). Sitting on chairs, which derive from thrones and the four legs of which recall the legs of animals, is another matter entirely. It expresses power in the action itself and over those who must stand by. "A man lying down is a man disarmed" (390). The spectacle of a person who has fallen arouses ambivalence: a feeling of superiority, but "also uneasiness at the fall of a fellow-man" (392). An active form of powerlessness, "kneeling is always in some sense a prelude to a last moment" (394). It flatters in extremis, for it implies that the supplicated one has the ability to redeem the supplicant from death.

Aspects of Power: "The Orchestral Conductor"

Every detail of the orchestra conductor's behavior illuminates the nature of power. He alone stands before an assemblage of seated musicians whom he transforms into a unit. Like a god, he sees and hears what every orchestra member does; and he knows what each should be doing. "He is the living embodiment of law, both positive and negative. His hands decree and prohibit. His ears search out profanation" (396). For as long as the performance lasts, the conductor rules the world. "The applause he receives is the ancient salute to the victor" (395). (It is also the discharge of the crowd that he has created.)

Aspects of Power: "Fame"

Promiscuous fame seeks to establish a name that will collect a crowd, any crowd. As a rich man collects treasure and a ruler collects people, "a celebrity collects a chorus of voices" (397). They may be the voices of the living, the dead, or the as yet unborn.

Aspects of Power: "The Regulation of Time"

Because communal activity must frequently be synchronized, "one might say that the regulation of time is the primary attribute of all government" (397). Peoples become nations when they adopt a uniform calendar and nations disintegrate when they no longer take their own chronology seriously. Rulers embody the time of their reign. (English-speaking historians traditionally divide certain periods into Elizabethan, Georgian, Victorian, Edwardian, and so on.)

Aspects of Power: "The Court"

The court derives from the idea of a center. Surrounding a ruler who beams forth "splendor, terror, and hope of favor," courtiers orbit as satellites between rulers and their other subjects. The court functions as a crowd crystal, appearing to the world as a single unit "radiating the loyalty they have in common" (400).

Aspects of Power: "The Rising Throne of the Emperor of Byzantium"

A kind of mechanical exaggeration of the posture of standing or of a startlingly abrupt change from sitting to standing upright, the rising throne of the Byzantine Emperor "symbolized the urge to increase in all power. Exhibited to the emissary of a foreign power its threat was unmistakable" (401).

Aspects of Power: "General Paralytics and Their Notions of Greatness"

Canetti discusses in this essay the manic mental illness characterized by the rapid proliferation of grandiose plans and an enormous self-conception. The notions of greatness in the delusions of such persons center less on absolute size than on growth. Unlike paranoiacs, they imagine the crowd as always loyal and compliant, tied to them by the inherent desire for growth that they share. "The greatness of which men dream contains both individual biological growth and the compulsive increase which characterizes crowds" (408).

Rulers and Paranoiacs: "African Kings"

Warning against dismissing African kings as irrelevant to modern experience or as inferior or primitive, Canetti observes that "it is not for a European of the 20th century to regard himself as above savagery. His despots may use more effective means, but their ends often differ in nothing" (411). The death of a king and the elevation of his successor in Gaboon exemplify a fluctuating series of crowd events that is intimately connected with power. A lamenting pack mourns the dead king, then turns from him to select his successor. Elected without his desire, assent, or even knowledge, the new king is physically and verbally abused by a mob which acts as a reversal crowd loosing the hostility once felt toward the old king. After suffering the abuse for an hour or so, he is crowned and a feast/increase crowd then celebrates his ascension for a riotous six days.

Throughout Africa, tribal kings function as providers and symbols of increase. The possessor of absolute control over the life and death of any subject, the African ruler lives apart in some sort of royal residence. As with the possessors of power everywhere, "uniqueness, isolation, distance and preciousness thus form an important group of attributes which can be recognized at sight" (416). Nothing the king does lacks importance. Indeed, in some cases "people regard his every movement and utterance as a *command*" (417); if he sneezes or coughs, those in his presence also sneeze or cough. His court serves as an increase pack and a crowd crystal. Some tribes incorporate safeguards to ameliorate the king's power and to prevent his passion for survival from becoming overween-ing—a permanent prime minister or council of advisors, for exam-ple, or a limited term (which often means a limited life span). Yet most African kings are institutionalized survivors, with the author-ity to issue a command "in its oldest and purest form, as the death sentence with which the lion threatens all weaker animals" (424). As is usually the case when Canetti turns to examples distant in time or place, this essay both underlines the universality of the il-lustrated phenomena of crowds and power and exposes them di-vested of familiar contemporary trappings.

Rulers and Paranoiacs: "A Sultan of Delhi: Muhammad Tughlak"

Talented, cultured, intelligent, and pious, Muhammad Tughlak was nonetheless profligate and cruel. "He is the purest case of a para-noiac ruler" (433). He was obsessed with four crowds: his army, his treasure, the corpses of the innumerable people he caused to be killed, and his court; "but he only succeeded in increasing one at the expense of another" (434). An insatiable survivor, he judged prisoners for execution daily and once wholly depopulated his cap-ital city of Delhi. Yet for all his murderousness and terror, he has been defended and justified by historians who eulogize power.

Rulers and Paranoiacs: "The Case of Schreber: I"

A distinguished and prominent citizen of Dresden at the end of the nineteenth century, Schreber left a detailed account of his descent into acute paranoia. Although he possessed gargantuan power only in his delusions, his *Memoirs of a Nervous Illness* nonetheless "lay bare the inner processes of power." Schreber's paranoid politics, the form and substance of his fantasies, coincidentally but revealingly became—"though in rather a cruder and less literate form"—"the creed of a great nation, leading, under 'a Mongol Prince,' to the conquest of Europe and coming within a hair's breadth of the con-quest of the world" (447). The likeness between Schreber's mad dreams and the ideology and aspirations of Hitler and Nazi Ger-many reveal only too clearly the essential pathology of power.

Although Canetti is reluctant "to blur the clarity of Schreber's vision" with "a conceptual analysis," he identifies in Schreber's elaborately systematized history of his delusions familiar and em-blematic instances of the dynamics of crowds and power. Increase, in the forms of *"growth"* and especially of *"extension,"* lies at the center of Schreber's narrative. His delusion models *"political* power, power which feeds on the crowd and derives its substance from it" (441). His personal place, as for all paranoiacs, "is of cardinal importance," for he feels surrounded and must constantly defend himself from the attacks of his enemies. Even his supreme antagonist, God, "sits in the web of (His) policy like a spider" (444).

Schreber's *Memoirs* are pregnant with a sense of catastrophe. Ultimately, he is left "as the sole survivor because this is what he himself wants. . . . To be the last man to remain alive is the deepest urge of every real seeker after power" (443). In Schreber's fantasy, religion and politics are inextricably intertwined; "the Savior of the World and the Ruler of the World are one and the same person." At the center of both roles is the desire for power. "Paranoia is an *illness of power*" (448).

The fact that Schreber did not attain the position his delusions led him to desire has no bearing on the invaluable understanding of the workings of power his *Memoirs* provides *from the inside.* The world is full of talented, wicked paranoiacs, some of whom have attained mighty positions. "A conscientious investigation of power must ignore success. . . . A madman, helpless, outcast, and despised . . . may, through the insights he procures us, prove more important than Hitler or Napoleon, illuminating for mankind its curse and its masters" (448).

(If Schreber's politico-religious system anticipated Nazism and Hitler, he also illuminates an aspect of us that we all share. Life, which begins with self-replication, soon turns to feeding on and thereby surviving other life. "We all eat. . . . Here each of us is a king in a field of corpses" [448]. To survive alone among all living things would return one to the state of the first life. "Two Paradises 'twere in one," as Andrew Marvell wrote, "To live in Paradise alone." The myth of the Garden before sin removes predation from feeding, allows naming without distance or questioning, and community without threat or domination. The German title for this essay, *"Der Fall Schreber,"* perhaps carries harmonic overtones of the Fall of Humankind, *"der Süderfall."*)

Rulers and Paranoiacs: "The Case of Schreber: II"

In addition to attempting to murder his soul and destroy his reason, Schreber's enemies wished to change him into a woman. Horrified at first, Schreber eventually embraced this fate both to propagate humankind—of which he was now the sole surviving example—and to win the love of God, the only possible father. This part of Schreber's *Memoirs* "has attracted the most attention, including a well-known attempt to find the origin of his particular illness, and of paranoia in general, in repressed homosexuality" (449). The "well-known attempt" is Freud's, unnamed by Canetti. "There could scarcely, however, be a greater mistake." For Canetti, the triggering cause of paranoia may be almost anything; processes of power are at the center of the malady, and particular cases are distinguished by "the *structure* of the delusional world and the way it is *peopled*" (450)—that is, by its crowds.

Attacked by questions and commands, Schreber's longing for *"freedom from words"* leads to an important general understanding of paranoia and, ipso facto, of power: "It is impossible to overrate the importance of words for the paranoiac. They are everywhere, like vermin, always on the alert. They unite to form a world order which leaves nothing outside itself. Perhaps the most marked trend in paranoia is that toward a complete seizing of the world through words, as though language were a fist and the world lay in it" (452).[1]

In the rigid, increasingly impoverished world of his delusions, a paranoid like Schreber both is forbidden transformation himself and dismisses it in others. He becomes obsessed with unmasking the hostile pack that surrounds him, whose members are all finally the same enemy.

In common with many entire civilizations, paranoiacs share a conception of power as sacred. Like rulers who are forbidden transformation, Schreber adopts extreme immobility. His devout stillness makes him invulnerable, an attribute that merges into his passion for survival. To survive, we recall, means not just to stay alive but to stay alive uniquely, to get other people out of the way in order to become the only one left. "'Everything that happens,' says Schreber, 'is in relation to me. I became for God *the* human being'" (462).

Epilogue: "The End of the Survivor"

The increase pack dominates the modern world. "If there is now one faith, it is faith in production, the modern frenzy of increase; and all the peoples of the world are succumbing to it one after the other" (465). As a result, more people are required both to consume and to produce; the increase pack returns to its original motive of multiplying the number of human beings. Enormous double crowds no longer want so much to destroy as "to *surpass* each other" (466). As a means to increase, war is obsolete. At the same time, the religions of lament, for all that they have declined, have contributed to the tendency toward increase by raising our sense of the value of the individual.

Although war may show signs of dying, "we still have to reckon with the *survivor*. . . . He is not yet extinct, nor ever will be until we have the strength to see him clearly, whatever disguise he assumes and whatever the halo of his glory. The survivor is mankind's worst evil, its curse and perhaps its doom" (467–68).

Into "the idea of the 'bomb'" humans have poured all their terror of a supernatural force that can come to everyone with universal punishment and destruction. From the point of view of most survivors, fortunately, this everyone may well include them. "Power is greater than it ever has been, but also more precarious. Today either everyone will survive or no-one" (469).

To deal with survivors, we must learn to understand and control their use of command, behind which still lies the death sentence. Desperate, a survivor-ruler may yet issue "the sudden command for mass death." The survivor by nature remains isolated, rigid, and paranoid—and therefore terribly dangerous. The threat of death and the sting lurking in command make it key to the passing on, continuance, and proliferation of power. "If we would master power we must face command openly and boldly, and search for means to deprive it of its sting" (470).

Notes

INTRODUCTION

1. Elias Canetti, *Crowds and Power,* trans. Carol Stewart (New York: Farrar, Straus and Giroux, 1962, 1973), 75. Originally published as *Masse und Macht* (Hamburg: Claassen Verlag, 1960). Henceforth, numbers in parentheses following quotations refer to Stewart's translation.
2. Quoted by Siegfried Kracauer in *Theory of Film: The Redemption of Physical Reality* (New York: Oxford University Press, 1960), 31.
3. Ibid., 51.
4. Stanley Cavell, *The World Viewed: Reflections on the Ontology of Film,* enlarged edition (Cambridge: Harvard University Press, 1979), 35.
5. Vanessa R. Schwartz, *Spectacular Realities: Early Mass Culture and Fin-de-Siècle Paris* (Berkeley: University of California Press, 1998), 179.
6. Lenelis Kruse, "Conceptions of Crowds and Crowding," in *Changing Conceptions of Crowd Mind and Behavior,* ed. Carl F. Graumann and Serge Moscovici (New York: Springer-Verlag, 1986), 127.
7. As noted, throughout this study I quote Carol Stewart's translation of *Masse und Macht.* This may be an appropriate moment, however, to note that the resonant German seems to me richer than its English reduction. The *Masse* of Canetti's title, accurately translated for its primary sense, also carries in German (as in English) the sense of physical mass. It then combines with *Macht* not only to signify the connection between crowds and power but to suggest an anthropological relation of terms as profound and elemental as that which represents part of the best-known revolution in twentieth-century science, the discovery of the equivalence between matter and energy summed up in the famous equation $E = MC^2$. The latter association disappears from the English title. The importance to Canetti's thought of twentieth-century physical science is discussed in Petra Kuhnau, *Masse und Macht in der Geschichte: Zur Konzeption anthropologischer Konstanten in Elias Canettis Werk Masse und Macht* (Wärzburg: Könighausen und Neumann, 1996), esp. 24–70, 204–7.
8. Elias Canetti, *Notes from Hampstead / The Writer's Notes: 1954–1971,* trans. John Hargraves (Munich: Carl Hanswer Verlag, 1994; New York: Farrar, Straus and Giroux, 1998), 8. Citations are to the 1994 edition.
9. See Ernest Becker, *Escape from Evil* (New York: Free Press, 1975) and *The Denial of Death* (New York: Free Press, 1973).
10. Irving Massey, *The Gaping Pig: Literature and Metamorphosis* (Berkeley:

University of California Press, 1976), 14.

11. Becker, *Escape from Evil,* 139.

12. Such an ambition for inclusiveness may, as George Toles remarked to me, "inevitably entail" some aesthetic sacrifices and risks. If the achievement of inclusiveness is perceived to fall short of the ambition, viewers are apt to be "left not indifferent, but enraged." In an explicitly antagonistic analysis of *Forrest Gump,* Robert Burgoyne concludes, "The film evokes the cultural encyclopedia of the sixties and seventies chiefly in order to construct a virtual nation whose historical debts have all been forgiven and whose disabilities have been corrected" (Burgoyne, *Film Nation: Hollywood Looks at U.S. History* [Minneapolis: University of Minnesota Press, 1997], 119). Speaking directly to the issue of presumptive inclusiveness, he cites Tom Conley's view that "the project of national reclamation . . . depends on the film's 'wiping the slate clean of female presence'" (108).

13. Jeffrey Richards, *The Age of the Dream Palace* (London: Routledge, 1987), 18. Cited in Mark Jancovich and Lucy Faire with Sara Stubbings, *The Place of the Audience: Cultural Geographies of Film Consumption* (London: British Film Institute, 2003), 87.

14. Bruce A. Austin, *Immediate Seating: A Look at Movie Audiences* (Belmont, Calif.: Wadsworth, 1989), 87.

15. Katie Hafner, "Let's All Gather Round the Screen," *New York Times,* February 5, 2004, E1, 6.

16. Ibid., E1.

17. Cavell, *World Viewed,* 40.

18. Jancovich and Faire, *Place of the Audience,* 169. This volume has an especially compendious bibliography—more than 500 items—of studies in film spectatorship and the development of moviegoing in the modern world.

19. Leo Charney and Vanessa R. Schwartz, eds., *Cinema and the Invention of Modern Life* (Berkeley: University of California Press, 1995).

20. David Bordwell, foreword to *Shared Pleasures,* by Douglas Gomery (Madison: University of Wisconsin Press, 1992), xiv.

21. Elias Canetti, "The Writer's Profession," in *The Conscience of Words* (New York: Seabury, 1979), 245.

22. Elias Canetti, *Comedy of Vanity and Life-Terms* (Munich: Carl Hanser Verlag, 1976; New York: Performing Arts Journal Publications, 1983), 85. Citations are to the 1983 edition.

23. Eric Rohmer and Claude Chabrol, *Hitchcock: The First Forty-Four Films,* trans. Stanley Hochman (New York: Frederick Ungar, 1979), 134.

CHAPTER 1

1. Vachel Lindsay, *The Art of the Motion Picture* (1915; reprint, New York: Liveright, 1970), 68.

2. Herbert Marshall, *The Battleship Potemkin: The Greatest Film Ever Made*

(New York: Avon, 1978).

3. N. Volkov and A. Gvozdev, quoted in ibid., 94 and 243, respectively.

4. Ibid., 312 (V. Pudovkin, "*The Battleship Potemkin* in Retrospect," quoting *Soviet Films, Principal Stages of Development* [Bombay: People's Publishing House, 1951]).

5. Ibid., 347 (quoting Parker Tyler, *Classics of the Foreign Film, A Pictorial Treasury* [New York: Citadel, 1962]).

6. David Bordwell, *The Cinema of Eisenstein* (Cambridge: Harvard University Press, 1973), 43.

7. Lindsay, *Art of the Motion Picture*, 68.

8. Bordwell, *Cinema of Eisenstein*, 63.

9. James Goodwin, *Eisenstein, Cinema, and History* (Urbana: University of Illinois Press, 1993), 57.

10. The epigraph is quoted by Steven P. Hill, who has also located the Trotsky article from which it was taken. Hill's essay, "The Strange Case of the Vanishing Epigraphs," appears in Marshall, *Battleship Potemkin*, 74–85. As Hill's research makes clear, the epigraph from Lenin that is now attached to prints of *Potemkin* was inserted "after Trotsky's fall from grace," sometime between 1929 and 1935.

11. Bill Buford, *Among the Thugs* (London: Secker and Warburg, 1991), 286.

12. Goodwin, *Eisenstein*, 64, details how "the citizenry gathered on the steps in part IV distinctly traverses all class and other discriminatory lines."

13. In *The Battleship Potemkin* (London: I. B. Tauris, 2000), Richard Taylor asserts, "The original Russian formulation is much stronger than the conventional English translation: The full force of '*Bie zhidov!*' is 'Kill the Yids!'" He goes on to provide illuminating background about "the significance of this remark in the Odessa of 1905" (33).

14. In addition to noting this invocation of the Fates, Miriam Hansen argues that "the heroine's [the Dear One] confrontation with the three Uplifters over the baby in the cradle . . . graphically underlin[es] the parallel between Uplifters and Fates." *Babel and Babylon: Spectatorship in American Silent Film* (Cambridge: Harvard University Press, 1991), 208–9.

15. Northrop Frye, *Anatomy of Criticism* (1957; reprint, New York: Atheneum, 1967), 44.

CHAPTER 2

1. See Ray Cywinski, *Preston Sturges: A Guide to References and Resources* (Boston: G. K. Hall, 1984). Although somewhat out of date on particular films, Cywinski's summary of critics who view Sturges as a cynic, a pessimist, or, at the least, as a filmmaker who characteristically tacked unconvincing happy endings on his movies still represents, as far as I can tell, a majority of commentators. Sturges "mocks the notion of the rosy Hollywood ending. . . . The resolutions, far from

being standard commercial cop-outs as some critics aver, may actually testify to the opposite—a part of Sturges that believes ultimate success is impossible" (32, 27). In *American Film Comedy* (New York: Prentice Hall, 1994), Scott Siegel and Barbara Siegel call Sturges's humor "cynical, sometimes savage SATIRE that usually undercut Hollywood conventions and expectations. . . . He often gave his audiences illogical happy endings" (267). Brian Henderson attributes this long-lasting view of Sturges's work to the ultimately distorting influence of James Agee's essays and reviews, persuasively arguing that most subsequent commentators have accepted "the Agee myth" of Sturges. Henderson disputes that understanding: "That Sturges compromised particular scripts or films in order to achieve success or, in general, that he had insufficient artistic ambition is not in keeping with the facts as we now know them." *Five Screenplays by Preston Sturges* (Berkeley: University of California Press, 1985), 22.

2. In her informative, detailed study of *Intolerance,* Miriam Hansen asserts, "Only the modern story ends happily." *Babel and Babylon,* 134. As must be clear from my discussion of that film, I find this to be a misunderstanding of the triumphant final sequence of the film (usually called "The Epilogue"), which I take to connect directly to the Judean story via both the tinting of its opening scenes and the heavenly cross at its end. In any event, describing the end of the Judean story, like the conclusions of the Babylonian and French ones, as characterized by "slaughter and catastrophe" fails to account for the Christian meaning of the crucifixion, which is the greatest of triumphs as well as a tragedy.

3. Manny Farber, *Negative Space* (New York: Praeger, 1971), 98. Cited by Brian Henderson in the introduction to *Sullivan's Travels,* in *Five Screenplays by Preston Sturges,* 522.

4. Stanley Cavell, *Pursuits of Happiness: The Hollywood Comedy of Remarriage* (Cambridge: Harvard University Press, 1981), 60.

5. Brian Henderson, introduction to *Hail the Conquering Hero* in Preston Sturges, *Four More Screenplays by Preston Sturges* (Berkeley: University of California Press, 1995), 529.

6. Cavell, *Pursuits of Happiness,* 60.

7. Lesley Brill, "Redemptive Comedy in the Films of Alfred Hitchcock and Preston Sturges," in *Alfred Hitchcock Centenary Essays,* ed. Richard Allen and S. Ishii-Gonzalès (London: British Film Institute, 1999), 205–20.

8. "Chaplin in Retrospect," in *Walter Benjamin: Selected Writings,* ed. Michael W. Jennings, vol. 2, 1927–34 (Cambridge: Harvard University Press, 1999), 224. The full sentence reads, "In his films, Chaplin appeals both to the most international and the most revolutionary emotion of the masses: their laughter."

9. In the service of interpreting the ending of *Sullivan's Travels* as "an example of comedy turning to horror before our eyes," Kathleen Moran and Michael Rogin read this closing montage against the

grain—unpersuasively, it seems to me. "Far from merry enjoyment, the maniacal laughter in the closing montage, like that of the prisoner audience, looks and sounds like hysteria." "'What's the Matter with Capra?': *Sullivan's Travels* and the Popular Front," *REPRESENTATIONS* 71 (Summer 2000): 127.

CHAPTER 3

1. Citations to *Macbeth* are from *The Complete Signet Classic Shakespeare,* ed. Sylvan Barnett (New York: Harcourt Brace Jovanovich, 1973).
2. Becker, *Escape from Evil,* xvii.
3. Ibid.
4. Sigmund Freud, *Collected Papers,* Vol. 4, ed. Ernest Jones (London: Hogarth, 1948), 396.
5. See Canetti's discussions of Chinese ancestor worship in *Crowds and Power,* 270–72, and of fame, 277–78.
6. A. Zambrano, although she misremembers the purpose of Asaji's errand, sees this sequence much as I do: "Asaji belongs to this supernatural world as much as the forest witch does. After Tsuzuki's death Asaji fetches water to cleanse herself of his blood, disappearing into the darkness of the next room and then emerging from the darkness as though she were a silent phantom who had vanished into hell and then returned." "*Throne of Blood*: Kurosawa's *Macbeth,*" *Literature/Film Quarterly* 2, no. 3 (1974): 269.
7. Peter S. Donaldson, *Shakespearean Films/Shakespearean Directors* (Boston: Unwin Hyman, 1990), 87.
8. Critics have generally asserted, as Jack Jorgenson put it, that "the central polarity in *Throne of Blood* is between the forest and the fortress" (*Shakespeare on Film* [Bloomington: Indiana University Press, 1977], 157). Similarly, Anthony Daves observes, "The major conflict in *Throne of Blood* is presented through the spatial polarity between the castle and the forest; the world of man and the world of nature" (*Filming Shakespeare* [New York: Cambridge University Press, 1988], 156). E. Pearlman argues that the world of nature triumphs: "The rigid and futile geometry of manufactured structures is continually contrasted to the fertility, magic, and riot of the forest" ("*Macbeth* on Film: Politics," *Shakespeare Survey* 39 [Cambridge: Cambridge University Press, 1987], 73). Closer to my reading of natural imagery is Brian Parker, "Nature and Society in Kurosawa's *Throne of Blood,*" *University of Toronto Quarterly* 66, no. 3 (1997): 517: "Nature and Society . . . are perceived ultimately as collaborating."
9. Garrett Stewart gives this image an extended discussion in *Between Film and Screen: Modernism's Photo Synthesis* (Chicago: University of Chicago Press, 1999), 179–86.
10. James Goodwin, *Akira Kurosawa and Intertextual Cinema* (Baltimore: Johns Hopkins University Press, 1994), 191.
11. Robert Warshow, *The Immediate Experience* (New York: Atheneum,

1970), 132, 133. Quoted in Gilberto Perez, *The Material Ghost* (Baltimore: Johns Hopkins University Press, 1998), 252.

12. Becker, *Escape from Evil*, 147.

CHAPTER 4

1. Andrew Sarris addressed this issue in *"Citizen Kane*: The American Baroque," *Film Culture* 2 (1956): 14–16. Reprinted in *Focus on Citizen Kane*, ed. Ronald Gottesman (Englewood Cliffs, N.J.: Prentice Hall, 1971). Sarris wrote, "In all respects, *Kane*'s technique is a reflection and projection of the inhuman quality of its protagonist" (107).

2. George Oppen, *The Collected Poems of George Oppen* (New York: New Directions, 1975). The lines are from stanza 37 of "OF BEING NUMEROUS."

3. Genee Kobacker Lesser, *"Citizen Kane* Hailed as Triumph of Cinema," *Columbus* (Ohio) *Citizen*, April 6, 1941; reprinted in *Perspectives on Citizen Kane*, ed. Ronald Gottesman (New York: G. K. Hall, 1996), 30.

4. Noel Carroll and Garrett Stewart have argued for understandings of "Rosebud" and of *Citizen Kane* closely related to but rather more dichotomized than mine. Carroll ("Interpreting *Citizen Kane*," originally published in *Persistence of Vision*, no. 7 [1989] and reprinted in Gottesman, *Perspectives on Citizen Kane*) divides all interpretations of Welles's film into two "incompatible" understandings, "the enigma of interpretation, on the one hand, and the Rosebud interpretation, on the other" (*Perspectives*, 254). In an essay written for the Gottesman volume, Stewart calls "the last word of the dying hero . . . by turns—or at once—overdetermined and insufficient" (*Perspectives*, 430).

5. James Naremore, *The Magic World of Orson Welles* (Dallas: Southern Methodist University Press, 1989).

6. Elias Canetti, *The Human Province* (New York: Seabury Press, 1978), 13.

7. When we first see the lighted window, the light goes out, then comes slowly back up, now behind a curving silhouetted object that appears to be just inside the window. Because the windows are matched, the light remains largely behind the object, and the curve of the silhouetted mass is also matched, we do not experience the dissolve as disorienting—even though it presents two points of view that are not logically compatible.

8. For informative details about the art production for *Citizen Kane*, see Robert L. Carringer, *The Making of Citizen Kane*, rev. ed. (Berkeley: University of California Press, 1996), 36–66.

CHAPTER 5

1. James Naremore, "Introduction: Spies and Lovers," in *North by Northwest: Alfred Hitchcock, Director*, ed. Naremore (New Brunswick, N.J.: Rutgers University Press, 1993), 11. Marian Keane observes in "The Designs of Authorship: An Essay on *North by Northwest*," *Wide Angle*

4, no. 1 (1980), that associations of ingestion are subtly raised by the statuette Vandamm uses to transport his information: "His secret is embodied in a little film, itself embodied, engorged, or swallowed, into the belly of a miniature demigod statue." Reprinted in Naremore, *North by Northwest*, 214.

2. Sidney Gottlieb, "Hitchcock and the Art of the Kiss," *Hitchcock Annual*, ed. Christopher Brookhouse, 1997–98, 75. Donald Spoto has observed that Hitchcock persistently associates in *Frenzy* the acts of eating and of sex: *The Art of Alfred Hitchcock* (Garden City, N.Y.: Doubleday, 1979), 435–45. Similarly, Tania Modleski in her discussion of the same film observes that "eating and copulating have frequently been posited as analogous activities in Hitchcock films" and relates this tendency to her general argument about the centrality of the "fear of the devouring, voracious mother . . . in much of Hitchcock's work." *The Women Who Knew Too Much* (New York: Routledge, 1989), 105, 107.

3. Maggie Kilgour, *From Communion to Cannibalism: An Anatomy of Metaphors of Incorporation* (Princeton, N.J.: Princeton University Press, 1990), 18.

4. Frye, *Anatomy of Criticism*, 189–92.

5. Thomas Leitch remarks that in "the film's color scheme . . . maternal figures are all associated with red, rust, and earth tones. . . . The film's complementary hues, blues and grays, are associated with male figures." *Find the Director and Other Hitchcock Games* (Athens: University of Georgia Press, 1991), 208.

6. Slavoj Žižek identifies Thornhill as one of a number of late Hitchcock heroes who display "the features of the 'pathological narcissist' dominated by the obscene figure of the maternal superego." Žižek, *Looking Awry: An Introduction to Jacques Lacan through Popular Culture* (Cambridge: MIT Press, 1991). Excerpted in Naremore, *North by Northwest*, 227.

7. Sigmund Freud, *Group Psychology and the Analysis of the Ego*, trans. James Strachey (New York: Liveright, 1967), 55.

8. Robin Wood, *Hitchcock's Films Revisited* (New York: Columbia University Press, 1989), 133.

9. Siegfried Kracauer, *The Theory of Film: The Redemption of Physical Reality* (New York: Oxford University Press, 1960), 27–28.

10. Fredric Jameson notices the emphasis on the trees of the pine forest and the "striations of the rock upon which the representational heads are embedded." But he does not, it seems to me, know quite what to make of them, suggesting rather inconclusively that "the very trunks of the trees seem to surcharge this scene with the sense of the 'aesthetic' as such," and that in the carving lines on the monument, "far more abstractly, we confront the same grid of parallel lines [as in the agricultural countryside at Prairie Stop]." "Spatial Systems in *North by Northwest*," in *Everything You Always Wanted to Know about Lacan (But Were Afraid to Ask Hitchcock)*, ed. Slavoj Žižek (Lon-

don: Verso, 1992), 63–64. I believe that Canetti's understanding of crowd symbols offers a more coherent way to look at these details. Such interpretative "advantages," it is only fair to note, may well be for Jameson no advantages at all, but ideologically motivated reductions or simplifications.

11. Leitch argues that the roles Thornhill plays as the "mad killer" at the United Nations, the hopeless drunk at Townsend's estate, and the disruptive bidder at the auction all show "the practical utility of acting" for his efforts to escape his pursuers. *Find the Director*, 212.

12. Lesley Brill, *The Hitchcock Romance: Love and Irony in Hitchcock's Films* (Princeton, N.J.: Princeton University Press, 1988), 13.

13. Discussing Cary Grant's star persona and his suitability as the director's surrogate within the film, Stanley Cavell remarks that *North by Northwest* seems "to redeem him from certain guilts." For Cavell, these guilts were acquired in previous Hitchcock films, which he calls "earlier environments." Cavell, "*North by Northwest*," reprinted in *A Hitchcock Reader*, ed. Marshall Deutelbaum and Leland Poague (Ames: Iowa State University Press, 1986), 251.

14. Murray Pomerance gives considerable attention to the interactions of Thornhill and his society. "*North by Northwest* is a profoundly social film," he writes, "by which I mean it reveals social structure and power." *An Eye for Hitchcock* (New Brunswick, N.J.: Rutgers University Press, 2004), 17. Similarly, Richard H. Millington argues that Hitchcock's film is "not only a psychological allegory of maturity but a historical or 'anthropological' allegory of the relation between character and culture." "Hitchcock and American Character: The Comedy of Self-Construction in *North by Northwest*," in *Hitchcock's America*, ed. Jonathan Freedman and Richard Millington (New York: Oxford University Press, 1999), 136.

15. Cavell, "*North by Northwest*," 263.

16. Elias Canetti, *The Memoirs of Elias Canetti* (1970; reprint, New York: Farrar, Straus and Giroux, 1999), 387.

CHAPTER 6

The context for this quotation in *Crowds and Power* has to do with the return of a person from a crowd to his home: "When he returns to his house, to *himself,* he finds them all there again, boundaries, burdens, and stings" (324).

1. According to an article in the *New York Times* (January 1, 1995), Burnett completed *Killer of Sheep* as his M.A. thesis at UCLA in 1974. Its copyright date, however, is 1977, and it seems to have made its first public appearances (outside of showings that may have occurred at UCLA) in 1978.

2. The National Film Registry lists the film as running eighty-three minutes.

3. Gaston Bachelard, *Lautréamont* (Dallas: Dallas Institute, 1986), 19.
4. Ibid., 4.
5. Frye, *Anatomy of Criticism*, 143.
6. Speaking (somewhat skeptically) from a structuralist viewpoint, Irving Massey offers an understanding of the relation between metaphor and metamorphosis that is at once congenial to a Canettian one and different from it. "Metamorphosis is itself a process of exchange, in which 'body' connects the two forms. In the sense that body, not language, binds its elements together, metamorphosis is the reverse of metaphor. . . . Man is reborn by himself without having made the excursion through the 'other' (through language). Metamorphosis is a process of change essentially unaccompanied by language." *Gaping Pig*, 51.
7. Alice Miller, *Banished Knowledge: Facing Childhood Injuries,* trans. Leila Vennewitz (New York: Doubleday, 1990), 35.
8. Stan Brakhage, "Metaphors on Vision," *Film Culture,* no. 30 (1963). Reprinted in Gerald Mast, Marshall Cohen, and Leo Braudy, eds., *Film Theory and Criticism* (New York: Oxford University Press, 1992), 71.
9. Canetti, *Human Province*, 221.
10. Ibid., 190.

CHAPTER 7

1. Kracauer, *Theory of Film,* 273.
2. Amy Taubin, "An Avant-Garde Master Finds Art in the Everyday," *New York Times,* December 9, 2001.
3. Stewart, *Between Film and Screen,* xi, 152.
4. Andre Bazin, "What Is Cinema?" reprinted in Leo Braudy and Marshall Cohen, eds., *Film Theory and Criticism* (New York: Oxford University Press, 1999), 198.
5. Jean Epstein, "The Cinema Continues," in *French Film Theory and Criticism, A History/Anthology, Volume II: 1929–39,* ed. Richard Abel (Princeton, N.J.: Princeton University Press, 1988), 64.
6. Stanley Cavell, "The Thought of Movies," *Yale Review* 72, no. 2 (1982): 181–200.
7. Malcolm Gladwell, "The Naked Face," *New Yorker,* August 5, 2002, 38–49.
8. Stewart, *Between Film and Screen,* 141.
9. Carol Watts, "From Looking to Coveting: The 'American Girl' in *The Silence of the Lambs,*" *Women: A Cultural Review* 4, no. 1 (1993): 68.
10. After a thorough cataloging of the avian imagery in *The Silence of the Lambs,* Jhan Hochman asserts that "birds are characterized by flight and vulnerability, both leading to their sacrificial status." "*The Silence of the Lambs: A Quiet Bestiary,*" *ISLE* 1 (1993): 59.
11. Thomas Harris, *The Silence of the Lambs* (New York: St. Martin's, 1988), 294.

12. Stephanie Wardrop offers two more alternatives: "Is it desire Bill expresses for us in that awkward moment when he reaches out his hand toward Clarice's hair and shoulder, or is it a sense of awe that she inhabits what society identifies as a more perfect version of the body he wishes to acquire?" *Literature Interpretation Theory* 5, no. 1 (1994): 102.

13. Most commentators on Demme's film have studiously ignored or dismissed this gesture toward heterosexual romance while arguing either for Clarice's lesbianism or for her "missing sexual affect" (Bruce Robbins, "Murder and Mentorship: Advancement in *The Silence of the Lambs,*" *Boundary 2: An International Journal of Literature and Culture* 23 [Spring 1996]: 72). Elizabeth Young, in *"The Silence of the Lambs* and the Flaying of Feminist Theory," *Camera Obscura: A Journal of Feminism, Culture, and Media Studies* 27 (September 1991): 11, writes that "she seems utterly indifferent to any suggestion of romance as the film poses it, in heterosexual terms." Julie Tharp dismisses the "entomologist [who] 'makes a pass' at Starling . . . as comedic." "The Transvestite as Monster: Gender Horror in *The Silence of the Lambs* and *Psycho,*" *Journal of Popular Film and Television* 19 (Fall 1991): 109. Harold Schechter—without, however, dismissing his importance to the film—notes that Clarice has "a cross-eyed boyfriend of almost comically exaggerated homeliness." *Literature Interpretation Film* 5, no. 1 (1994): 26.
As Robbins observes, Clarice at the end of Harris's novel emphatically finds romance with the entomologist.

14. Harris, *Silence of the Lambs,* 239.

15. Ibid., 148.

16. Karen B. Mann, "The Matter with Mind: Violence and *The Silence of the Lambs,*" *Criticism: A Quarterly for Literature and the Arts* 38, no. 4 (1996): 601.

17. "Lechter's role in the film," observes David Sundelson, "is perfectly ambiguous." "The Demon Therapist and Other Dangers," *Journal of Popular Film and Television* 21, no. 1 (1993): 13.

18. Judith Halberstam notes that Gumb "is waiting . . . for his beautiful metamorphosis" and that "Hannibal too attempts a transformation." "Skinflick: Posthuman Gender in Jonathan Demme's *The Silence of the Lambs,*" *Camera Obscura* 27 (September 1991): 48.

CONCLUDING THOUGHTS

1. Frye, *Anatomy of Criticism,* 163–85.

2. *Aristotle's Poetics,* trans. Hippocrates G. Apostle, Elizabeth A. Dobbs, Morris A. Parslow (Grinnell, Iowa: Peripatetic Press, 1990), 5.

3. Canetti, *Memoirs,* 280. We know little of what Canetti thought about the cinema per se, but two recent books, which appeared too late to

be discussed in this study, may offer hints. He reportedly speaks of film in an interview in *Aufsätze, Reden, Gespräche* (Munich: Carl Hanser Verlag, 2005); and Sven Hanuschek reports in his new biography that Canetti intended to discuss film in public lectures that were planned but never delivered (*Elias Canetti* [Munich: Carl Hanser Verlag, 2005], 307).

4. J. S. McClelland calls *Crowds and Power* the first masterpiece of crowd theory, in *The Crowd and the Mob from Plato to Canetti* (London: Unwin Hyman, 1989), 1.

AFTERWORD

1. McClelland, *Crowd and Mob*, 1.

2. Richie Robertson, "Canetti as Anthropologist," in *Elias Canetti, Londoner Symposium*, ed. Adrian Stevens and Fred Wagner (Stuttgart: Verlag Hans-Dieter Heinz, 1991), 132.

3. *Einladung zur Verwandlung Essays zu Elias Canettis Masse und Macht* [Introduction to transformation essays on Elias Canetti's *Crowds and Power*], ed. Michael Krüger (Munich: Carl Hanser Verlag, 1995).

4. David Darby, ed., *Critical Essays on Elias Canetti* (New York: G. K. Hall, 2000).

5. "Elias Canetti, The Anthropology of Evil and Metamorphosis," *Running New* 99, no. 129 (2002).

6. Kuhnau, *Masse und Macht in der Geschichte*, 1 (see Introduction, note 7, above). My translation.

7. Frye, *Anatomy of Criticism*, 311.

8. Ibid., 16–17.

9. Among the commentators with whom I am familiar, the one who most closely approaches my understanding of *Masse und Macht* is Michael Mack, who argues, "The question of genre is best addressed when one reads *Masse und Macht* as a piece of satirical writing" ("Canetti's Response to the Shoah: *Masse und Macht*," in *A Companion to the Works of Elias Canetti*, ed. Dagmar C. Lorenz [Rochester, N.Y.: Camden House, 2004], 290). Mack does not appear to be familiar with the categories of the anatomy or Menippean satire, but his understanding of the genre of Canetti's magnum opus partly approaches the formal description critics give to those species of writing.

10. David Denby, "Learning to Love Canetti," *New Yorker*, May 31, 1999, 106–7. A hard but ultimately affectionate understanding of humankind, it seems to me, characterizes Canetti's attitude toward humanity in general. It is to understand only half of Canetti to suppose him afflicted by "pervasive pessimism"—Dagmar C. G. Lorenz—or "attempt[ing] to plunge his readers into despair"—Michael Mack (both in *A Companion to the Works of Elias Canetti*, 247 and 309, re-

spectively).

11. Canetti, *Memoirs*, 331.
12. Frye, *Anatomy of Criticism*, 311.
13. Canetti, *Human Province*, 2.
14. Ibid., 29.
15. Ibid., 215.
16. Roberto Calasso, *"Bibliographische Bekenntnisse,"* in Krüger, *Einladung zur Verwandlung* (Munich: Carl Hanser Verlag, 1995), 23. My translation.
17. Youssef Ishaghpour, *Elias Canetti: Metamorphose et identité* (Paris: La Différence, 1990), 105. All translations from Ishaghpour's French are mine.
18. Canetti, *Memoirs*, 511.
19. Canetti, *Notes from Hampstead*, 37.
20. Ibid., 8.
21. Canetti, *Memoirs*, 387.
22. Freud, *Group Psychology*, 34.
23. Canetti, *Memoirs*, 407–8.
24. Freud, *Group Psychology*, 25.
25. Norman O. Brown, *Life against Death* (Middletown, Conn.: Wesleyan University Press, 1959), 269.
26. Norman O. Brown, *Apocalypse and/or Metamorphosis* (Berkeley: University of California Press, 1991), 8.
27. Northrop Frye, *Fables of Identity: Studies in Poetic Mythology* (New York: Harcourt, Brace and World, 1963), 152.
28. Brown, *Apocalypse and/or Metamorphosis*, 20.
29. Ibid., 134.
30. Becker, *Escape from Evil*, xvii.
31. Ibid., 1.
32. Quoted in ibid., 108.
33. Siegfried Kracauer, *The Mass Ornament Weimar Essays*, translated, edited, and with an introduction by Thomas Y. Levin (Cambridge: Harvard University Press, 1995), 300.
34. Jessica Benjamin, *The Bonds of Love: Psychoanalysis, Feminism, and the Problem of Domination* (New York: Pantheon, 1988), 219.
35. Ibid., 41.
36. D. W. Winnicott, *Human Nature* (London: Free Association, 1988), 158.
37. Ibid., 121.
38. Alice Miller, *Banished Knowledge: Facing Childhood Injuries*, trans. Leila Vennewitz (New York: Doubleday, 1990), 35.
39. Richie Robertson, "Canetti and Nietzsche: An Introduction to *Masse und Macht*," in *Companion to the Works of Canetti*, 203.
40. Mack, "Canetti's Response to the Shoah," 290ff.
41. Johann P. Arnason and David Roberts, *Elias Canetti's Counter-Image of Society* (Rochester, N.Y.: Camden House, 2004). The quoted phrase occurs on 139.

42. Canetti, *Conscience of Words*, 14 (see Introduction, note 21).
43. Ishaghpour, *Canetti: Metamorphose et identité*, 32.
44. Ibid., 49.
45. Ibid., 33–34.
46. Canetti, *Memoirs*, 491.
47. Edward Piel, "Putting an End to Power: Canetti's Archetypal Images and New Myth," in *Essays in Honor of Elias Canetti*, trans. Michael Hulse (1985; reprint, New York: Farrar, Straus and Giroux, 1987), 154.
48. Canetti, *Conscience of Words*, 47.
49. Canetti, *Human Province*, 215.
50. Ibid., 124.
51. Canetti, *Notes from Hampstead*, 164.

APPENDIX

1. One might here reflect on theories that inform much of contemporary study in the humanities. Proponents of these theories often exhibit a logocentric preoccupation with power and obsessively discover and expose malignant conspiracies and institutions. After reading Canetti, one is apt to conclude that current academic disciplines in the humanities have been substantially shaped by paranoia.

Index